PARTIES AND POLITICS IN AMERICAN HISTORY

GARLAND REFERENCE LIBRARY
OF THE HUMANITIES
VOL. 1724

PARTIES AND POLITICS IN AMERICAN HISTORY

A Reader

edited by

L. Sandy Maisel
William G. Shade

GARLAND PUBLISHING, INC.
New York & London / 1994

Library of Congress Cataloging-in-Publication Data

Parties and politics in American history : a reader /
edited by L. Sandy Maisel and William G. Shade.
     p.   cm. — (Garland reference library of the
humanities ; vol. 1724)
   Includes bibliographical references (p.).
   ISBN 0–8153–1690–9. — ISBN 0-8153-1323-3 (pbk.)
   1. United States—Politics and government. 2. Political parties—United States—History.   I. Maisel,
Louis Sandy, 1945– . II. Shade, William G. III. Series.
E183.P32   1994
320.973—dc20   94-8022
                                                  CIP

Paperback cover design by Patti Hefner

Printed on acid-free, 250-year-life paper
Manufactured in the United States of America

To Charles W. Bassett

Colleague and Friend, Scholar and Editor,
but primarily and always
a consummate teacher and mentor

Contents

About This Reader

This reader has a somewhat unusual history. Three years ago Garland published *Political Parties and Elections in the United States: An Encyclopedia*, a 1,200-entry reference book edited by L. Sandy Maisel. The entries in the encyclopedia were of two types: traditional short articles, providing biographical data on key individuals or descriptions of concepts or events; and longer, analytical essays by contributing editors, examining time periods or broader questions.

Bill Shade, one of the contributing editors, noted that taken together a group of these longer articles would constitute a fairly complete examination of the history of parties and politics in the United States, with commentary provided by some of the nation's leading historians. Thus this anthology was conceived.

This book contains nine articles (some updated) from the original encyclopedia (chapters 1–6, 8, 10, and 11), one significant revision and updating of an encyclopedia article (chapter 9), and three original essays (the Introduction and chapters 7 and 12). In style we have followed the encyclopedia's format, eliminating footnotes except when absolutely necessary, but including a larger number of references.

These essays were not written to stand as a unified whole. However, as we have compiled this collection and read and edited the chapters, we are pleased with the coherence of the result and are confident they comprise a good introduction to the history of parties and politics in American history.

Acknowledgments

We want to acknowledge the efforts of the many people who contributed to this work. First, we want to thank the authors who allowed us to use their essays in this collection for their aid to future generations of students of American politics. We also want to thank the staff at Garland Publishing: Kennie Lyman, editor of the original encyclopedia and a constant support on this work; Chuck Bartelt, whose technical assistance was invaluable; and Tony Cape for professional copyediting.

Bill Shade would like to acknowledge the efforts of Lewis Gould, Ron Formisano, and Frank Colon.

Sandy Maisel continues to extend his thanks to Patricia Kick, whose skill as a secretary and document manager increases from year to year. He also wants to thank Chris Selicious for serving as a research assistant in the final stages of preparing this manuscript.

Finally, this volume is dedicated to Charles W. Bassett. Charles edited every article in the original encyclopedia on which this book is based—as he has edited every word Sandy Maisel has published over twenty years. This book is dedicated to him not only because he is an editor, colleague, and friend, but because it is appropriate to dedicate a book for classroom use to one whose career exemplifies the contributions to young adults made by a dedicated and talented teacher.

LSM
WGS

Contributors

Richard Beeman
   Department of History
   University of Pennsylvania

Allan G. Bogue
   Department of History
   University of Wisconsin, Madison

David W. Brady
   Department of Political Science and the
      Graduate School of Business
   Stanford University

William Crotty
   Department of Political Science
   Northwestern University

John Ettling
   Department of History
   University of Houston

William E. Gienapp
   Department of History
   Harvard University

L. Sandy Maisel
   Department of Government
   Colby College

David R. Mayhew
    Department of Political Science
    Yale University

Samuel T. McSeveney
    Department of History
    Vanderbilt University

Richard G. Niemi
    Department of Political Science
    University of Rochester

William G. Shade
    Department of History
    Lehigh University

Joel H. Silbey
    Department of History
    Cornell University

Harold W. Stanley
    Department of Political Science
    University of Rochester

Martin P. Wattenberg
    Department of Political Science
    University of California, Irvine

Elections, Parties, and the Stages of American Political Development

William G. Shade

In recent years, the decrepit state of American political parties has become the subject of satirical humor as well as serious analysis. If parties should continue their present course toward oblivion, future historians may find themselves ill-prepared to comprehend whatever institutions emerge to take their place to organize the governing process; and generations reared with little experience of parties may have great difficulty making sense of most of the political histories written in this century. The overwhelming importance, however, of "parties" and "party conflict" as analytical tools for the modern student of American political history can hardly be questioned.

This emphasis on "the party battle" came into professional historical writing at the moment of its conception—a period of our national history in which virile parties dominated the political arena. Most of the basic questions that historians continue to ask about political parties originated in the writings of the "progressive" historians, most importantly Charles Beard, whose model of political development dominated the histories of American elections and parties in the first half of this century and continues to hold sway over the historical memory of most political scientists. Raised in the heyday of American partisanship, they debated its value, but never doubted the importance of the party conflict—between liberal and conservative forces— as the appropriate focus of their study of the American past.

The progressive historians traced the lineage of contemporary parties back into the colonial era and registered few doubts that the Federalists and the Republicans functioned as fully developed political parties—the first in modern history. Their critics, the "consensus" historians of the 1950s and 1960s, disputed the grounds of difference between these parties and tended to dismiss pre-1789 groups as mere "factions," but accepted the 1790s as the decade when modern parties were born. While some historians and political scientists have decried their emergence, most have credited the peaceful evolution of the American political system to their existence.

Recently, however, students have vigorously debated not only the role, but the actual existence of modern parties in the half-century following the Revolution. The political culture was hostile to such organizational structures and eighteenth-century references to "party" bore a distinctly different meaning than the term would assume a century later because it associated partisanship with self-interest hostile to the common good. An anti-party animus dominated early American political culture and provided the subject of Richard Hofstadter's enlightening study of the Founding Fathers' hostility toward parties, *The Idea of a Party System* (1969).

Modern Political Parties

What, in fact, constitutes a political party is far more elusive than most commentators care to admit. Both scholarly literature and popular usage provide a wide variety of definitions. Usually these have been infused with a strong normative dimension that clouds the present debate and inhibits longitudinal analysis. To deny that James Madison and Thomas Jefferson created a "modern" party in the 1790s or to suggest that Andrew Jackson may not have been an effective "party leader" would diminish their "true" stature. Once the dramatic moment of modernization arrived, further development involved little more than fine-tuning and decay proved nearly impossible to describe in an operational fashion, leaving the 1850s particularly with an anomalous partisan history.

In *Party Politics in America* (1968), Frank Sorauf portrayed parties as tripartite structures made up of three distinct elements—party organization; the party-in-the-electorate; and the party-in-office—with each involving different roles played by individuals as cadres, voters, and politicians. Among each group there is a hierarchy based on the relative importance of individuals in that role. Here one contrasts cadres and party managers, nonvoters, regular participants, and "influentials," and run-of-the-mill legislators and "cue givers." Since each of these three elements of a party can be discerned at each of the levels of political activity in the American system, any schematic depiction would become hopelessly complicated. Yet, there is a certain consensus that the term "party" describes exactly the sort of enigmatic institution that provides an orderly integration of these various roles in an effort to attain the goal of wielding political power. Development involves the degree of integration of these elements. The effects of the federal system on American parties complicate the task since they need to function not only over a vast geographic expanse, but also at a variety of levels of authority. Not only is there inherent tension between the spheres of federal and state authority, but the tripartite separation of powers and functions that characterizes the federal Constitution is replicated fifty times over in the states. Local government adds a further layer of complexity. A highly institutionalized two-party system would serve to coordinate behavior of the various sectors of partisan activity, override the constitutional separation of powers, and transcend the federal system in order to give consistent organization to governance and elections at all levels of the political system and in all areas of the country. Other than its freedom from sectional influences, such a system would involve almost exactly the kind of parties the Founding Fathers struggled to suppress.

In order to examine the subject, historians must not only look for the usual "symptoms" of party in traditional sources such as the presentation of candidates, the formation of corresponding committees, organized propaganda, and nominating conventions, but also construct methods of measuring the relative level of development of each of the party systems at any time in the past. Most historians have taken a surprisingly ahistorical stance in which they have focused upon dichotomous indicators such as those mentioned above. If some evidence of the existence of parties could be found, scholars have tended to assume that these parties were sufficiently developed to perform most of the functions associated with modern parties. Consequently, they have characterized important changes in the American political system—following the appearance of modern parties in the 1790s—solely in terms of an altered relationship between the major parties. Some attention has been given to the shifting social makeup of the parties, voter turnout, tenure of office-holding and patterns of recruitment, but the important questions relating to the institutionalization of party systems and political development at various times have been ignored.

Looking at the American past one can discern "one-party" periods, the appearance of "third" parties, and multi-party elections, but most scholars have been struck by the pattern of long epochs of stable two-party competition punctuated by short-lived but intense periods of realignment. This has led to the concept of the "normal vote," and the familiar typology of elections as "maintaining," "deviating," "reinstating," "converting," and "realigning," and the characterization of American electoral history in terms of five distinct party systems coinciding with stable periods since the appearance of the Federalists and the Republicans in the 1790s.

The Party Systems Model

The progressive historians conceived of themselves as political scientists and at the time disciplinary lines were loosely drawn. In the 1930s, Charles Beard served successively as president of the American Historical Association and, two years later, as president of the American Political Science Association. The standard text of mid-century, *American Political Parties: Their Natural History* (1943), was written by Wilfred E. Binkley, primarily a political scientist who had a joint appointment in history. Following World War II, Louis Hartz, who taught political theory in the government department at Harvard, played a crucial role in constructing the "consensus" interpretation of

American political history with his brilliant and often misunderstood book *The Liberal Tradition in America* (1955). His previous work was better known to historians than political scientists.

The behavioral revolution in political science and the divergence of that discipline from history, however, produced an explosion of theoretical creativity that led to the development of "realignment theory." While consistent with the central premise of the "consensus" historians, this approach to electoral analysis evolved with a totally different methodological and conceptual focus that emphasized quantitative analysis and a positivistic approach to social science. The main figures in its development were V.O. Key and the authors of *The American Voter*—Angus Campbell, Philip E. Converse, Warren E. Miller, and Donald E. Stokes. Key was responsible for the introduction of the "theory of critical elections," while the latter group at the University of Michigan developed the central concept of "party identification" and the initial typology of elections that extended Key's insight.

As realignment theory unfolded, the "party systems" perspective replaced the "presidential synthesis" that postulated each new election as a relatively independent decisionmaking process involving a "rational" electorate motivated by economic interest weighing each voting decision anew. In its stead historians and political scientists in the 1960s perceived long periods of electoral stability in which psychologically based partisanship established a "normal vote" punctuated by short-term "critical periods" of realignment in which the coalitional structure of the parties was altered and a new equilibrium emerged.

In line with the theory of voting behavior based upon party identification, critical realignment was associated with a traumatic event like the Great Depression or the emergence of an emotionally powerful cross-cutting issue such as slavery in the territories that caused a significant number of voters to alter their behavior. In fact, this view of the past coincided with, and sometimes was confused with, traditional interpretations of the presidential elections of 1828, 1856, 1896, or 1932, but it provided an explanation for the continuing commitment to party allegiances patterned in a moment of crisis.

Presidential elections could be characterized as belonging to one of four types. "Maintaining elections" continued the "normal" pattern of the system as when an incumbent or his hand-picked successor won (1832 and 1836 or 1904 and 1908). "Deviating elections" were elections in which the "normal" minority party gained the presidency for a short period (the Whigs in 1840), before a "reinstating election" (1844) returned the "normal" majority party to power. "Critical elections" produced permanent realignment within the electorate by reshuffling of the coalitional structures of the two parties, which yielded a new majority and essentially new parties, even if labels remained the same (1896 and 1932).

As the model evolved, each party system assumed a life cycle that entailed an initial realignment followed by years of stability (the "normal" phase) and included a mid-sequence adjustment before entering into a season of decay. With the passage of time, the crisis that produced the realignment waned in voters' memories and the effectiveness of these issues, personalities, and symbols dissipated for both the electorate and the political elite. New issues arose to disrupt the "normal" agenda and, in time, new voters with little personal experience of the realignment crisis entered the electorate. They were more receptive to new issues and often responded to the populist appeals of third parties that tend to appear in the period of partisan dealignment.

The studies upon which the party systems model was based referred to presidential elections, but it is possible to think in terms of systemic partisan realignment involving a large-scale coordinated shift in the elements of the entire government complex as put forward by Jerome M. Clubb, William H. Flanigan, and Nancy H. Zingale in *Partisan Realignment* (1980). A rational extension of this typology of electoral behavior would include the impact of realignment on the policymaking agenda effecting both congressional and state legislative behavior and, with a certain lag (because of its long tenure), of judicial behavior as well. This would be consonant with the idea that the economic crisis that produced the New Deal created a policy agenda dominated by disputes primarily over economic policy between liberal Democrats and conservative Republicans that penetrated into the state capitols and even local government. This is of course not far from the popular journalistic view of the situation from the 1930s through the 1960s.

The First Party System: Hamiltonian Federalists and Jeffersonian Republicans

After 1789 the Constitution created a new arena that made possible the emergence of modern parties, although the new frame of government grew out of a political culture hostile to parties and was designed to thwart their appearance. The architects of the First Party System tended to believe that the ad hoc structures they constructed would quickly wither away. Nevertheless contesting congressional blocs did form which represented the "Friends of Government" who supported the administrations of Washington and Adams and the "Republican interest" that stood in opposition and eventually organized sufficiently to win the presidency in 1800 and long-term control of the Congress. While the Virginia dynasty of Jefferson, Madison, and Monroe established itself in the federal government, the formerly dominant Federalists were forced to regroup as the relatively loyal opposition until 1815 when the coincidence of the Peace of Ghent, the Battle of New Orleans, and the Hartford Convention swept away the vestiges of Federalism. The Era of Good Feelings yielded a decade of no-party government in which each and all affirmed allegiance to Republicanism.

Viewed more formally, the years 1789 to 1816 reflect the low level of development of this First Party System. Labels were never really clear and modern structures of organization were nonexistent. The "symptoms of party" described by traditional historians did exist, but the party disease was not very well advanced. In the first Washington administration, conflicts over the economic policies of the vigorous young Secretary of the Treasury Alexander Hamilton caused sectionally based, or actually state-based, controversies within the Congress. The idea of a systematic approach to tariff protection and state aid to internal improvements never rose above the bickering of state interests.

Consistent bloc voting dominated Congress with the emergence of foreign policy questions generated by the Atlantic World War that arose from the French Revolution. As Richard Beeman emphasizes in his essay, "Republicanism and the First Party System," the period's passionate politics emerged from the ideological hothouse of the Revolutionary era. The debate over foreign affairs both rekindled fears of "faction" which might endanger the continuance of the Republican experiment and led the Republican interest in Congress to gain increasing coherence and spread its influence unevenly into state legislatures and the electorate.

The patterns of the late 1790s, however, quickly disappeared during the period of peace that made possible Jefferson's highly successful first term and saw the virtual disappearance of the "symptoms" of party that had appeared by 1800. When Europe returned to war, foreign policy again divided the Congress into those favoring the English and those favoring the French. Administration policies, particularly the Embargo, bred both factionalism among the Republicans and the re-emergence of a Federalist or "American" opposition in the electorate.

On the state level, party organization tended to be limited to the small states and the more developed areas of the large states, and where it appeared, party activity was sporadic. Interstate cooperation hardly existed at all, and there was little consistent intrastate relationship between state and federal politics, although some ties formed since state legislatures chose the United States senators and a majority chose the presidential electors as well.

Voter turnouts varied greatly from election to election and state to state. State elections drew more voters than presidential elections and turnouts tended to depend on the presence of competition that was irregular in most constituencies. Politics retained much of the elitist flavor that had brewed during the colonial era although the Revolution had produced modest democratization of the system and radicalized the political culture. The erratic and incomplete nature of party development makes generalization about the social bases of the parties in the electorate impossible beyond allusions to conflicts between the center and the periphery within some of the larger states such as Massachusetts and Virginia that the Turnerians had described in terms of intrastate sectionalism.

The Second Party System: Jacksonian Democrats and Democratic Whigs

The election of 1824—best remembered because it was decided in the House of Representatives—epitomized the no-party nature of the Era of Good Feelings. While a congressional caucus of the administration (Republican) party met, it was not well attended and the caucus candidate, Secretary of the Treasury William H. Crawford, ran a poor third in the electoral college and fourth among the popular vote-getters. The other candidates were all connected with the Monroe administration: ex-General Andrew Jackson, hero of the Battle of New Orleans and the Indian wars, was a senator from Tennessee; John Quincy Adams was Secretary of State; and Henry Clay served as the extremely popular Speaker of the House. A fifth candidate, Secretary of War John C. Calhoun, whose support extended well beyond his native South Carolina, settled for the vice-presidency. The divisions in Congress at the time were rooted in state interest although they sometimes took on a regional configuration. Much the same was also true of the popular vote in 1824. While Jackson received a plurality, nearly half of his popular vote came from only three states. Most states voted heavily for the regional favorite although in the Old Northwest the various candidates' support was clearly related to the origins of the settlers.

The outlines of the emerging two-party system appeared in 1828 and during Jackson's presidency. Short-lived working-men's parties appeared in the cities and the Antimasons were sufficiently strong in several northern states to mount a serious challenge in the presidential election of 1832 before most of the movement's followers moved into the new Whig party in the mid-1830s, but the degree of institutional development continued to be confined through the election of 1836. The election 1832 was a three-way race in which Jackson faced both Henry Clay and William Wirt—the candidate of the short-lived Antimasonic party; all three groups held national conventions. Four years later the election of 1836 was even more chaotic. The administration's supporters, calling themselves Democratic Republicans, held a convention to ratify Jackson's choice of

Martin Van Buren as his successor and to pick a running mate. But even this did not assure unanimity since the choice of Richard M. Johnson was particularly distasteful to the Virginians who eventually cast their electoral votes for William Smith of South Carolina. However, the opposition was disorganized. Three candidates—William Henry Harrison, Hugh Lawson White, and Daniel Webster—were nominated in traditional fashion by state legislatures. An array of vice-presidential candidates appeared with little or no coordination. In the end, five men received electoral votes for president and four for vice-president, although these were paired in seven different combinations. The choice of the second office went to the Senate for the only time in American history.

While there were rather clear-cut conflicts between the Jackson administration and its opponents in Congress over such matters as Indian policy and the Bank of the United States, during his second administration party lines in Congress emerged clearly and the opposition adopted the Whig label. Turnout for the presidential election of 1836 remained about the same as it had been in 1828 and 1832, but the pattern of the vote for the victorious Van Buren differed markedly from that given to Jackson. State elections drew more voters to the polls than the presidential elections and the returns from the different levels of the federal system were not correlated closely until the 1840s. As William G. Shade argues in his essay "The Jacksonian Party System," there were two distinct phases of development in which the major parties reached different levels of organization and had different coalitional structures.

The Panic of 1837 and the subsequent depression precipitated the organizational development of the Second Party System and the advent of modern mass political parties—at least for the white male population. Nominating conventions became commonplace as did platforms or at least relatively clear policy statements. Both major parties developed extensive grassroots organizations and a network of political newspapers usually featuring special election editions, which served as the backbone of what is today called a "media blitz," and also included extensive speechmaking by both office holders and party loyalists.

Voters responded by turning out in record numbers—in 1840 over 80 percent of the eligible voters marched to the polls. Various county and state committees coordinated federal and state elections to an unprecedented degree. In the 1840s not only Congress but also the state legislatures worshiped at the "shrine of party." Similar policy agendas drew the lines of battle between Whigs and Democrats from Maine to Mississippi. While the clearest evidence of partisan dissimilarity involved economic policy, other issues concerning constitutional questions and social policies drew contrasting responses from the politicians of the major parties. The organizational phase of the Second Party System initiated what some historians call the "party period" of American politics as modern party structures penetrated into the nooks and crannies of the American political system.

The most interesting contrasts between the more recent literature produced by the now middle-aged, "new" political history and the more traditional "Age of Jackson" view involve the social basis of the Whigs and Democrats and the virility of the Second Party System. In *The Concept of Jacksonian Democracy*, Lee Benson introduced the idea that in the 1840s the voters' ethnic and religious associations were relatively more important than occupation or wealth in determining party identification. Subsequent scholars have extended this perspective to other states in the North although somewhat different patterns appeared at the time in the southern states. Community studies of the South tend to find that neighborhood and kin groups— often clustered about competing churches—were the most important local influences on party choice while in general the Whigs were more popular in the areas experiencing the most rapid economic development. The voting patterns in the upper South were much more like those in the southern band of the North than those found in the Cotton South.

Patterns created in the 1830s—not the 1820s—reached their institutional maturity in the mid-1840s and lasted into the 1850s. In the states of the upper South these electoral patterns contin- ued until the Civil War. The famous antislavery third parties of these years—the Liberty party of 1840–44, the Free Soilers of 1848, and the Free Democrats of 1852—are notable for their weakness and for their contrasting coalitional makeup and policy orientation. Party loyalty for Whigs and Democrats was extremely tenacious and people would rather not vote than switch allegiances. In "Party Organization in Nineteenth-Century America," Joel H. Silbey details the manner in which this phase initiated the elaborate organization and the partisan control of political information that continued through the century.

The Third Party System: Republicans, Democrats, and Civil War

The Third Party System featured the disappearance of the Whigs and the emergence of an entirely new party—the Republican party of Abraham Lincoln. While recent studies of this system emphasize its continuance of many of the most modern elements of the Second Party System, they tend to break with the traditional view on a number of important particulars. The first involves several matters of dating. It is very difficult to push the sectionalization of politics back into the 1840s since it is clear that Texas annexation and the Mexican War were the products of partisan policy rather than sectionalism and that "Manifest Destiny" itself was a propaganda device invented by the editors of the *Democratic Review*—the national organ of the party that now called itself "The American Democracy." High turnouts and consistent patterns of party preference in national politics held into the early 1850s and were accompanied by the dominance of partisan responses in congressional roll-call voting. The softening of electoral loyalty to the Whigs in the lower South at the end of the 1840s and the weakening of partisan cohesion in the state legislatures at the same time signaled the system's decomposition.

The Whigs and Democrats, however, contested the election of 1852 on far more even terms and with greater vigor than textbook accounts concerned with the coming Civil War would have us believe. As an antislavery third party, the Free Democrats drew about half the support given to Free Soilers in 1848. The losing Whig candidate General Winfield Scott managed to retain 45 percent of the popular vote. The turnout fell to a fraction below 70 percent of the eligibles primarily because of the abnormally low votes in the Gulf states. Both parties, however, chose to support the Compromise of 1850, run sectionally balanced tickets and emphasize traditional issues and symbols— the Democratic platform of 1852 differed little from the primary statement of party principles laid out in 1840 and repeated throughout the decade. In most of the states the configuration of the vote correlated with the previous three elections. Nine months after the election, in July 1853, the usually sensitive Richmond *Enquirer* reported "a calm, comparatively, in the political world."

Thus, while the late 1840s had produced strains in the Jacksonian party system, its collapse in the mid-1850s and the appearance of the new Republican party in the presidential election of 1856 was relatively sudden. Aside from the issue of slavery in the territories, rapid economic growth and an array of social issues related to the surge of immigration that swept across the country between 1845 and 1855 disrupted the Second Party System. While traditional historians have emphasized the effect of the Kansas-Nebraska Act, William E. Gienapp's essay "Formation of the Republican Party" details the crucial role in the realignment of the 1850s played by the American, or Know-Nothing, party that ran former President Millard Fillmore in the election of 1856 and received 22 percent of the popular vote.

Although the modern Republican party was born in the 1850s and managed to win the presidency in 1860, it was a distinctly sectional organization with practically no support at all below the Mason-Dixon line. The first phase of the Third Party System was inherently unstable including as it did the American Civil War and the disjointed years of Reconstruction. The election of 1856 had three major candidates; in 1860 there were four. Lincoln faced the Northern Democrat Stephen Douglas, the Southern Democrat John Breckenridge, and the Constitutional Unionist John Bell. The winner Abraham Lincoln received slightly less than 40 percent of the popular vote in a high turnout election. The election of 1864 occurred during the final months of the war and the post-war elections were characterized by boycotts, fraud, and violence.

The Republicans became the dominant party in the North, controlling a sizable portion of the counties in the region, and from 1868 into the early 1870s the party also controlled most of the Southern states. Associated with antislavery and emancipation, the Radicals were able to build the short-lived Republican coalition of northern-born "carpetbaggers," southern white "scalawags" and the mass of black Freedmen in the reconstructed South. The Democrats, who remained rabidly racist and opposed the Thirteenth as well as the Fourteenth and Fifteenth Amendments to the Constitution, emerged as the self-proclaimed "defenders of the white South." They regained control of the House of Representatives in the off-year elections between 1872 and 1876 and maintained a majority in all but two of the next ten Congresses.

The process of stabilization and the mid-sequence readjustment in the Third Party System involved the rejection of the Radical southern policy by the dominant "Half-Breed" faction within the Republican party led by James G. Blaine and the "Redemption" of the South by white (generally ex-Confederate) Democrats who gradually undermined the political influence of the mass of black voters loyal to the party of Lincoln. During the Gilded Age, an extremely close balance between the Democrats and the Republicans characterized the Third Party System. While Republicans generally held the White House, the Democrats gained a larger popular vote in every election from 1876 to 1892 except that in 1880. National politics was characterized by stalemate that has created the impression of a do-nothing government.

Turnouts, however, were extremely high and party structures dominated both electoral and congressional behavior. The Gilded Age represented the high point in party domination of the American government as Allan G. Bogue clearly shows in "Legislative Government in the United States Congress, 1800–1900." The system contrasted sharply with its predecessor in its sectional imbalance. The South was solidly Democratic while the North was predominately Republican. Only a handful of states—Connecticut, New York, New Jersey, Virginia, West Virginia, and Indiana—were closely contested. Party identification was rooted in culturally homogeneous local communities. The Republicans appealed to northern evangelical Protestants, respectable middle-class WASPs, and those southern blacks who continued to vote, while the Democrats gained the support of Roman Catholics and German Lutherans in the North and nearly all southern whites. Ethno-religious differences were the relatively best predictor of voting behavior at the time. The Democrats were the party of individual liberty, laissez-faire, negative government, and states rights while the Republicans were the party of economic and moral progress and of national consensus. The GOP accepted the idea of an active government both to support veterans and their dependents and to encourage economic development by cooperating with the private sector to achieve these goals.

The Fourth Party System: Progressivism and the New Era of the 1920s

During the late nineteenth century, political protests tended to take the form of third party activity. All of the elections of the Gilded Age featured small but tenacious single-issue groups such as the Greenback, Greenback/Labor, and the Prohibition parties. The last of these constantly put forward the most reformist platform although the tiny Equal Rights party ran the most radical ticket in 1872 when it paired Victoria Woodhull, an advocate of Free Love, with the great African-American leader Frederick Douglass. In 1892, however, the appearance of the People's Party of America signaled the realignment of the mid-1890s that ushered in the Fourth Party System and the Progressive era. The Populists were extremely strong in the South, where they challenged Democratic dominance, and in several agricultural north central states, where they successfully challenged Republican rule at the state level.

The decade of the 1890s, troubled by the severe depression that lasted from the Panic of 1893 into mid-1897, spawned a new party system with characteristics slightly different from those of the nineteenth-century systems. Rather than introducing yet another new party, this realignment involved a shift from the period of party equilibrium to one in which one party, the Republicans, became clearly dominant. From 1896 to 1932 only the two terms of Woodrow Wilson disrupted the Republican hold on the White House and in both 1912 and 1916 the winning Democrat failed to receive a majority of the popular vote. During these years, the Democrats held majorities in the House four times and the Senate three times in eighteen consecutive Congresses, constituting a brief "abnormal" interval between two subsystems dominated by the GOP.

The Progressive era witnessed a precipitous decline in partisanship and an attack on the power of the urban and state bosses who had emerged within the Gilded Age party system by the reform-minded Muckrakers in the popular press. William Crotty's "Urban Political Machines" demonstrates that the machine involved patronage and corruption as the reformers charged, but at the same time served the disorganized urban population in a relatively democratic fashion. Progressive political culture took an antiparty turn that involved various efforts to undercut the influence of parties through registration and ballot reform, nonpartisan local elections and city commissions, and the introduction of referendum, initiative, and recall in the states.

As Samuel T. McSeveney details in his essay "The Fourth Party System and Progressive Politics," the decline in turnout and the increase in antiparty feelings accompanied the emergence of professional organizations as a source of external pressure on the political system and the concomitant appearance of the "administrative-regulatory state" that enhanced the power of bureaucratic agencies at both the state and federal level. Progressives tended to equate efficiency with democracy and looked to the application of technique and academic expertise to social problem-solving in the name of the public good.

Their effort to clean up politics included not only the passage of the Seventeenth, Eighteenth, and Nineteenth Amendments to the Constitution that provided for popular election of senators, prohibition, and women's suffrage, but also the erection the southern system of racial segregation that accentuated the importance of the solid (and uniformly Democratic) South. As a result of this complex of systemic changes that weakened party control, turnout in the electorate declined dramatically. Partisan behavior in Congress also deteriorated with the challenges to party control, represented by the changes in House rules in the Sixty-first Congress (1909–1911) that removed Speaker Joseph G. Cannon from the Rules Committee and generally disconnected committee leadership from party leadership. David W. Brady and John Ettling reveal the transitional nature of the Fourth Party System in "The Party System in the United States House of Representatives," which effectively contrasts the nineteenth-century organization of Congress with that of the twentieth century. As the House of Representatives matured as an institution, the relative importance of partisanship in its deliberations declined from the pinnacle reached in the previous era.

The significance of economic conflicts in effecting electoral behavior grew and the saliency of ethno-religious differences declined as the major native-born ethnic and religious groups lost some of their previous coherence. As the party of the metropolitan center, the Republicans were connected to industrial development, the solid middle class, and those among the workers who aspired to that status. The Democrats as the party of the semi-colonial periphery continued a strong agriculturally oriented or what came to be popularly called "agrarian" constituency in the staple-crop South. But most western farmers were Republicans and many of the urban immigrants who came to the United States in the "new" immigration from southern and eastern Europe threw their support to the Democrats, creating an anomalous coalition of radically different social groups—described as "an aggregation of local interests" resembling "the Old Austrian Empire"— whose internal tensions were publicly displayed at the party's 1924 convention that took 103 ballots to chose a corporation lawyer, John W. Davis—who would later both oppose the New Deal as a founder of the Liberty League and defend school segregation before the Supreme Court in 1952 as the counsel for South Carolina.

Third parties during the Progressive era included both the continuing activity of the Prohibitionists and the appearance of distinctly working-class organizations, Socialist Labor, and the Socialists, who ran Eugene Debs as their perpetual candidate. The most important challenges to the two-party system, however, came in 1912 with Theodore Roosevelt's Progressive or

"Bull Moose" candidacy and in 1924 when Robert La Follette also ran as a Progressive.

The election of 1928, that pitted the feisty Irish Catholic New York State Governor Al Smith against the immensely popular ex-Progressive Secretary of Commerce Herbert Hoover, is sometimes looked upon as a critical election, because Smith symbolized the power of the "new" immigrants in the Democratic party and the "rise of the city." The attractiveness of the Republican candidate and the general prosperity of the country, however, maintained Republican control through the mid-term congressional elections of 1930 that produced a Democratic majority in the House for the first time since World War I and began an era of Democratic control of that body that has lasted to the present day.

The Fifth Party System: Era of the New Deal, the Fair Deal, and the Great Society

The realignment that spawned the Fifth or New Deal system came in response to the stock market crash of 1929 and the Great Depression of the 1930s. In the election of 1932, voters disenchanted with the Hoover administration either switched their long-term allegiance and voted for Franklin Roosevelt or stayed home. Turnout that year was down from 1928 and it was only in 1936 that the outlines of the new party coalitions became clear. Although no new party in name emerged, the Fifth Party System differed from the Fourth. The Democrats surged into dominance with a thoroughly overhauled ideology and a transformed electoral base. The party of provincialism, state rights, and laissez-faire became the champion of strong executive leadership, the welfare state, and internationalism in foreign affairs as those in power struggled to respond to the economic crisis at home and the rise of fascism abroad.

The party of FDR retained the loyalty of southern whites, northern Catholics, the descendants of the "new" immigrants in the cities, but Jews and African-Americans switched allegiance and eventually became the most loyal members of the New Deal coalition. New voters, whose allegiance was born of the economic crisis, contributed the key to realignment and the strength of the Democrats for the next three decades. During the 1930s and 1940s, the long-term decline in turnout was reversed and over two-thirds of the electorate regularly voted in both presidential and congressional elections.

Given the crucial nature of the economic crisis it is not surprising that the Fifth Party System was more clearly rooted in economic class conflict than any of its predecessors. The New Deal provided the legal environment for the widespread unionization of industrial labor and the workers responded with disproportionate support for the Democrats. The president's personal attacks on business leaders and media images cultivated by party propagandists so thoroughly reinforced this association that the sociologist Paul Lazarsfeld, one of the authors of the seminal voting study *The People's Choice*, confessed his initial unwillingness to accept the data which showed that religious and ethnic attachments continued to play a significant role in determining electoral behavior. In the post-war era, groups such as Irish Catholics and Jews continued to be strongly Democratic although they were no longer predominantly working class. The anomalous position of white southerners, most of whom were evangelical Protestants, produced another distinctive aspect of the Fifth Party System: the Conservative bloc in Congress made up of Southern Democrats and Northern Republicans.

In 1948 Harry Truman, who had become president somewhat to his own shock when Roosevelt died, faced not only the moderate Republican governor of New York Thomas Dewey, but two factional off-shoots of his own party. On the Right, Strom Thurmond ran as the candidate of the States' Rights or "Dixiecrat" party that rejected the regular Democrats' modest embrace of civil rights. On the Left, Henry Wallace, the former vice-president, ran as a Progressive, opposed to containment and the Cold War hostility to Russia, and in favor of greater commitment to racial justice. The pre-election polls predicted that Truman would be roundly rejected. Nearly every textbook still features the picture of Truman holding aloft the early edition of the Chicago *Tribune* that proclaimed Dewey's victory, but the embattled incumbent won, because his opponent was unable to gain a greater share of the vote than he had held when he lost to FDR in 1944. While in the 1950s the Democrats lost the presidency to the popular (and apolitical) war hero General Dwight D. Eisenhower, they generally continued to control Congress and the majority of voters continued to identify themselves as Democrats.

Realignment theory and the general approach to electoral analysis put forward in *The American Voter* emerged at this time as a direct response to the voting patterns of the New Deal system. Party identification formed the basis of the model underlying the party systems approach to American political development in the 1960s. The victory in 1960 of the wealthy Boston-Irish Catholic John F. Kennedy, and the 1964 landslide for Lyndon Johnson following Kennedy's murder, only served to build confirming evidence. Although turnout continued to fall, the normal Democratic majority had reasserted itself. By the late 1960s realignment theory became increasingly nuanced and seemed to provide the key to the history of American political parties and elections in the United States. The title of W. Dean Burnham's *Critical Elections and the Mainsprings of American Politics* (1970) reflected this conviction.

The End of Realignment?

The upheavals of the sixties—Vietnam, racial conflagration, the counterculture of "sex, drugs, and rock-and-roll"— followed rather quickly in the 1970s by Watergate and the failure of Keynesian fine-tuning to sustain painless economic growth, led to an unexpectedly long dealignment of the Fifth Party System. It unraveled rather than ended with the expected bang, and its successor, like the enigmatic Godot of Samuel Beckett's play, has failed to appear. In 1980 Burnham published a new book, *The Current Crisis in American Politics*, that again caught the mood of his colleagues in history and political science troubled by the sharp decline in turnout, the evaporation of partisanship, the increasing power of PACs and other lobbying groups, and the ossification of the bureaucracy that were all becoming the hallmarks of American government.

If the traditional generational pattern had held, the late 1960s should have produced an realignment and some of the signs were there. The election of 1968 featured factionalism among the Democrats and a classic populist third party challenge. Richard Nixon won the presidency with a plurality of 43 percent of the popular vote by appealing to traditionalists upset by the challenges posed by racial integration and antiwar protests. Harold W. Stanley and Richard G. Niemi examine "Partisanship and Group Support over Time" in their essay, introducing a new analytic technique designed to avoid the pitfalls of earlier studies. Whites in the South, union members, men in general, and even Jews moved toward the "emerging Republican majority" in presidential elections. As a consequence, the party's liberal wing was purged and its presidential aspirants took on the protective coloring of cultural conservatives and the defenders of traditional values.

One characteristic of the new electoral order has been the revival of the long-standing American ambivalence toward political parties. In the 1950s Americans talked about voting for the man rather than the party, but tended to vote straight party tickets. The two-party system seemed synonymous with democratic government. Since 1972 increasing numbers of Americans are willing to tell pollsters that parties are neither meaningful nor even useful, let alone essential. More and more people believe that interest groups better represent their political needs; fewer and fewer Americans bother to vote.

Not only did the proportion of the electorate participating in presidential elections decline between 1960 and 1988 from two-thirds to one-half, but party discipline at the polls deteriorated and ticket-splitting increased markedly. In 1900 one could predict the vote for governor from a knowledge of the vote for president; the correlation was almost perfect. By 1980 it was nonexistent. Obviously presidential votes today do not correlate with votes for the House, but these relationships have been a key behavioral element in our operational definition of what party politics meant in its classic form. These arguments are detailed in Martin P. Wattenberg's essay "Dealignment in the American Electorate," which also reveals a simultaneous decline in party identification. The percentage of Independents has increased and many more people are neutral about the major parties, including even those who consistently vote for one of the major parties.

In recent years social science historians and historically oriented political scientists have debated the "end of realignment." In his essay "Party Organization in Historical Perspective," David R. Mayhew takes an entirely different approach to the fragmented state of present-day parties. He defines American parties as patronage-based organizations and attempts to explain why since 1960 only thirteen states have retained traditional party structures by stressing the relative weakness of entrenched socio-economic hierarchies that has characterized their historical development.

The failure of the last two decades to usher in the anticipated Sixth Party System has led other scholars to propose the substitution of the idea of political eras in place of party systems. Certainly the essays by Silbey, Bogue, Crotty, and Brady and Ettling could be easily fitted into a model that perceives four "political eras" since 1789: the pre-party period from 1789–1838; the classic party era, 1838–1893; a half-century of realignment and dealignment from the mid-1890s to the early 1950s; and the post-alignment period that has continued to the present. The advocates of this scheme argue that it better captures the "profoundly different qualities" of politics at the time than the party system model. Another alternative suggests there are a set of twelve "keys" to interpreting presidential elections. Each of these approaches, while they do emerge from valid criticisms of the party systems model, remains too vague to represent much of an improvement for the political historian and each seems to return in the direction of the discredited, traditional approach of the progressive historians in their emphasis on the distinctiveness of each election and the dominance of short-term economic effects on electoral outcomes.

References

Anderson, Kristi. 1979. *The Creation of a Democratic Majority, 1928–1936.* Chicago: U. of Chicago Pr.

Beard, Charles A. and Mary R. Beard. 1927. *The Rise of American Civilization.* 2 vols. New York: Macmillan.

Broder, David. 1972. *The Party's Over.* New York: Harper & Row.

Bryce, James. 1888. *The American Commonwealth.* 2 vols. New York: Macmillan.

Burner, David. 1968. *The Politics of Provincialism.* New York: Knopf.

Burns, James McGregor. 1973. *The Deadlock of Democracy: Four-Party Politics in America.* Englewood Cliffs: Prentice-Hall.

————. 1982–89. *The American Experiment.* 3 vols. New York: Knopf.

Chambers, William W. 1963. *Political Parties in a New Nation.* New York: Oxford U. Pr.

————, and W.D. Burnham. eds. 1967. *The American Party Systems.* New York: Oxford U. Pr.

Duverger, Maurice. 1954. *Political Parties.* New York: Wiley.

Eldersveld, Samuel. 1964. *Political Parties: A Behavioral Analysis.* Chicago: Rand, McNally.

Epstein, Leon D. 1986. *Political Parties in the American Mold.* Madison: U. of Wisconsin Pr.

Fiorina, Morris P. 1981. *Retrospective Voting in American National Elections.* New Haven: Yale U. Pr.

Formisano, Ronald P. 1982. *The Transformation of Political Culture.* New York: Oxford U. Pr.

Ginsberg, Benjamin, and Martin Shefter. 1990. *Politics By Other Means.* New York: Basic Books.

Gosnell, Harold F. 1937. *Machine Politics.* Chicago: U. of Chicago Pr.

Gould, Lewis L. 1986. *Reform and Regulation: American Politics from Roosevelt to Wilson.* New York: Knopf.

Hays, Samuel P. 1980. *American Political History as Social Analysis.* Knoxville: U. of Tennessee Pr.

Hofstadter, Richard. 1948. *The American Political Tradition.* New York: Knopf.

Holt, Michael F. 1993. *Political Parties and American Political Development from the Age of Jackson to the Age of Lincoln.* Baton Rouge: Louisiana State U. Pr.

Key, Jr., V.O. 1949. *Southern Politics in State and Nation.* New York: Knopf.

————. 1966. *The Responsible Electorate: Rationality in Presidential Voting, 1936–1960*. Cambridge: Harvard U. Pr.

Kleppner, Paul. 1979. *The Third Electoral System: Party Votes and Political Cultures*. Chapel Hill: U. of North Carolina Pr.

————. 1982. *Who Voted? The Dynamics of Electoral Turnout, 1870–1980*. New York: Praeger.

————. 1987. *Continuity and Change in Electoral Politics*. Westport, CT: Greenwood Pr.

————, et al. 1982. *The Evolution of American Electoral Systems*. Westport, CT: Greenwood Pr.

Ladd, Jr., Everett Carll, and Charles D. Hadley. 1975. *Transformations of the American Party System*. New York: Norton.

Lichtman, Allan J. 1990. *Thirteen Keys to the Presidency*. Lanham: Madison Books.

Lubell, Samuel. 1965. *The Future of American Politics*. New York: Harper & Row.

McCormick, Richard L. 1986. *The Party Period and Public Policy*. New York: Oxford U. Pr.

McCormick, Richard P. 1966. *The Second American Party System*. Chapel Hill: U. of North Carolina Pr.

McGerr, Michael E. 1986. *The Decline of Popular Politics: The American North, 1865–1928*. New York: Oxford U. Pr.

McSeveney, Samuel T. 1972. *The Politics of Depression: Voting Behavior in the Northeast, 1893–1896*. New York: Oxford U. Pr.

Mazmanian, Daniel. 1974. *Third Parties in Presidential Elections*. Washington, DC: Brookings.

Nie, Norman H., Sidney Verba, and John R. Petrocik. 1976. *The Changing American Voter*. Cambridge: Harvard U. Pr.

Ostrigorski, Moisi Y. 1902. *Democracy and the Organization of Political Parties*. New York: Macmillan.

Patterson, James T. 1967. *Congressional Conservatism and the New Deal*. Lexington: U. of Kentucky Pr.

Phillips, Kevin. 1969. *The Emerging Republican Majority*. New Rochelle, NY: Arlington House.

Ranney, Austin. 1975. *Curing the Mischiefs of Faction: Party Reform in America*. Berkeley: U. of California Pr.

Reichley, A. James. 1992. *The Life of the Parties*. New York: Free Pr.

Rosenstone, Steven J. 1980. *Who Votes?* New Haven: Yale U. Pr.

Sabato, Larry. 1988. *The Party's Just Begun*. Glenview, IL: Scott Foresman.

Schattschneider, E. E. 1942. *Party Government*. New York: Reinhart.

———. 1960. *The Semi-Sovereign People*. New York: Holt, Reinhart, and Winston.

Schlesinger, Jr., Arthur M. 1945. *The Age of Jackson*. Boston: Little Brown.

———. 1986. *The Cycles of American History*. Boston: Houghton Mifflin.

Silbey, Joel. 1985. *The Partisan Imperative: The Dynamics of American Politics Before the Civil War*. New York: Oxford U. Pr.

———. 1992. *The American Political Nation, 1838–1893*. Stanford: Stanford U. Pr.

———, Allan Bogue, and William Flanigan. eds. 1978. *The History of American Electoral Behavior*. Princeton: Princeton U. Pr.

Shafer, Byron E. ed. *The End of Realignment? Interpreting American Electoral Eras*. Madison: U. of Wisconsin Pr.

Sisson, Daniel. 1974. *The American Revolution of 1800*. New York: Knopf.

Stave, Bruce. 1970. *The New Deal and the Last Hurrah*. Pittsburgh: U. of Pittsburgh Pr.

Sundquist, James. 1968. *Politics and Policy*. Washington, DC: Brookings.

———. 1983. *Dynamics of the Party System: Alignment and Realignment of Political Parties in the United States*. Washington, DC: Brookings.

Young, James Sterling. 1968. *The Washington Community, 1800–1828*. New York: Columbia U. Pr.

CHAPTER 1

Republicanism and the First American Party System

Richard Beeman

While many issues were left unsettled at the Constitutional Convention of 1787, all of the delegates present agreed that they were creating a "republican" form of government. The meanings that those delegates attached to their republican faiths differed significantly, but at least a few essential components of republican ideology were embraced by virtually everyone at the Convention. At its core the republican consensus was a negative one, embodying the rejection of two important principles that lay at the foundation of the Americans' English heritage—the principles of hereditary monarchy and hereditary aristocracy. The republican alternative to those hereditary norms was "representative democracy," but within that concept lay a multitude of alternative meanings, ranging from direct democracy to a system in which the people's role in the selection and oversight of public officeholders was extremely limited.

The end toward which republican governments were to be directed was the public good. As John Adams noted, "There must be a positive Passion for the Public Good [and] the Public Interest . . . established in the Minds of the People, or there can be no Republican Government, nor any real liberty." In fact, considerable debate split Americans over the best means by which to balance the public good with personal liberty (and, indeed, debate over what the proper doses of those commodities should be), but most of the revolutionary leaders present in the Constitutional Convention had a relatively traditional view of that equation. Reacting to the threat posed by Shays's Rebellion, the delegates wished to create an "energetic" government capable of maintaining the public order in the face of the licentious behavior of the great mass of the citizenry. And, believing in the principle of the "filtration of talent," they created governmental structures—for example, the indirect election of the U.S. Senate and of the chief executive—that gave a broad popular base to the central government and at the same time removed officeholders in certain arms of the government from the direct influence of the passions of the people.

In the dozen years following the adoption of the Constitution in 1788, as the new central government began to operate, the framers' original conception of that Constitution underwent a dramatic transformation. This transformation would significantly alter the structures of many of the essential governmental agencies created by the framers; it would change the relationship between those serving in the government and their constituents; and, most important, it would reshape Americans' understanding of what "republicanism" really meant. The agencies for these dramatic changes were the Republican and Federalist parties, entirely novel entities unimagined by and distasteful to the framers of 1787.

The initial differences over public policy that would lead to the development of institutionalized political parties were provoked by differing conceptions of the meaning of "federalism" as articulated by the Founding Fathers. As the new federal government began to do its job, and as the policies and ideological perspectives of President George Washington's Secretary of the Treasury Alexander Hamilton appeared to veer toward a definition of federalism in which the balance of power between the central and the state governments shifted dramatically in favor of the central, opposition within the halls of Congress and occasionally within the legislatures of the individual states began to surface.

The initial core of opposition to Hamilton's policies consisted of those Anti-Federalists who had feared the Constitution's centralizing tendencies from its very inception. Those Anti-Federalists were joined, however, by growing numbers of former Federalists, who had come to recognize that many of the Anti-Federalists' warnings about the powers of the new government were justified. The ranks of former Federalist supporters of the Constitution in the new U.S. Congress were seriously split during the debate over Hamilton's plan calling for the central government not only to fund the continental debt at full value plus interest, but also to assume responsibility for the payment of the Revolutionary War debts of the individual states. Opposition to the proposal was particularly strong in the South, and even such staunch nationalists as James Madison came to oppose Hamilton's plan. The grounds for opposition were complex: Some opposed the funding proposal because it failed to distinguish between original holders of the continental debt and those speculators who had purchased it subsequently at depreciated prices; nearly all who opposed the assumption of state debts did so on the grounds that it was unconstitutional, believing that to give to the central government the power to meddle in the financial affairs of the individual states would, in the words of Virginia Senator William Grayson, leave the states with little else to do "but to eat, drink, and be merry." Hamilton's proposals ultimately won congressional assent, but only after some behind-the-scenes negotiating that guaranteed to southern congressmen a more southerly location for the nation's capital in the newly created District of Columbia, rather than near Philadelphia, as previously planned.

The divisions in Congress over funding and assumption became even sharper in the aftermath of the debate over Hamilton's proposal for a national bank. The bill chartering the First Bank of the United States passed Congress by a nearly two-to-one margin, but opponents of the Hamiltonian plan had raised questions about whether the central government was constitutionally empowered to give a monopoly to a private, profit-making corporation simply because the existence of such a corporation might facilitate the government's financial business. At this point, President Washington issued his well-known request to both his Secretary of Treasury and his Secretary of State Thomas Jefferson for opinions on the bank bill's constitutionality. Both Hamilton and Jefferson based their opinions on the "necessary and proper clause" of the Constitution, but each read that clause in a radically different way: Jefferson arguing for a "strict construction" doctrine and Hamilton for a "broad construction" of those powers necessary and proper to effect the explicitly enumerated powers granted to the Congress.

Jefferson's and Hamilton's opposing interpretations of constitutional doctrine reflected sharply diverging understandings of the meaning of "federalism," and their understandings would in some important respects prefigure the shape of the debate between nationalists and the defenders of state rights for decades to come. Furthermore, and important to note, is that the terms of the debate were still couched in a traditional republican language and within equally traditional understandings of the way governments were supposed to function. It was a debate carried out primarily among well-established members of the political elite, who differed among themselves on how they might best order the affairs of their country. Few people on either side felt any need to resort to appeals beyond the bounds of the national legislature, for they all tended to share a common assumption that the country's political destiny was best left to disinterested, wise, and virtuous leaders like themselves and not to the great mass of the citizens whom they served.

The language that the proponents of each side in the debate used was, quite strikingly, the language of traditional republicanism. Hamiltonian "broad" constructionists argued that payment of the continental and state debts was a matter of "morality and justice"; a failure to honor those financial obligations would be to "render all rights precarious and to introduce a general dissipation and corruption of morals." Hamiltonians defended the national bank in similarly moralistic terms, calling it essential for the defense of the national credit, a "sacred" obligation. Opponents were equally hyperbolic in identifying the "unrepublican" features of Hamilton's plans. Jefferson charged that the "ultimate object of [Hamilton's financial system] is to prepare the way for a change, from the present republican form of government to that of a monarchy," and both he and Madison argued that the bank and the funding and assumption bills would lead toward a "consolidated government" that would sacrifice the public interest to those of the monied aristocracy.

The early debates in Congress over the precise meaning of the new Federalist system, however acrimonious they may have been, certainly did not suggest the abandonment of one conception of politics for another. While Madison and Jefferson were inclined to be increasingly critical of Hamilton's personal motives as well as of the substance of his policies, such personal animus was inseparable from the traditional, elite-dominated political discourse of the age. And as much as Jefferson and Madison may have lamented their defeats at Hamilton's hands, they were nevertheless generally comfortable with the traditional structure within which their contests with Hamilton took place. Nevertheless, in a few years, with the injection of issues of foreign policy and national defense into the political arena, the grounds of debate would shift well beyond the constitutional imperatives of "federalism" to embrace such fundamental issues as the future of America's experiment in independence and the very meaning of revolutionary republicanism itself.

At first glance it would seem puzzling that political divisions over matters of foreign policy would provide the catalyst for the conversion from elite-dominated to mass-based democratic politics in America. The American people in the late eighteenth century were hardly a cosmopolitan lot and they had certainly not kept a close eye on the actions of other nations around the world in the past. Yet the foreign policy issues of the 1790s—and questions of America's proper relationship with the two major European powers, England and France, in particular—would cause the narrowly defined constitutional and sectional divisions in the First and Second Congresses to be transformed into intensely emotional, broadly based popular divisions in the years between 1793 and 1801. The only way to explain the intensity and pervasiveness of the ideological debate generated during that period is to understand the conflict over American foreign policy not merely as a set of diplomatic policy decisions facing the young nation but, more importantly, as a searching debate about the meaning of America's revolutionary experience itself, a debate that would in the final analysis transform the structure of American political life and at the same time alter the definitions that many Americans gave to their republican faith.

In April 1793, with the outbreak of yet another armed conflict between England and France, the newly formed government of the United States found itself, quite against its natural predilection, thrown into the balance of power struggles in Europe. America's revolutionary ally, France, by the terms of the Franco-American treaty of 1778, believed that it had a right to expect substantive aid from the Americans in its struggle against their mutual enemy. George Washington's Secretary of State Thomas Jefferson was inclined to agree; while he did not advocate direct military involvement for America, Jefferson did believe that America's diplomatic and spiritual ties to the republican government of revolutionary France at least required some public expression of support for the people of that nation.

Others in the Washington administration had different ideas. Hamilton, arguing forcefully that treaties should remain in force only so long as they served a nation's interest, insisted that the government should "temporarily and provisionally suspend" the Franco-American alliance. Washington, as he did in nearly all of the important decisions during his two administrations, reached an independent judgment on the matter; nevertheless, he took a position much closer to Hamilton's than Jefferson's. The Proclamation of Neutrality of 1793 declared America's intention to conduct itself in a manner "friendly and impartial toward the belligerent powers," but, given the reality of America's well-established economic relationships with England, the Proclamation was justifiably viewed by many as a betrayal both of existing treaty obligations and, more important, of America's commitment to the principles of revolutionary republicanism. For the rest of the decade, in reaction first to the Proclamation of Neutrality, then to the treaty of "amity and commerce" that Federalist John Jay negotiated with Great Britain in 1794, and finally in the repercussions flowing from that treaty in 1797 and 1798 (when France pursued an exceedingly belligerent policy toward American shipping on the high seas) Americans would debate their relationship with those two European powers.

The rhetorical ingredients of that debate suggest that Americans were still a long way from reaching a common understanding about where the logic of their revolutionary republican ideology was taking them. Some of the features of the debate suggest that both the Federalists and the emerging Jeffersonian Republican party were still working within the same traditional/classical republican framework and drawing on precisely the same themes based on that language for their attacks on their opponents. Both a preoccupation with "virtue" and corruption and an abhorrence of "party" and "faction" infected the debate; Federalists and Republicans alike seemed obsessed with the notion that their opponents had lost their virtue and denounced their adversary's attempts at political organization as a sure sign of the corrosive effects of a lust for power.

Other aspects of the debate suggest that Republicans and Federalists were drawing on different aspects of the same traditional language. The Federalists, committed to the notion that the public good required the restraint of private interests and private passions, condemned the disorderly and self-interested opposition of the Republicans. They were particularly alarmed at the Republicans' attachment to revolutionary France, believing that anarchy, atheism, and the consequent destruction of virtue among that country's citizenry were the inevitable results of excessively popular modes of government. Beginning with the passage of the Alien and Sedition Acts in 1798 and continuing through the election of 1800, the Federalists became even more hysterical in their fear that the combination of Republican loyalty to revolutionary France and the disorderly character of the Republican opposition to government policy at home would lead to anarchy within America. For their part the Republicans tended to draw on the antimonarchical, antiaristocratic aspects of traditional republican language, condemning the Federalists for their close ties with the "monocrats" of England and arguing that their opponents were using their control of the executive branch to install themselves as a permanent, hereditary cabal.

Both the Republican and Federalist languages were what a historian might expect to emerge from political combat anywhere in the Anglo-American world at nearly any time in the eighteenth century, yet indications were that some within the emerging Republican party had begun to employ a new language—one predicated on a new set of assumptions about the relationship between a government and its citizenry. It is more closely related to what analysts have come to identify as liberal capitalism than to the traditional concerns of classical republicanism. Some Republicans explicitly rejected the Federalists' call for an "energetic" government, claiming that such government accounted for "all those rigid codes of law that have subverted the natural liberties of mankind." Rejecting the classical republican assumption that private interests must be suppressed in the name of the public good, many Republicans came to the conclusion that the collective actions of "free and independent men," unimpeded by the weight of government regulation and repression, would in themselves result in the greatest public good for the greatest number. Individualistic, utilitarian, and egalitarian, theirs was a doctrine pointing in a very different direction from the one impelling men like John Adams or Alexander Hamilton to call for restraints on personal liberty for the sake of public order.

Students of the period must be careful not to draw too sharp a distinction between Republican and Federalist ideological perspectives, for not all Republicans during the 1790s were not ideologically wedded to "liberalism." Ample evidence points to the fact that many Republicans as well as Federalists were slow to abandon classical republican notions of virtue, disinterestedness, and opposition to party in their rhetorical stances, and some would argue that the economic policies of Hamilton rather than those of Jefferson were in the forefront of the development of liberal capitalism in America. Whatever the ambiguities in the Republicans' and Federalists' own understanding of what they were doing and where they were heading, their actual behavior—first in Congress and ultimately among the electorate at large—was clearly leading them in very new directions.

As early as 1793 opposition leaders like Jefferson and Madison were referring to a "republican interest" in the country, and while they hotly denied charges that they were fomenting a "party spirit" in the country, their actions displayed a self-consciousness of purpose that was hardly in keeping with traditional republican notions of disinterested, elite decisionmaking. The contradictions between the Republican opposition's rhetoric and the reality of their organizational efforts is ironic. Clear in both the private correspondence and the public statements of opposition leaders is their rejection of a mass-based, popular party system. Rather, as a minority faction in the national Congress (and likely to remain a minority so long as George Washington continued to lend his considerable prestige to the policies of Hamilton), the Republicans turned to popular appeals to the electorate out of desperation. The methods they used would eventually become the standard devices of political organization throughout America: town and county meetings in which the opinions of the citizenry on American foreign policy were shaped, collected, and mobilized; the self-conscious use of the press to promote the policies and candidates of their party; and, finally, the creation of extragovernmental institutions (congressional nominating caucuses, state and local party committees, legions of precinct workers) to recruit ordinary citizens at the local level into the political process.

The broad outlines of the institutional development of the first American party system are now well established. As indicated above, a growing consciousness of basic constitutional divisions between strict constructionists and broad constructionists appeared as early as the First Congress, but voting in that Congress was strictly factional; moreover, the factional alignments in the First Congress according to broad issues of ideology and national policy were short-lived. The overall levels of agreement among former Federalists and former Anti-Federalists in the First Congress stood only at about 55 percent, just a few percentage points higher than the levels of agreement *between* members of those two camps (49 percent). By contrast, cohesion among the various regional and sectional voting blocs in the First Congress was much more striking and durable.

By the period 1794–1797, however, the transition from factions to parties is clear in the voting behavior of the representatives to Congress. During those years shifting factional alignments gave way to voting behavior that was much more consistently partisan. More and more often, congressmen self-consciously identified themselves as either Federalists or Republicans, and levels of voting agreement among members of each of those camps rose to about 75 percent. At this stage in the evolution of parties in Congress, the range of issues capable of producing partisan behavior was still relatively circumscribed, encompassing primarily those issues of economic and foreign policy that touched obviously on the Federalists' and Republicans' differing views of America's future.

During the period 1797–1801 the consistency of party voting in Congress increased markedly; during the two Congresses preceding the presidential election of 1800, party cohesiveness within Federalist and Republican ranks had increased to 85 percent, a level of partisan voting behavior that exceeds even present-day patterns. As an interpreter might expect from these rates of party cohesion, the range of issues affected by partisan voting had widened considerably, including not only questions of foreign policy, economic policy, and constitutional interpretation but also a number of purely "partisan" questions relating to the aggrandizement of political power within the bureaucratic structures of the executive, legislative, and judicial branches.

These developments have persuaded most students of the period that parties in Congress were well developed by the end of the eighteenth century. Great debate, however, continues over whether a fully developed party system reaching down into the electorate had come into being. Many scholars, pointing to the incomplete character of the party structures at the local level and the persistence of antiparty rhetoric among leaders of both the Federalist and Republican parties, have concluded that while some "party voting" took place in Congress, a full-fledged "party system" did not come into being in America during the 1790s.

To some extent these questions are semantical ones, depending upon the definition of "party," but the heart of the problem is whether the more partisan character of political debate and political organization in the 1790s caused a fundamental transformation in people's conceptions of the political process itself. And the evidence on that question is mixed.

The transformation of American politics was closely tied to two concepts—democracy and nationalism—and both of those concepts came to play an increasingly important role in the political process well before the new government commenced operation in 1789. The forces working for democratization of the political process had been at work in America long before the Revolution, and to some considerable extent the acceptance of a tradition of popular politics was an important precondition to the development of popular political parties. The extent to which democratic styles of politics were accepted varied considerably from region to region; however, and not surprisingly, the extent to which "party" politics filtered down to the electorate at large depended in large measure on the extent to which the various regions had a previous tradition of popular politics.

New York and Philadelphia, for example, had already taken important steps toward a nondeferential, issue-oriented system of politics before the new national government started operation, and when the divisive issues of the 1790s first appeared, the organizers of the Federalist and Republican "interests" mobilized the electorate in support of their respective positions relatively easily. By contrast, the southern states had a long tradition of deferential, elite-dominated politics. As a consequence, while southern representatives were among the most aggressive in promoting the Republican interest in Congress during the 1790s, the conduct and content of the political discourse at the local level continued to display many "preparty" features. While many of the structures of partisan politics (party newspapers, state and county committees) came into being in the southern states, the actual conduct of elections in the South continued to be dominated by traditional factors of personality and prestige.

The change in focus from a provincial to a national politics within America was much less well advanced by the 1790s, but that process was nevertheless underway well before the framers met in Philadelphia to deliberate on a national government. The imperatives of resistance and, finally, of revolution, forced

Americans out of a purely provincial view of their political destinies. Indeed, many of the debates of the 1790s—particularly those centering on the strict constructionist/broad constructionist division on constitutional interpretation and those relating to America's relationship with the European powers—were in a significant way extensions of debates begun during the period of the Revolution. Obviously, the creation of a strengthened central government provided a much more clearly focused forum for the resolution of those long-standing questions, and the subsequent emergence of parties in the national Congress would accelerate the tendency to place "national" rather than "local" issues at the center of the political consciousness of Americans. Indeed, one of the ironies of the development of the first American party system is that the principal initiators of that system—the Republican party—stood unambiguously for the return of power to state and local agencies of government, but the very necessity to organize politically in order to deal with issues coming out of the national Congress would itself tend to direct the popular sensibility toward a "national" rather than a "local" agenda.

As was the case in the democratization of American politics, the nationalization of the political discourse occurred unevenly throughout the country. The residents of America's urban and commercial centers were probably the first to fix their sights firmly on the central government and on issues of national policy as the primary focus of attention, while citizens of the vast expanse of backcountry, stretching from northern New England down into the Carolinas, remained determinedly provincial long after the structures of party organization had been put in place.

The events during the 1790s that did the most to accelerate both the democratization and nationalization of American politics and, indeed, to change radically the way in which Americans regarded their relationship with the government, were the presidential elections of 1796 and 1800. When the Founding Fathers created the electoral college, they had in mind a system of indirect election whereby virtue and disinterestedness would triumph over passion and interest; but beginning in 1796, and reaching a white-hot fever of partisan vituperation and mobilization in 1800, the leaders of the

Federalist and Republican parties directed all of their energies to creating a system in which the role of ordinary voters in the election of the president was direct and immediate. Likewise, the role of the disinterested and virtuous electors envisioned by the framers ended up being reduced to that of mere agents of the will of the party. Although the rhetoric of those elections continued to resonate with traditional themes of personal virtue and disinterested pursuit of the public good, and though leaders of each of the parties continued to preach an antiparty ideology, the extent of popular mobilization around a set of national issues and national symbols that occurred during these elections was absolutely unprecedented.

The role of "party" in American politics reached a temporary high point during the election of 1800. After Jefferson's election and with the subsequent demise of the Federalists, party cohesiveness in Congress would decline markedly during the first two decades of the nineteenth century. The emergence of even more elaborately organized party structures during the period of the Second Party System would of course reverse that trend, but even during that better-developed phase of party organization, personal, sectional, and purely local considerations would confuse and confound party discipline. Throughout the period of the Second Party System, and, indeed, throughout all of American political history subsequently, presidential elections have served as the occasions when the efforts of party both in and out of Congress have been most concerted and most effective.

When Thomas Jefferson delivered his inaugural address on the steps of the still-unfinished national capitol in March 1801, he evoked themes that clearly exhibited the mixture of traditional and modern ideas that would guide American politics for the next several decades. The recurrent refrain of his address—his commitment to both "union and republican government"—tended to look backward to the antimonarchical, antiaristocratic heritage of the Revolution. And the most oft-quoted words in the address—"We are all Republicans, we are federalists"—expressed his desire to quell the spirit of "party" that had infected the political debate of the previous decade; though Jefferson's peaceful accession to power in 1801 would do much to establish the tradition of a "loyal opposition" in American politics, even Jefferson himself would continue to manifest an uneasiness about the party system that he had helped bring into being.

But while Jefferson and most other American politicians in the nineteenth century would continue to use the antiparty and antipower language of classical republicanism, the actual conduct of nineteenth-century politics suggests that a very different set of assumptions were at work. The outcome of elections to the Congress and, even more dramatically, to the chief executive's office, would increasingly be determined by concerted, partisan effort by professional politicians rather than by the inherent virtue of individual contestants. The principle of the "filtration of talent," whereby the voice of the people in the selection of public officials was to be muted and refined, was increasingly sacrificed to the practical needs of popular, partisan mobilization. While neither the Federalists nor the Republicans may have intended to give the American electorate such a direct and active role in the selection of public officials, that electorate, once empowered in such fashion, would be reluctant to resume its previous, deferential role. Thomas Jefferson, a well-born and wealthy gentryman born into a society that was wedded to "republican" virtues, probably greeted partisan popular politics with a mixture of anticipation and concern. Andrew Jackson, the product of a different culture in a different age, would embrace the imperatives of democratic partisan politics less equivocally.

References

Appleby, Joyce. 1984. *Capitalism and the New Social Order: The Republican Vision of the 1790s.* New York: New York U. Pr.

Bailyn, Bernard. 1967. *Ideological Origins of the American Revolution.* Cambridge: Belknap Pr.

Bell, Rudolph M. 1973. *Party and Faction in the House of Representatives.* Westport, CT: Greenwood Pr.

Buel, Richard. 1972. *Securing the Revolution: Ideology in American Politics.* Ithaca, New York: Cornell U. Pr.

Charles, Joseph. 1961. *Origins of the American Party System: Three Essays.* Williamsburg, VA: Institute of Early American History and Culture.

Cunningham, Noble. 1957. *The Jeffersonian Republicans: The Formation of Party Organization, 1789–1801.* Chapel Hill: U. of North Carolina Pr.

Hoadley, John F. 1986. *Origins of American Political Parties, 1789–1803.* Lexington: U. Pr. of Kentucky.

Hofstadter, Richard. 1969. *The Idea of a Party System: The Rise of Legitimate Opposition in the United States, 1780–1840.* Berkeley: U. of California Pr.

Miller, John C. 1960. *The Federalist Era, 1789–1801.* New York: Harpers.

Nichols, Roy F. 1967. *The Invention of Political Parties.* New York: Macmillan.

CHAPTER 2

The Jacksonian Party System

William G. Shade

The idea of a Jacksonian party system like that of "the Age of Jackson" is rather abstract. Andrew Jackson was, of course, the hero of New Orleans and a well-known Indian fighter. Although he was clearly the most popular of the four candidates in 1824, the House of Representatives chose John Quincy Adams to be President. Four years later, however, Jackson defeated Adams and began an eight-year term that divided the country on major issues such as Indian policy, money and banking, internal improvements, the tariff, land policy, and the federal government's response to the abolitionists. The opposition to Jackson on these matters gave rise to the Whig party that would contend with the Democrats over these same issues until the 1850s. This "Great Man approach," however, does little to show the organizational development of the American political system during these years. Parties and elections in the United States between 1824 and 1852 may also be looked upon in terms of the invention of modern parties through the evolution of the Second Party System.

Probably the best way to begin is with a narrative of generally accepted facts before attempting a general interpretation. Most historians have focused on presidential elections. In 1824 the four main candidates were all closely connected with James Monroe's administration. The poorly attended congressional caucus—led by Martin Van Buren—threw its support to the Secretary of the Treasury William H. Crawford. Various state legislatures nominated the Secretary of

State John Quincy Adams; the Speaker of the House Henry Clay; and Jackson, who was a senator from Tennessee at the time. After failing to obtain the necessary support in the Middle States, the former Secretary of War John C. Calhoun was nominated by Pennsylvania as the sole candidate for vice-president. When none of the four presidential candidates received a majority in the electoral college, the election devolved upon the House, which chose Adams, despite Jackson's plurality of both popular and electoral votes.

Jackson felt cheated by a "corrupt bargain" after the newly elected president chose Clay, who had thrown his support to Adams in the House, to be Secretary of State—the traditional stepping stone to the presidency. Jackson vowed to defeat Adams in 1828 and in the course of the intervening years gained the support of Van Buren and those who had supported Crawford. With an improved organization and united support of the congressional "opposition" to the Adams administration, Jackson won the election with 56 percent of the popular vote and more than twice the electoral vote of Adams. Calhoun was reelected to the vice-presidency over Richard Rush who was running with Adams.

Four years later Jackson, running with Van Buren, defeated Clay and John Sergeant. This election also included the first real "third party" in a presidential election and the introduction of the national nominating convention at which the "Democratic Antimasons" chose William Wirt and Amos Ellmaker as their candidates. Actually, Clay and Sergeant were anointed by a convention of "National Republicans." Finally, the "Republican Delegates of the states of the Union" met in Baltimore to nominate a vice-presidential candidate, in this case Van Buren, to run with Jackson. Calhoun had broken with Jackson and eventually resigned the vice-presidency to return to the Senate and defend Nullification.

While Jackson received only slightly fewer popular votes than he had in 1828, the returns were complicated by the participation of the Antimasons. Eight states saw three different tickets in the field, and in others deals were made between Clay and the Antimasons. In the electoral college Jackson won by a much larger margin over Clay than he had over Adams. South

Carolina cast its votes for Virginia governor John Floyd and Henry Lee of Massachusetts. Pennsylvania's electors voted for Jackson but rejected Van Buren in favor of a favorite son.

Such party confusion multiplied during the election of 1836. In preparation for the election, the "Democratic Republicans" met in a rather irregularly attended convention in 1835 to support the elevation of Van Buren and to choose a running mate. Against the wishes of Virginia, they selected Jackson's favorite, Richard Mentor Johnson of Kentucky, equally famous for possibly killing the Indian chief Tecumseh and for having a mulatto mistress. From 1834 on, the diverse opponents of "King Andrew" began to refer to themselves as "Whigs." In 1836 this coalition called no convention, set no platform, and organized no national party. Traditional methods of nomination produced three opposition candidates who together received 49 percent of the popular vote. The name Whig was not universally used by the opposition and one candidate, Hugh Lawson White, even denied being a Whig. The electoral college saw further confusion when South Carolina exercised her right of eccentricity and Virginia's Van Buren electors refused to support Johnson. In all, five presidential candidates and eight tickets received electoral votes. For the only time in American history, the Senate was asked to choose the vice-president and, by a vote of 33 to 16, picked Johnson who had a clear plurality among the electors.

Although famous for log cabins and hard cider, buncombe and ballyhoo, the election of 1840 ushered in a new period in the organization of presidential politics as well as a new style of campaigning. Both major parties held conventions. Whigs meeting in Harrisburg in 1839 overlooked their party's best-known figure, Henry Clay. Instead they chose William Henry Harrison of Ohio and the Virginian John Tyler. Harrison had been the leading opposition candidate in 1836, and Tyler had received 47 electoral votes for the vice-presidency that year. Although the Whigs nominated a balanced ticket, they foreswore writing a platform. When the Democrats met the following year, they renominated Van Buren and drew up what most historians consider to be the first modern platform designed to propound the principles of limited government and to allay southern fears about a northern candidate. The Democrats, however, did not pick a vice-presidential candidate. Opposition to Johnson led them to leave the choice up to each state's electors. Harrison swept the famous log cabin campaign, polling nearly four times more electoral votes than Van Buren, although he only took 53 percent of the popular vote.

After that date, presidential and vice-presidential nominations were usually contested within party conventions, and generally uniform partisan support was given to the chosen candidates. Conventions also adopted the practice of drawing up platforms formally expressing the party's basic principles, a feature clearly evident in the election of 1844. In convention, "the American Democracy" rejected their front-runner, Van Buren, in favor of a dark horse, James K. Polk, and drew up a platform that included, along with traditional party principles, the famous demand for "the reoccupation of Oregon and the re-annexation of Texas." The Whig convention nominated Clay and New Jersey minister and congressman Theodore Frelinghuysen, on a rather brief quasi-platform reiterating the principles associated with their candidate. By far the longest platform in 1844 was that of the Liberty party. This third party had grown out of the abolitionist movement of the 1830s and had made a modest effort in the election of 1840; it also met in convention to pick as candidates a former Alabama slaveholder, James G. Birney, and Thomas Morris of Ohio. Although they won only slightly over 2 percent of the popular vote, the Liberty party decisively affected the election by drawing enough votes away from Clay in New York to give the state and the election to Polk. Not one elector in the electoral college deviated from supporting his party's ticket.

This pattern was repeated in both 1848 and 1852, and so for the most part were the other changes just mentioned. At the same time, national committees began to play a role. By 1848 the Mexican War and the Wilmot Proviso (outlawing slavery in any acquired territory) had split both parties but most particularly, the Democrats. To reunify the party, the Democratic convention produced a moderate and balanced ticket of northerner Lewis Cass and southerner William O. Butler and a platform steering away from the proviso in the direction of popular sovereignty. The Whigs, meeting in Baltimore, followed a different strategy, putting forward Mexican War hero Zachary Taylor, a slaveholder from Louisiana, and New York moderate Millard Fillmore. They chose not to write a platform given the fact that their candidate Taylor had never voted in a national election, although he assured party leaders that he was a Whig "in principle." The proviso controversy involved a crucial split in the Democratic party that was not patched over by the convention. A significant number of Democrats—mostly New York Van Burenites who were called "Barnburners"—joined with Whig dissidents and former supporters of the Liberty party to form the Free Soil party. At their New York City convention, the Free Soilers named a ticket of ex-President Van Buren and Charles Francis Adams, John Quincy's son, and drew up a platform that reflected their motto "Free Soil, Free Speech, Free Labor, and Free Men." While Van Buren's 10 percent of the popular vote won the Free Soil ticket no electoral votes, it eased Taylor's victory.

Most of the administrations of Taylor (who died in 1850) and Fillmore were taken up with the debates that led to the Compromise of 1850 and the subsequent struggle between Unionists and radicals in the southern states. Both Democrats and Whigs attempted to silence agitation over the slavery question and to bring about both national and party unity. After 49 ballots, the Democratic convention in 1852 settled on Franklin Pierce—the "Young Hickory of the Granite Hills"—for president and William R. King of Alabama as his running mate on a platform affirming the Compromise of 1850. The Whigs once again looked to a Mexican War hero, General Winfield Scott, as their presidential candidate. William A. Graham of North Carolina was their vice-presidential candidate. The Whigs' somewhat unusual platform tilted in the direction of states' rights and in extremely convoluted language supported the compromise and opposed agitation of the slavery question in the interest of "the nationality of the Whig Party and of the Union." The remnant of the Free Soil party minus the New York Barnburners met in Pittsburgh to nominate John P. Hale, who had stepped aside in favor of Van Buren four years earlier, and George W. Jullian, both northerners. The platform of the "Free Democracy" differed radically from those of the major parties in that it repudiated the Compromise of 1850 and called slavery "a sin against God and a crime against man." This platform was also much more comprehensive in the discussion of policies unrelated to slavery. Hale was able to gain only a bit over 5 percent of the popular vote, and the Free Democrats seem to have had little impact on Pierce's overwhelming victory. While the popular vote was much closer, Pierce and King received 254 votes in the electoral college in contrast to 42 cast for Scott and Graham. The presidential election of 1852 would be the last to feature a contest between Democrats and Whigs.

The presidential elections from 1824 to 1852 fall into two groups, each of which represents a distinctly different phase of party development. The correlation among the areas that showed support for Jackson in the first three of these elections— Phase I (1824–1832)—was relatively high, but bore little relation to the areas of Van Buren's strength in 1836. That election began a new and relatively stable era—Phase II (1840–1852)—in which the distributions of Democratic strength from one election to the next were highly intercorrelated.

The election of 1836 was a transitional one that reflected some of the characteristics of both phases. Turnout in the last two elections of Phase I and in 1836 was moderately high (approximately 55 percent of those eligible), but it lagged below that for state elections. Phase II initiated a fifty-year period of high and consistent popular interest in American presidential elections. Accompanying the jump in turnout (to 78 percent of those eligible in 1840) was a shift in the sectional patterns of party support. The elections of Phase I were distinctly sectional; the candidates obviously appealed to different parts of the country. New England went radically one way in each of these elections while the slave South leaned in the opposite direction. The Second Party System evolved with each successive presidential election, spreading from the Middle States where it appeared in 1828, to New England in 1832, and penetrating the South finally in 1836.

But historians following Frederick Jackson Turner have generally overemphasized the political importance of "sections" in the 1820s and 1830s. States were the most important entities, and most evidence of sectionalism—with the exception of slavery—represented only short-term shared interests of sets of contiguous states. In the first place most states gave their vote heavily to one candidate, with little intrastate competition. Where competition did exist, it did not reflect the development of two national parties. In 1832 the voters of four states split their votes among three candidates. Voters in only six states in that election decided real two-ticket contests, but the same tickets did not battle in each of these states. Four years later, the number of two-ticket contests doubled, and the confusion of tickets increased.

A new phase characterized by high turnout and two-party competition in all of the states (except South Carolina) appeared in 1840: The nature of the presidential contest changed from one rooted in cohesive state interests to one structured by national parties that penetrated into the states. This change came in two distinct steps: competition appeared in most states between 1832 and 1836; and participation increased between 1836 and 1840. While the latter was undoubtedly influenced by the economic miseries attending the Panic of 1837, shifts in the partisan allegiances of social classes had little to do with these changes.

Between 1824 and 1832 the vote for Jackson fluctuated widely from state to state—in fact, he received no votes in New Hampshire in 1824 and all of those cast in Mississippi in 1832. A similar wide range characterized Van Buren's vote in 1836; after 1840 the difference between the states giving the highest and lowest Democratic vote seldom exceeded 10 percent, and generally it was within a 5 percent range. Similarly, the Adams vote in 1828 correlated only moderately with both the Adams vote in 1824 and the Clay vote in 1832, and the later was not correlated with the vote for any of the candidates in 1836. In contrast, relatively high correlations existed between elections for both parties from 1840 to 1852.

If one moves from the nation with the states as the units of analysis to the states with the counties as the unit of analysis, then the difference between the two phases becomes even clearer. While a variety of patterns existed in both phases, what stands out is the diversity of these patterns in the first phase and their basic similarity in the second phase. The seeming stability of the presidential elections in Phase I masks intrastate volatility through 1836. Only after the late 1830s did American parties exhibit the stability that historians invariably have associated with them. In terms of the development of the Second Party System, Phase I was characterized by a diversity of responses in turnout and distribution of the vote within the states, while Phase II witnessed a uniformity of voter behavior throughout the country. Phase II did not owe to sectional responses but rather to the growth of party development within each state. Not only did New Jersey differ from Pennsylvania in Phase I, but both also differed from New York. Missouri and Alabama followed fairly similar patterns in the presidential elections of Phase I, but each differed from the neighboring states of Illinois and Mississippi. Virginia differed from North Carolina.

Although state gubernatorial and legislative elections did not occur at the same time as presidential elections, they also reflect two phases of development that roughly coincide with those discussed above. State politics in Phase I was for the most part a factional and personal politics that was dominated by intrastate regional conflict. Elections and legislatures were dominated by cliques such as the Albany Regency in New York (although Tammany Hall controlled New York City), the Richmond Junto in Virginia, and the Nashville Junto in Tennessee. Pennsylvania politics pitted the "Family party" against the "Amalgamation party." Georgia was run by the "Royal party." In Arkansas, opponents charged that the territory was in the hands of a clique colorfully designated "Ambrose Seivers' Hungry Kin." Similar groups often emerged to oppose the establishment, usually in the name of republicanism. In 1824 the People's party was organized in New York to demand popular election of presidential electors. In Kentucky the New Court "party" favored relief of debtors. In New York City the Workingmen's party was formed to oppose Tammany, and it served as a model for sporadic workingmen's parties in other cities and towns. The most successful of such groups was the Antimasons. In many states dubious organization generated gubernatorial elections that were contested by three or more candidates. By the late 1820s the convention system provided some formal organization for state parties in the Middle States where the idea of conventions had first taken root. In New

England, conventions coexisted with other forms of nomination beginning in the early 1830s, but not until the end of that decade did the system penetrate most southern and western states. Although the patterns of state party development differed from state to state, most state parties exhibited remarkably similar characteristics by 1840.

Historians have assumed a close relationship between state and federal elections. Local leaders sided with one candidate or the other, and it is well known that the Jacksonian candidacy in 1828 depended heavily on the alliance of the Albany Regency and the Richmond Junto. Generally, however, state and federal elections in Phase I were not closely correlated because of multiple candidacies in state elections and a general lack of continuity of organization from one election to the next. Several states at this time practiced what has been called "dual" politics, in which separate organizations contested state and federal elections. Gradually this situation gave way to a more stable relationship in Phase II. After the mid-1830s voters began to respond to candidates at both levels in a partisan fashion. Emerging was a sense of party identification that transcended the popularity of an individual; voters went to the polls with the conviction that they were either Democrats or Whigs.

The effect of partisanship in Congress fits roughly with the two phases found in the response of the electorate. While the party association of many congressional leaders was clear, the partisan affiliation of many congressmen is difficult to ascertain until at least the middle of Jackson's second term. From Monroe's presidency until the last two years of Jackson's (Phase I), patterns of voting behavior in Congress reflected high cohesion within state delegations, and given the kinds of issues under consideration—Indian removal, internal improvements, public lands, the Bank of the United States, and the tariff—one can readily understand why. Historians have had less difficulty comprehending this pattern or understanding why the Turnerians confused it with sectionalism than they have had explaining why they have come to favor a pattern structured by party. While Jackson, for example, wished to alter traditional policies in several areas, "Jacksonian" Congresses did not always go along. All in all we have little evidence to suggest that party structured the roll-call behavior of congressmen. After 1835 and throughout Phase II, party cohesion and competitiveness were generally high, although some fluctuation and slightly different patterns marked relations between the Democrats and the Whigs. Such partisanship reflected developing party institutions. In the late 1820s New Jersey, Delaware, and Ohio initiated the nomination of congressional candidates by party conventions, and the procedure gradually spread during the next decade. With the Twenty-fourth Congress in 1835, contests for the speakership of the House generally became two-party affairs. After that date only the elections of 1839 and 1849 (ones with sectional overtones) disrupt the pattern of well-managed party control. Finally, in 1846 the Senate made party organizations responsible for committee assignments. With these changes an altered conception of representation and a new legislative style emerged; independence gave way to party discipline. In dealing with one another, these "new" politicians demonstrated a flexibility in compromising on issues and a keen respect for manipulation of parliamentary procedures. In the mid-1840s, the Democrats annexed Texas, lowered the tariff, reinstituted the Independent Treasury, and prosecuted the Mexican War. These were party measures, and roll calls showed high Democratic cohesiveness and sharp conflict with an equally unified Whig opposition. Party unity and competitiveness were at their height in Congress in the mid-1840s. Even after 1849, when sectionalism increasingly intruded into congressional business, partisanship remained extremely important.

Generalizing about state legislative behavior is more difficult during these years, since relatively little systematic work has been done. While some locally popular candidates continued to run unopposed, the majority after the middle 1830s ran as major party candidates in fairly competitive elections. The scattered available roll calls tend to conform to the idea that, during Phase I, party as such had little effect upon any state legislation except appointments. Gradually, in Phase II partisan perspectives came to dominate in several areas (most particularly money and banking) before declining in relative importance at the end of the 1840s. At their height party cohesion and party dissimilarity in state legislatures were not equal to the levels in Congress. The difference between Phase I and Phase II can also be seen in constitutional conventions. The state constitutional conventions that created the western states in the 1810s and those up to that in Virginia in 1829 and 1830 were dominated by intrastate sectionalism. While sectionalism was never entirely absent and there was a good deal of antiparty rhetoric especially among the Whigs, partisanship dominated the Pennsylvania convention that met in 1837 and those of the other states that followed it in the 1840s and early 1850s. From the mid-1840s on, the *Democratic Review* laid out a nationwide program of reform that included an elective judiciary, biennial sessions of limited duration, limitations on spending, a strong veto, and opposition to banks that formed a basic part of the agenda in most of the conventions. During Phase II, especially in the mid-1840s, partisan conflict in state legislatures and constitutional conventions took on remarkably similar outlines from state to state.

In each state the Democrats and the Whigs assumed positions shared by their fellow partisans throughout the country. The behavior of the voters, however, reflected the unique social and economic situations within each of the states. The social basis of party politics in the South differed from that in the North. Yet, in distinct contrast to traditional views, recent voting studies from all parts of the country suggest that the relative wealth of citizens had little to do with their party preference.

In the North some occupational and status difference occurs between Whigs and Democrats; a strong Whiggish bias marked the wealthy in northern cities. But the major distinctions between the rank and file of Whig and Democratic voters grew from their relation to certain ethno-religious communities. For the most part recent studies counsel caution on such traditional conceptions as an "immigrant vote"; historians now reject as reductionist a stance that views denominational affiliation as an indicator of economic class only. Immigrants divided their vote in New York and Pennsylvania. In these states the "invisible immigrants"—the English, Scots, and Welsh—were Whigs. While the Irish and the German newcomers better fit the traditional picture of strong Democratic support, both groups were split by religious differences. The political behavior of Irish Catholics who were Democrats, virtually to the man, stood in sharp contrast to that of the Irish Protestants who were predominantly Whigs. Among Germans the minority sects, such as the Brethren and the Moravians, bitterly opposed the majority who were Lutheran, German Reformed, or Catholic. Such denominational differences continued to affect members of these ethnic groups even though they had lived in the United States for several generations. For all that, political behavior was also related to doctrinal disputes within denominations, a split that reflected differences in religious style. Most northern Presbyterians tended to be Whigs, but in the Middle States the Old School "party" leaned toward the Democrats. In Illinois, Baptists favoring home missions tended to be Whigs, while those who opposed home missions supported Jackson and his followers. Often these differences in religious style were only aspects of other forms of group hostility. In the lower Midwest, settlers from the upland South almost invariably clashed with the Yankees who moved into the area in the 1820s and 1830s. Generally these group conflicts had economic overtones as well, but the shared values and group perspectives of certain ethnocultural communities enabled their members to comprehend the meaning of political action in personally relevant terms. Even partisan response to economic issues must be understood in relation to the economic orientation consonant with the group's values.

In the South wealth seems to have had only a minor relation to political preference. The allegiance to the Democrats of the Germans in Virginia, the Catholics and foreign-born in Louisiana, the handful of Episcopalians and Presbyterians in Georgia and Arkansas, as well as the contrasting roles of the Germans and native-born Presbyterians in Missouri all point to the relevance of ethnic and religious differences in these states. But the dominance of Anglo-Protestants, particularly Methodists and Baptists, in most of the South, and the compartmentalized nature of religious outlooks in that section have frustrated historians' attempts at developing an ethno-religious synthesis. Studies of Mississippi, Alabama Georgia, Tennessee, North Carolina, and Virginia have connected Whig sentiments with those flourishing economic areas that had a commercial orientation toward the outside world. For example, southern cities and towns had a distinct Whiggish cast. Whigs often predominated in nonagricultural occupations, while those isolated completely from market forces were more likely to be Democrats. Yet leaders of both parties who were drawn from the social and economic elite retained a personal following that involved a combination of deference and the response of leaders to local needs. County studies emphasizing the importance of kin relationships—"friends and neighbors politics"—and the continuing impact throughout the South of intrastate regionalism suggest that certain aspects of Phase I were simply extended and redefined during Phase II to relate to national issues and the relevant market perspectives shared with their northern counterparts.

Hindsight enables historians to see that the presidential election of 1852 represented the last hurrah of the Whigs and that the Second Party System was in shambles by the end of 1854. Turnout had declined and competition was becoming less marked, especially in the Gulf States. Antisouthernism seemed to be on the rise in the North. At least one historian has equated the growth of the Second Party System to the spread of favorable attitudes toward party conflict and its decline to the widespread belief that the Whigs and Democrats presented an echo rather than a choice. Yet, on most grounds, the Whigs and the Second Party System seemed to remain viable, even after the defeat in 1852. The Whigs had received more votes than ever before and a larger percentage of the vote in the North. The party was still strong in Congress, the upper South, and in the North; it was more than a respectable minority. Shrewd politicians such as William Seward and Abraham Lincoln were not about to desert the ship, although both would soon become leaders of the Republican Party and the latter its first president.

Although some historians of the Jacksonian party system have understood the mid-1820s in terms of partisan realignment and 1828 as a critical election, others have pointed to some of the problems involved in applying twentieth-century concepts to the early nineteenth century. If the term "party" is applied loosely, however, it can be used to describe what was happening. The election of 1828 featured two candidates with a certain amount of new organizational support and a significant increase in voter interest. Although traditional party conflict, as it existed in the days of the Federalists and the Republicans, had been dormant for over a decade, former partisans split their allegiance between the two candidates. The followers of Jackson formed the core of what would become the Democratic party while the supporters of Adams would become the nucleus of the Whig Party. Jackson's presidency, moreover, did bring major changes in several areas of public policy that lasted until the Civil War. Yet the system went through two stages of development and, in Phase I, was hardly a "system" at all. Partisanship barely extended beyond presidential elections into Congress and had minimal impact on state government. During Phase II modern parties emerged and penetrated into the electoral and legislative politics of the states. While Jackson was no longer on the scene, he remained a symbolic presence.

References

Alexander, Thomas P. 1967. *Sectional Stress and Party Strength: A Study of Roll-Call Voting Patterns in the House of Representatives.* Nashville: Vanderbilt U. Pr.

Benson, Lee. 1961. *The Concept of Jacksonian Democracy: New York, a Test Case.* Princeton: Princeton U. Pr.

Chase, James S. 1973. *Emergence of the Presidential Nominating Convention, 1789–1832.* Urbana: U. of Illinois Pr.

Formisano, Ronald P. 1971. *The Rise of Mass Political Parties: Michigan, 1827–1861.* Princeton: Princeton U. Pr.

———. 1983. *The Transformation of American Political Culture: Massachusetts Parties, 1790s–1840s.* New York: Oxford U. Pr.

Levine, Peter. 1977. *Behavior of State Legislative Parties in the Jacksonian Era: New Jersey, 1829–1844.* Rutherford, NJ: Fairleigh Dickinson U. Pr.

McCormick, Richard P. 1966. *The Second American Party System: Party Formation in the Jacksonian Era.* Chapel Hill: U. of North Carolina Pr.

Remini, Robert. 1963. *The Election of Andrew Jackson.* Philadelphia: Lippincott.

Schlesinger, Arthur M., Jr., ed. 1973. *History of U.S. Political Parties.* 4 vols. New York: Chelsea House.

————, and Fred L. Israel, eds. 1971. *History of American Presidential Elections.* 3 vols. New York: Chelsea House.

Shade, William G. 1972. *Banks or No Banks: The Money Issue in Western Politics, 1832–1865.* Detroit: Wayne State U. Pr.

Sharp, James Roger. 1970. *The Jacksonians Versus the Banks: Politics in the States After the Panic of 1837.* New York: Columbia U. Pr.

Thornton, Mills, III. 1978. *Politics and Power in a Slave Society: Alabama, 1800–1860.* Baton Rouge: Louisiana State U. Pr.

Watson, Harry L. 1981. *Jacksonian Politics and Community Conflict: The Emergence of the Second American Party System in Cumberland County, North Carolina.* Baton Rouge: Louisiana State U. Pr.

CHAPTER 3

Formation of the Republican Party

William E. Gienapp

Since its formation more than a century ago, the Republican party has gained a durable place in American political life. Born during the political realignment of the 1850s, it was the first antislavery party in American history to win substantial popular support, and it quickly became a major political force. By the end of 1856, it had assumed the Whig party's former position as the major opposition party to the Democrats; four years later, in 1860, it was the strongest party in the nation and elected Abraham Lincoln as its first president. Since then, it has been a fixture in the American two-party system.

Viewed from the perspective of the war that loomed like a dark cloud on the political horizon during the 1850s, the rise of the Republican party seemed almost predestined. The party's formation, according to the traditional interpretation, was a direct response to the passage in May 1854 by the Democratic-controlled Congress of the Kansas-Nebraska Act, which repealed the 34-year-old Missouri Compromise's ban on slavery in the northern part of the Louisiana Purchase. Angered by this unexpected destruction of the compact of 1820, indignant Whigs, Democrats, and Free Soilers in the North flocked to the new Republican party, which took as its platform opposition to the expansion of slavery. According to the usual scenario, the party quickly replaced the crumbling Whig organization as the main anti-Democratic party in the nation, and after a narrow defeat in 1856, it swept to victory in 1860. In short, sectionalism, and especially the slavery expansion issue, galvanized by the Kansas-

Nebraska Act and reenforced by the ensuing violence in the
Kansas Territory, accounts for both the party's formation and its
widespread popular support.

In reality, however, the Republican party faced a difficult
struggle to survive, and during the first years of its existence,
like all previous antislavery parties, it seemed destined for an
early death. In 1854 and 1855, in those states where it existed, the
party met defeat almost everywhere. Instead, during these years
the fastest growing party in the North and in the nation—and
the primary rival to the Democrats—was the secret nativist
American party, popularly known as the Know-Nothings. Thus
the shift from Whiggery to Republicanism was not a
straightforward process, and the formation of the Republican
party was a much more complex, drawn out process than it is
usually portrayed.

The rise of the Republican party occurred in two stages,
each of which, while crucial to the party's ultimate success,
posed distinctly different problems. In the first stage, which
extended from the party's beginning through the presidential
election of 1856, the Republicans waged a desperate and, at first,
seemingly hopeless battle with the rival American party to
assume the position of the defunct Whig organization as the
major anti-Democratic party in the country. The Republicans'
amazing showing in that election sealed the doom of the
American organization and established the Republican party as
the second party in the two-party system. During the next stage,
which extended from the party's defeat in 1856 through the 1860
campaign, leaders sought to broaden the Republican coalition by
moderating and expanding the party's appeal and by bringing
additional groups into its ranks. Further conversions would
occur after 1860, but Abraham Lincoln's victory represented the
culmination of the Republicans' rapid rise to power. In many
ways, that the Republican party survived was more remarkable
than that it eventually succeeded.

Voting patterns reveal that the realignment in the North
began before the Kansas-Nebraska Act was introduced, and it
began at the state and local level, not the national. The most
important cause of the realignment was the emergence after 1850
of a set of ethno-cultural issues, particularly temperance and

nativism, that cut across traditional party lines and thus had unusual potential to disrupt the Whig and Democratic coalitions. By the end of 1853, party lines were in complete disarray in many northern states and the process of party decomposition was well advanced. Voters' ties to parties were weaker than observers could ever remember, and party support fluctuated widely from one election to the next.

At this point, Congress passed the Kansas-Nebraska Act. Sensitive that this issue had split northern congressional Democrats down the middle, a number of antislavery leaders believed that the repeal of the Missouri Compromise would at last precipitate the creation of a powerful antislavery sectional party. This expectation was negated, however, by the emergence in the spring of 1854 of the anti-Catholic, anti-immigrant American party, or Know-Nothings, as a powerful independent organization. Political observers were astounded by this secret society's rapid growth in the summer of 1854, as countless Whigs, Democrats, and Free Soilers joined the new lodges. Combining opposition to the expansion of slavery with virulent anti-Catholicism and support for temperance, the Know-Nothing movement capitalized on the forces that undermined the Second Party System and won over many voters discontented with the existing parties and eager for reform, at the same time that it mobilized legions of those who had never voted.

The power of the Know-Nothings, the hostility of eastern Whigs who still clung to their sinking party organization, and the continuing animosity among Whigs, Free Soilers, and anti-Nebraska Democrats blocked formation of the Republican party in most free states in 1854. Efforts by antislavery men to organize a new party failed in such important states as New York, Pennsylvania, Massachusetts, and Illinois. In Ohio and Indiana, opposition forces combined in a temporary People's party that was dominated by the Know-Nothings; in Vermont and Iowa, anti-Democratic groups united behind a common ticket but did not organize a new party. Only in Michigan and Wisconsin did the Republican party take shape in 1854. In both states, the new party adopted a strong antislavery platform that was too extreme for more conservative latitudes.

The 1854 state elections in the North, many of which presented the voters with a bewildering array of choices, were a crushing defeat for the Democratic party. Yet which party had triumphed in these contests was not clear to contemporaries. Although the Republican party was victorious in Michigan and Wisconsin, in general the Know-Nothings, by combining nativism, anti-Nebraska sentiment, temperance, and opposition to the existing parties, were the most potent force in the northern elections. Because these other issues—and not just the Nebraska question—were central to the 1854 upheaval, the northern Whig party, despite its clear anti-Nebraska stance, suffered an even more devastating blow than did the Democrats. Thousands of rank-and-file Whigs abandoned their traditional loyalty for the American party. After the election, a despondent New York Whig, J. W. Taylor, concluded in a November 11 letter to Hamilton Fish, "This election has demonstrated that, by a majority, Roman Catholicism is feared more than American slavery" (Hamilton Fish Papers, Library of Congress). Battered first by temperance and then nativism, the Whig party abruptly collapsed.

With the Know-Nothings riding a crest of popularity, antislavery politicians launched the Republican party. The Republican movement combined Whigs, anti-Nebraska Democrats, and Free Soilers who wished to make antislavery, not nativism, the dominant element in northern politics. Some of these groups were adamantly hostile to nativism while others, particularly Free Soilers, had previously supported the Know-Nothings; whatever their views on other questions, however, Republican party members gave greater importance to sectional matters. While the Republican party confronted a number of major obstacles at its birth, its most serious problem was the power of the Know-Nothings. In most northern states, and especially in the most populous ones with the greatest strength in the electoral college, the Republican party could not be victorious without substantial Know-Nothing support. The major task confronting the Republicans, therefore, was to win over the bulk of the northern Know-Nothings and thus replace the American party as the primary opponent of the Democrats.

Over the next two years, Republicans and Americans battled for control of the anti-Democratic majority in the North. In analyzing the complex maneuvering among anti-Democratic factions during this period, historians have traditionally interpreted this struggle strictly in terms of antislavery versus nativism, seeing it solely as a contest over which idea would prevail and which would be shunted aside politically. Yet antislavery, anti-Catholicism, and hostility to alcohol were not neatly segregated attitudes in the antebellum electorate. In some ways nativism and antislavery competed with each other, but strong links also existed between the movements psychologically and in terms of mass support. For the most part, northern Know-Nothings were anti-Nebraska and opposed the extension of slavery. In addition, Know-Nothings more often than not favored temperance, as referenda in this decade clearly establish. Thus a strong though not perfect congruence existed among these attitudes, an affinity that greatly complicated the process of realignment in general and the formation of the Republican party in particular. Had a majority of northern voters from the start given greatest priority to the slavery issue or had antislavery voters been indifferent to nativism and temperance, the creation of the Republican party would have been immensely simplified.

The first significant steps to organize the Republican party occurred in 1855. Hoping to reorient northern politics around sectional questions, antislavery leaders took heart from the disruption of the national American party in June. When the American party's national convention adopted a platform endorsing the Kansas-Nebraska Act, a majority of the northern delegates walked out. Even more crucial to Republican hopes was the situation in the territory of Kansas. By the summer of 1855, the rivalry between free state and slave state partisans had led to a complete breakdown of order in the territory. Alarmed by northern efforts to save Kansas for freedom by sending settlers to the territory, proslavery partisans from neighboring Missouri invaded the territory before the March 1855 election, seized control of the polling places, and stuffed the ballot boxes, giving proslavery men firm control of the first territorial legislature. Proslavery leaders in the legislature then made the situation worse by expelling the few legally elected antislavery members and passing a draconian legal code designed to protect the institution of slavery and silence its critics. Antislavery partisans responded by organizing a separate "state" government and petitioning Congress for the admission of Kansas as a free state. With each government denouncing the other and denying the validity of its acts, sporadic fighting soon broke out between proslavery and antislavery partisans. Republican leaders anticipated that affairs in Kansas would significantly strengthen the movement to organize a northern antislavery party.

New York and Ohio offered contrasting visions of how to build a powerful Republican party. In Ohio, antislavery men led by Salmon P. Chase united with the Know-Nothings, who were the strongest element in the Republican coalition. In exchange for Chase's nomination for governor, the Know-Nothings received the remaining seven spots on the Republican ticket. In addition, the Republican platform was silent on the question of nativism, hoping thereby to appeal to both German Protestants and Know-Nothings. In New York, in contrast, the Republican party under the leadership of William H. Seward and Thurlow Weed, who recognized that the Know-Nothings were controlled by their enemies, assumed a clear antinativist stance. New York's was the only Republican state platform in 1855 to explicitly condemn the Know-Nothings and their proscriptive principles.

Although the Know-Nothing national council in June adopted a pro-Nebraska platform, the American party in every northern state repudiated this platform and reaffirmed its opposition to the extension of slavery. Thus wherever they ran a separate ticket, the Know-Nothings continued to exploit both nativism and antislavery sentiment. Republican leaders, in contrast, believed that the continuing violence in Kansas between proslavery and antislavery factions would enable the party to ride to victory on a strictly antislavery platform. Instead, the 1855 elections documented the continuing power of ethno-cultural concerns in northern politics. In Ohio, where the Republican party won its one significant victory, Republicans had united with the Know-Nothings on a common ticket. In states such as New York and Massachusetts, where the

Republicans rejected fusion with the Know-Nothings, the party went down to defeat. In the face of the Republican challenge with its overriding emphasis on the slavery issue, a substantial majority of eastern Know-Nothings remained loyal to the American party with its more broadly based appeal, a development that doomed the Republicans to defeat. The 1855 results demonstrated that, together, anti-Catholicism and antislavery represented the strongest political program in the North. "The people will not confront the issues we present," Edward L. Pierce, a despondent Massachusetts Republican, shrewdly observed in a November 9 letter to Salmon P. Chase. "They want a Paddy hunt & on a Paddy hunt they will go" (Salmon P. Chase Papers, Library of Congress).

Chase's victory in Ohio in 1855 was the Republicans' one bright star in an otherwise dismal political sky that year. Bolstered by his narrow victory, Chase launched a movement to organize a national Republican party on what Seward, an opponent of nativism, in a letter to Thurlow Weed on the last day of the year, scorned as "the Ohio plan, half Republican and half Know-Nothing" (Thurlow Weed Papers, University of Rochester). As a result of his efforts, Republicans held a national organizing convention in Pittsburgh in February, where they laid the groundwork for a national nominating convention in June. As plans proceeded to field a national ticket, Republican prospects still remained decidedly bleak, for the spring elections produced additional discouraging results. In the most important of these elections in Connecticut, where the Republicans for the first time ran a state ticket, the party polled a discouraging 10 percent of the popular vote. Experienced politicians predicted that the party would finish a distant third in the 1856 presidential election and then quickly fade from the political scene. As one veteran Democratic editor in the *Albany Argus* on October 20, 1855, commented, "Nobody believes this Republican movement can prove the basis of a permanent party."

Against this background, the 1856 presidential election produced one of the most remarkable turnarounds in American political history. The weakest party at the beginning of the year and seemingly headed for oblivion, the Republicans were by the time of the election in November the dominant party in the

North and the second strongest party in the nation. Several factors contributed to the party's amazing success after two years of frustration. By forming an alliance with northern Know-Nothings and electing Nathaniel P. Banks, a Massachusetts Know-Nothing-Republican, Speaker, the Republican minority gained control of the U.S. House of Representatives and forged the first national bonds of union with antislavery Know-Nothings. In addition, the American party convention ruptured for the second time in two years when the delegates adopted a pro-Nebraska platform and nominated Millard Fillmore to head their national ticket. A majority of northern delegates walked out, repudiating the platform and the ticket. But the most important reason for the Republican party's sudden growth was two incidents that occurred virtually simultaneously in May at almost opposite ends of the country: the attack on the Lawrence, Kansas, headquarters of the free-state movement by a proslavery mob (Bleeding Kansas); and the caning of Republican Senator Charles Sumner of Massachusetts, a prominent antislavery spokesman, by Congressman Preston S. Brooks of South Carolina in the Senate chamber (Bleeding Sumner). Of the two events, the assault on Sumner was decidedly the more important. It inflamed northern public opinion, provided a particularly dramatic example of alleged southern aggression, and brought thousands of moderate and conservative northerners into the Republican ranks.

The Republicans' first national nominating convention met in Philadelphia in June 1856. Stimulated by the recent violence in Kansas and Washington, an atmosphere akin to a religious revival prevailed on the convention floor. The 1856 Republican national platform was largely devoid of the evasions and ambiguities typical of such pronouncements: it focused on the slavery issue in particularly forceful language. Proclaiming that it was both the right and the duty of Congress to prohibit slavery from all the territories, it denounced slaveholding as "a relic of barbarism." The longest section detailed the violations of the rights of free-state settlers in Kansas and demanded the admission of Kansas as a free state. Except for calls for construction of a transcontinental railroad by a northern route and for federal aid to internal improvements, economic issues—

over which party members were badly divided—were ignored. A carefully crafted final plank on nativism sought to mollify both former Know-Nothings and naturalized voters.

The convention selected the famous western explorer, John C. Frémont, as the first Republican presidential candidate. Frémont had a rather undistinguished antislavery record, but he enjoyed a popular image as a dashing figure of romance and had a sufficiently malleable record for the party's purposes. Frémont was more a symbol than a real Republican leader; he took no active role in the campaign, which was run by an inner circle of party managers.

It was in 1856 that the party's ideology finally crystallized. Republicans continued to emphasize opposition to the expansion of slavery, but they put this question in a larger ideological context. Throughout the decade, some Republican leaders forcefully spoke out against the morality of slavery. In his famous debates with Stephen A. Douglas, Abraham Lincoln declared, "The real issue in this controversy . . . is the sentiment on the part of one class that looks upon the institution of slavery as a *wrong*, and of another class that *does not* look upon it as a wrong. . . . The Republican party . . . look upon it as being a moral, social and political wrong" (Basler, vol. 3, pp. 312–313). Other Republicans, exploiting widespread racist sentiment in the northern electorate, denied any humanitarian concern for the welfare of blacks and advocated preserving the western territories for whites by keeping out all blacks, free or slave. "The Republicans mean to preserve all of this country that they can from the pestilential presence of the black man," announced the *Hartford Courant*, while in 1860 a Republican banner in Illinois proclaimed, "NO NEGRO EQUALITY IN THE NORTH" (Holt, 1978, p. 188). More important was the ideal of free labor, which extolled the values of economic opportunity, personal liberty, and social mobility. Portraying the South as an aristocratic and economically stagnant society in which slavery degraded labor, Republicans celebrated the superiority of northern institutions and the North's fluid, progressive society.

Yet none of these ideas stood at the core of the party's ideology, which was more negative than positive in its emphasis and evidenced less concern for the welfare of blacks than the rights of northern whites. The Lawrence and Sumner incidents, which allowed Republicans to attack the South rather than slavery, provided Republicans with the necessary material to fashion an effective appeal.

Giving less emphasis to the moral question of slavery, Republicans focused on the threat to the liberties of northern whites posed by the aggressive Slave Power, by which they meant the political power of slaveholders. The issues of Bleeding Kansas and Bleeding Sumner were ideal for Republicans' purposes, for they enabled Republicans to agitate the slavery question without addressing the issue of black rights. Throughout the summer of 1856, Republican spokesmen insisted that slaveowners were engaged in a gigantic conspiracy to expand slavery everywhere and destroy northern white liberties. To northern whites, this threat seemed much more personal than whether slavery would exist in some distant territory. Slaveholders would stop at nothing, Republican leaders cried, to ensure that their power remained supreme, not just in the South but in the nation as well. As the famous black leader Frederick Douglass aptly noted, "The cry of Free Men was raised, not for the extension of liberty to the black man, but for the protection of the liberty of the white" (Gienapp, 1986a, p. 61).

In fashioning their ideology, Republicans made use of the tradition of republicanism, which had been central to American politics since the Revolution. While the force of republicanism waned after 1815 in competition with liberalism, which placed economic individualism at the center of society, this body of thought remained influential until at least the end of the Civil War. The ideology of republicanism, as handed down from the Founders, posited that republicanism was a particularly vulnerable form of government and that there always existed conspiracies of those with power to destroy liberty. The raid on Lawrence and the assault on Sumner, like the Kansas-Nebraska Act before them, were pieces of this grand design, Republicans contended, and unless northerners acted quickly, any hope of thwarting the Slave Power would be gone. Following the caning of Sumner, on June 5, the Concord (NH) *Independent Democrat*, a Republican newspaper, declared, "The liberties of our country are in tenfold more danger than they were at the commencement of the American Revolution. We then had a distant foe to contend with. Now the enemy is within our borders."

To the modern observer, such claims seem fantastic, but antebellum Americans were thoroughly accustomed to such rhetoric. Voters *expected* to find conspiracies; they were a political fact of life. Republicans merely modified republican thought to fit the political crisis of the 1850s by identifying the South and more especially slaveowners as the internal threat to the Republic and its promise of liberty and opportunity. On November 26, 1856, the Columbus (OH) *Ohio State Jurnal* quoted the address of the Ohio Republican State Central Committee, in words that echoed those of the 1760s and 1770s, as it proclaimed, "Every despotism is aggressive, and the despotism of the Slave Power is no exception to the universal rule. The price of Liberty is eternal vigilance."

Republicans also broadened their appeal beyond the slavery issue by catering to nativist (especially anti-Catholic) sentiment in the North. Tactical considerations made an emphasis on opposition to foreigners undesirable, but anti-Catholicism entailed little political risk: the Catholic vote was solidly Democratic and hatred of Catholics was one policy on which both Know-Nothings and Protestant immigrants could unite. Republican newspapers and spokesmen denounced Catholics and linked the Church with the Slave Power in a combined assault on the country's republican heritage. Charging that "Popery and Slavery [had] banded together for a common object—the attainment of political power," the *Chicago Tribune* (February 4, 1856), insisted that "the Republican party, which is the avowed mortal enemy of chattel bondage, is not less the opponent of the partisan schemes of political Catholicism." Republican ideology thus depicted a dual threat to northern whites' liberties—the Slave Power and the Papal Power—and though they gave greater emphasis to the former and considered it the more serious danger, they by no means ignored the latter. Republicans were also careful to reach out to disaffected Americans in 1856. They united with the northern American party on a national ticket, nominated Know-Nothings for state and local offices, gave them a prominent place in the campaign, and did not require any renunciation of past opinions.

Despite a crusading enthusiasm that recalled the rousing contest of 1840, the first Republican presidential campaign confronted insoluble difficulties. The party was hurt by the fear among conservatives that it was a threat to the Union, but the most damaging accusation brought against it in the 1856 election was that its standard-bearer was a Catholic. In actuality, Frémont was an Episcopalian, but Democrats and American party leaders never tired of inventing new stories and publishing new testimonials that Frémont was a Catholic. Throughout the campaign, Republicans failed to devise an effective answer to this charge, and to the very end a large number of northern voters remained suspicious of Frémont's true religious affiliation. This accusation was especially damaging among Know-Nothings, who held the key to the 1856 outcome. In the end, the Republican party was unable to solve this problem, along with the organizational difficulties that any new party confronts.

Even so, aided by the rising sectional animosity, the Republicans' performance in the 1856 election was little short of astounding. Although James Buchanan, the Democratic nominee, was elected, Frémont ran ahead of both Buchanan and Millard Fillmore, the American party candidate, in the North and carried all but five free states: Pennsylvania, New Jersey, Indiana, Illinois, and California. Despite having virtually no support in the South, Frémont finished second in the electoral college and polled 33 percent of the popular vote. Had Frémont carried Pennsylvania and one of the other four free states that he lost, or had he carried these four without Pennsylvania, then he would have been elected. In their first national effort, Republicans had come within an eyelash of winning.

The Republican coalition in 1856 was strikingly diverse. The party won the bulk of the former Whigs and all the Free Soilers, a substantial proportion of Know-Nothings (the large majority in some states like Massachusetts, Connecticut, Ohio, and Indiana), a number of Protestant immigrants, and a disproportionate share of young voters and previous nonvoters. In general, Republican strength among Democrats has been exaggerated; only in a few states such as Ohio, Connecticut, and New York did the Republican party win a significant proportion of former Democrats, and the bulk of these Democratic converts seem to have entered the Republican camp through the secret Know-Nothing lodges rather than the much-emphasized anti-Nebraska movement. Republican strength among the foreign-born also varied from state to state, although everywhere Catholics, and especially Irish Catholics, voted overwhelmingly Democratic. Republicans won lopsided majorities among British, Scandinavian, and Scotch-Irish voters, all of whom had no particular liking for slavery and were also strongly anti-Catholic (many had voted Know-Nothing earlier, though they were ineligible for membership in the order); they adhered to the Republican party as the enemy of the Irish Democracy as long as it avoided an antiforeign stance. Republicans garnered fewer votes among the Germans, on whom they lavished particular attention, than party leaders had hoped, but in some states such as Illinois, where the party kept free from prohibition and relegated nativism to the background, the Republicans seem to have won a slight majority of German voters.

Among native-born voters, the clearest division was between southern-stock voters and New Englanders. Whereas the Democrats had previously won many Yankee voters, they now swung sharply to the Republicans. After the election, on November 11, former Senator Daniel S. Dickinson, a prominent New York Democrat, groaned to James Buchanan, "Wherever the *New England* people have sway, they came down like an avalanche,—men, women, and children,—priest, & people, & church, aggregate, and a train of frightened Buffaloes would be no more deaf to reason or argument" (James Buchanan Papers, Historical Society of Pennsylvania). At the same time, southern-stock voters in the Ohio valley gave very little support to the Republican party, which they viewed as a fanatical crusade against their native South and its institutions. Some southern-born Whigs crossed over the Democratic party, but many more voted for Fillmore. Because of the Republicans' weakness among southern-stock voters, the party did not present a solid evangelical front. In fact, many evangelical voters continued to oppose the party, and Frémont won many votes from those not formally affiliated with any church.

In assuming the Whigs' place in the two-party system, the Republicans did not simply inherit the old Whig voting base. Ethnically the Republican coalition was less homogeneous: While the Republicans had not done as well among the foreign-born as they had hoped, they nevertheless won a greater share of naturalized voters than the Whigs ever had. In addition, a larger proportion of Yankee Protestants voted for Frémont, as Yankee Free Soilers and Democrats switched parties; at the same time, the Republicans won substantially less support among southern-stock voters in the North than the Whigs had, and the Republicans were also weaker among the wealthy business class in large cities. These changes in voting patterns between the second- and third-party systems produced a fundamentally different anti-Democratic coalition than existed earlier and in the process reduced the Democrats to a minority party in the North.

The Republican party's remarkable performance in November 1856 marked the close of the first phase of the Civil War realignment: The Whig party had disappeared, the American party was on its deathbed, and the Republican party was the Democrats' primary opponent. Republicans had successfully met their first significant challenge: They had displaced the American party as the second party in the two-party system. Defeating the Know-Nothings to become the dominant opposition party was the most important victory that the Republican party would ever win in its long and storied history.

But if the Republican party were to survive, it had to win national power. For all their postelection elation, Republican leaders remained keenly aware that Frémont had received only a plurality of the vote in the free states, and their next objective was to create a northern Republican majority and elect a president in 1860 by retaining the party's previous supporters while picking up additional support from other groups, particularly the Fillmore voters. As before, Republicans continued to emphasize the threat of the Slave Power. In advancing this argument, the party was immensely aided by the events of the next four years and by James Buchanan's incompetent leadership.

In Buchanan's star-crossed presidency, the first event that strengthened the Republicans was the Dred Scott decision, rendered by the Supreme Court just two days after Buchanan's inauguration. In this decision, which concerned the status of a Missouri slave named Dred Scott who had lived previously in the free state of Illinois and the free territory of Wisconsin, the Court by a seven-to-two vote declared the Missouri Compromise of 1820 (which had been repealed by the Kansas-Nebraska Act three years earlier) unconstitutional. Congress, the Court declared, had no power to prohibit slavery in the territories, which was the major principle of the Republican party.

Intended to give additional protection to slavery, the Court's ill-conceived decision instead unleashed a storm of protest. "There is such a thing as the slave power," raged the Republican *Cincinnati Commercial* (March 12, 1857) after the decision was announced. Far from settling the slavery extension question, as the court majority intended, party and sectional differences intensified. More important, Republican leaders now perceived an expanded threat facing the North: they raised the cry that slavery threatened not just the territories, but the free states as well. All that was needed, Lincoln explained, was one more Supreme Court decision that a state could not ban slavery, and it would be a national institution, legal in the North as well as the South. "We shall *lie down* pleasantly dreaming that the people of *Missouri* are on the verge of making their State *free*," he argued, "and we shall *awake* to the *reality*, instead, that the *Supreme* Court has made *Illinois* a *slave* State" (Basler, vol. 2, p. 467). At the same time, since all five southern justices had joined in the majority decision, it strengthened northerners' fears of the Slave Power and added credibility to Republican claims that the federal government was entirely controlled by the slaveowning interest.

If the Dred Scott decision were not enough, a financial panic began in October 1857. As the party in power, the Democrats were hurt by the ensuing depression, which lasted until 1861. Seeking to capitalize on the situation, Republicans added several economic planks to their program, including a mildly protective tariff and a homestead law to give free farms to western settlers. Southern opposition in Congress, however, blocked passage of most economic legislation, and Buchanan vetoed a homestead bill in 1860. Economic questions increasingly became sectional rather than partisan issues, and with growing success Republicans appealed to conservative Whig business-men on economic grounds.

The most important boost that the Republican party received, however, came from the Kansas controversy, which now entered its final phase. In 1857, in large part because the free-state majority refused to vote, proslavery forces won control of a convention called to draft a state constitution for the territory prior to its admission as a state. This convention, which met at the capital in Lecompton, drafted a constitution recognizing the institution of slavery. Because the delegates were afraid that the free-state majority would reject the constitution, they refused to submit it for popular ratification. Instead, voters were given the choice of voting for the constitution with the right to bring in more slaves or for the constitution with only the slaves already in the territory. They could not vote for the constitution without slavery or reject the constitution entirely. Denouncing this choice as a sham, free-state men again boycotted the election, and the constitution with more slavery was approved.

Warned by the territorial governor that the Lecompton Constitution was a fraud and represented the wishes of only a small minority of the residents of Kansas, James Buchanan nevertheless urged Congress to approve the proposed constitution and admit Kansas as the sixteenth slave state. In the ensuing struggle in Congress, Buchanan pulled out all the stops, including resorting to outright bribery, in an effort to push the Lecompton Constitution through. His efforts split the Democratic party, as Senator Stephen A. Douglas of Illinois, the leading northern Democrat, broke with the administration and opposed the Lecompton Constitution. Upholding the idea that the residents of a territory should be allowed to decide the status of slavery for themselves without congressional interference, Douglas charged that the Lecompton Constitution made a mockery of this doctrine of popular sovereignty, which the Democrats had endorsed in both the Kansas-Nebraska Act and its 1856 national platform. Ultimately, the House rejected the

Lecompton Constitution, and then in a face-saving compromise sent the issue back to the people of Kansas by asking them to vote on whether they would accept admission under the Constitution with a reduced land grant. In the election in August 1858, the voters of Kansas overwhelmingly rejected the Lecompton Constitution. This vote, in effect, ended the Kansas controversy in national politics. No doubt remained that Kansas would be admitted as a free state as soon as it reached the requisite population, and it entered the Union in January 1861.

The Lecompton struggle left the Democratic party wrecked beyond repair. Championing the principle of popular sovereignty, Douglas spoke for the northern wing of the Democratic party, while southerners, furious over his apostasy, bitterly denounced him and insisted that they would never accept his nomination as president. Some southern radicals, angry that the Dred Scott decision had given the South no real benefits, now took up the demand for a congressional slave code to protect slavery in the territories, a measure that would surely encourage expansion of the institution. At the same time, Republicans experienced a resurgence in the wake of the popular outcry in the North against the bare-faced attempt of the South to force slavery on the unwilling residents of Kansas. The Lecompton crisis fed northern fears of an aggressive slaveocracy, willing to stop at nothing to protect its power. Here seemed additional direct proof of the existence of a Slave Power conspiracy and its designs on northern liberty. More and more northern conservatives gravitated toward the Republican party in response to the Buchanan administration's proslavery policies, and also its corruption, which congressional Republicans took great pains to expose and publicize.

Employing various strategies in different states, the Republican party scored impressive gains in the most populous northern states in the 1858 state elections. It regained power in Ohio and New York, increased its hold on Massachusetts, and added to its vote in New Jersey, Indiana, and Illinois. Moreover, by exploiting the Lecompton controversy and stressing the tariff issue and the need to aid the state's iron and coal industry, a coalition of Republicans and American party members under the banner the People's party carried Pennsylvania for the first time with 53 percent of the vote (compared to only 32 percent for Frémont in 1856).

The 1858 contest that attracted the most national attention, however, was the senatorial race between Stephen A. Douglas and Abraham Lincoln. Throughout the campaign, Lincoln hammered away at the idea, developed at length in his famous "House-Divided" speech in June when accepting the Republican nomination, that the Democratic party was an agent of the Slave Power, committed to spreading slavery throughout the country. He insisted that the crisis between the sections would not end until "either the *opponents* of slavery, will arrest the further spread of it, and place it . . . in course of ultimate extinction; or its *advocates* will push it forward, till it shall become alike lawful in *all* the States, *old* as well as *new*—*North* as well as *South*" (Basler, vol. 2, pp. 461–462).

In the end, the legislature returned Douglas to the Senate, vindicating his opposition to the Lecompton Constitution, but Republicans knew that Lincoln had won a moral triumph: Republicans noted that the total votes cast for candidates pledged to Lincoln exceeded those for Douglas's supporters, and they also believed that Lincoln had bested Douglas in their debates. Douglas's margin of victory rested on Democratic holdovers and a malapportionment of the legislature. Lincoln's strong showing in the 1858 Illinois senatorial contest catapulted him into serious consideration for the Republicans' 1860 presidential nomination.

By 1860 the political tide was running strongly in the Republicans' direction. The Democratic party split at its national convention in Charleston, unable to agree on a platform or a candidate. In the end, the northern wing nominated Douglas with a platform endorsing popular sovereignty, while most of the southern delegates, joined by supporters of the Buchanan administration, nominated John C. Breckinridge of Kentucky, Buchanan's vice-president, on a platform demanding a congressional slave code for the territories. In addition, a new party, the Constitutional Union party, which represented another effort to form a national conservative party, selected John Bell of Tennessee as its candidate.

Republicans assembled in Chicago in May for their second national convention. The 1860 Republican platform provided evidence of the party's growing moderation. While Republicans continued to oppose the expansion of slavery, the harsh indictment of the institution contained in the 1856 platform was dropped. In addition to reaffirming the party's endorsement of a transcontinental railroad, the Republican platform contained several new economic planks, including a demand for a homestead law and a moderately protective tariff. Finally, with an eye to the foreign vote, the platform opposed any alteration of the naturalization laws.

The front-runner for the presidential nomination was Senator William H. Seward of New York, the most prominent Republican in the country. But a number of Republicans, especially in the doubtful northern states that the party had lost in 1856, believed that Seward could not win. He had a reputation as a radical on the slavery issue and, most important, was bitterly hated by the former Know-Nothings because of his courageous denunciation of nativism earlier in the decade. Seward's major rival was Lincoln, who enjoyed several advantages. He came from a doubtful state, was a moderate on the slavery issue, was acceptable to both the Germans and Know-Nothings, and as a southern-born old Whig could appeal to those conservatives in the lower North who had backed Fillmore in 1856. On the third ballot, Lincoln received the Republican nomination.

A triumph of expediency and availability, Lincoln's nomination represented an act of grave irresponsibility. Dismissing southern threats of secession as mere bluster, Republicans paid little heed to the crisis that was likely to ensue if the party triumphed. The delegates had no way of knowing that Lincoln, who had been out of public office for more than a decade and had never held an administrative office, had the requisite ability to meet the challenge of civil war. Once in office, Lincoln would demonstrate his extraordinary political skills, but of these the delegates were not only blithely ignorant but also unconcerned. To them, Lincoln seemed to have the best chance of winning, and that was sufficient.

With victory seemingly all but certain, Republicans downplayed the issues in the 1860 campaign and conducted what has aptly been called a hurrah campaign. Parades with banners and transparencies saluted Honest Abe and Lincoln the Railsplitter, and campaign pageantry dominated the canvass. The Wide Awake Society, made up primarily of young men who marched with capes and lanterns singing party songs, chanting Republican slogans, and performing intricate maneuvers, was the most remembered feature of the campaign.

With the opposition divided, Lincoln easily triumphed in the electoral college, even though he won less than 40 percent of the popular vote. He carried every free state except New Jersey, whose electoral votes he split with Douglas. Even had the votes for his three opponents been combined, Lincoln would still have been elected, since he had absolute majorities in all the free states except Oregon, California, and New Jersey. He won all the doubtful states that the Republicans lost in 1856, while holding all the states Frémont had carried. Lincoln won 500,000 more votes than the party's total in 1856.

Lincoln's improved showing over Frémont's performance four years earlier stemmed from support from three major groups. First, Lincoln won a number of Fillmore voters, especially in the southern counties of Indiana and Illinois, eastern Pennsylvania, and New Jersey, and in the major metropolitan areas. Many of these midwestern voters had been born in the South, and Lincoln ran much stronger among southern-stock voters than had Frémont. Bell, in contrast, was much weaker in the North compared to Fillmore, winning only one-fifth as many votes. Lincoln also did better among foreign-born voters, especially Germans. Republican efforts to woo immigrant voters paid dividends in 1860, especially in states like Pennsylvania where the so-called Pennsylvania Dutch now swung to the Republicans. Finally, Lincoln did especially well among young men, many of whom cast their first presidential vote in 1860, after having been mobilized by the Wide Awake clubs. Together, these three groups, coupled with the party's retention of most of Frémont's supporters, provided the Republicans' margin of victory.

Having elected their first president in 1860, Republicans had no idea what they would do with their new-won power. Since its founding, the party had emphasized the necessity of displacing the South from control of the federal government as the way to preserve republicanism, and following Lincoln's victory, Seward announced that "the battle for Freedom had been fought and won" (Holt, 1978, p. 217). Party members were deeply divided over the slavery issue and economic matters. Moreover, the party did not control either house of Congress and had only one member of the Supreme Court. But the secession of the Deep South in response to Lincoln's election drastically altered the political situation. Lincoln took office determined to maintain the Union, and six weeks after his inauguration, the Civil War began.

Secession and war would convert the Republican party into the party of the Union and of emancipation. Under Lincoln's leadership, the Republicans would abolish slavery, push the military effort through to victory, and preserve the Union. After 1865, the party was tied increasingly to northern industrial and corporate interests and promoted quite different policies than it had in the 1850s, when the Republicans' main principles had been to stop the expansion of slavery and check the South's political power.

In the short span of six years, the Republican party had gained national power and established itself as the most powerful party in the nation. It was a truly remarkable achievement. Perhaps the clearest measurement of the Republican party's accomplishment is that it was the last new party to carry a presidential election in American history.

References

Anbinder, Tyler. 1992. *Nativism and Slavery: The Northern Know Nothings and the Politics of the 1850s.* New York: Oxford U. Pr.

Baringer, William E. 1937. *Lincoln's Rise to Power.* Boston: Little, Brown.

Basler, Roy, ed. 1953. *The Collected Works of Abraham Lincoln.* 8 vols. New Brunswick, NJ: Rutgers U. Pr.

Baum, Dale. 1984. *The Civil War Party System: The Case of Massachusetts, 1848–1876.* Chapel Hill: U. of North Carolina Pr.

Berwanger, Eugene H. 1967. *The Frontier Against Slavery: Western Anti-Negro Prejudice and the Slavery Expansion Controversy.* Urbana: U. of Illinois Pr.

Booraem, Hendrik. 1983. *The Formation of the Republican Party in New York: Politics and Conscience in the Antebellum North.* New York: New York U. Pr.

Crandall, Andrew Wallace. 1930. *The Early History of the Republican Party 1854–1856.* Boston: Gorham Press.

Craven, Avery O. 1957. *The Coming of the Civil War.* 2nd ed. rev. Chicago: U. of Chicago Pr.

Crenshaw, Ollinger. 1941. "Urban and Rural Voting in the Election of 1860." In Eric F. Goldman, ed. *Historiography and Urbanization: Essays in American History in Honor of W. Stull Holt.* Baltimore: Johns Hopkins U. Pr.

Fehrenbacher, Don E. 1961. "The Republican Decision at Chicago." In Norman A. Graebner, ed. *Politics and the Crisis of 1860.* Urbana: U. of Illinois Pr.

———. 1962. *Prelude to Greatness: Lincoln in the 1850s.* Stanford, CA: Stanford U. Pr.

———. 1965. "Comment on Why the Republican Party Came to Power." In George H. Knoles, ed. *The Crisis of the Union, 1860–1861.* Baton Rouge: Louisiana State U. Pr.

———. 1978. *The Dred Scott Case: Its Significance in American Law and Politics.* New York: Oxford U. Pr.

Fogel, Robert William. 1989. *Without Consent or Contract: The Rise and Fall of American Slavery.* New York: Norton.

Foner, Eric. 1970. *Free Soil, Free Labor, Free Men: The Ideology of the Republican Party Before the Civil War.* New York: Oxford U. Pr.

Formisano, Ronald P. 1971. *The Birth of Mass Political Parties: Michigan, 1827–1861.* Princeton: Princeton U. Pr.

Gara, Larry. 1969. "Slavery and the Slave Power: A Crucial Distinction," 15 *Civil War History* 5.

———. 1991. *The Presidency of Franklin Pierce.* Lawrence, KS: U. Pr. of Kansas.

Gienapp, William E. 1979. "The Crime Against Sumner: The Caning of Charles Sumner and the Rise of the Republican Party." 25 *Civil War History* 218.

————. 1986a. "The Republican Party and the Slave Power." In Robert H. Abzug and Stephen E. Maizlish, eds. *New Perspectives on Race and Slavery in America: Essays in Honor of Kenneth M. Stampp.* Lexington: U. Pr. of Kentucky.

————. 1986b. "Who Voted for Lincoln?" In John L. Thomas, ed. *Abraham Lincoln and the American Political Tradition.* Amherst: U. of Massachusetts Pr.

————. 1987. *The Origins of the Republican Party, 1852–1856.* New York: Oxford U. Pr.

Holt, Michael F. 1969. *Forging a Majority: The Formation of the Republican Party in Pittsburgh, 1848–1860.* New Haven: Yale U. Pr.

————. 1978. *The Political Crisis of the 1850s.* New York: Wiley.

————. 1992. *Political Parties and American Political Development from the Age of Jackson to the Age of Lincoln.* Baton Rouge: Louisiana State U. Pr.

Huston, James L. 1987. *The Panic of 1857 and the Coming of the Civil War.* Baton Rouge: Louisiana State U. Pr.

Johannsen, Robert W. 1991. *Lincoln, the South, and Slavery.* Baton Rouge: Louisiana State U. Pr.

Kleppner, Paul. 1979. *The Third Electoral System, 1853–1892: Parties, Voters, and Political Cultures.* Chapel Hill: U. of North Carolina Pr.

Kremm, Thomas W. 1977. "Cleveland and the First Lincoln Election: The Ethnic Response to Nativism": 8 *Journal of Interdisciplinary History* 69.

Levine, Bruce. *Half Slave and Half Free: The Roots of the Civil War.* New York: Hill and Wang.

Luebke, Frederick C., ed. 1971. *Ethnic Voters and the Election of Lincoln.* Lincoln: U. of Nebraska Pr.

Luthin, Reinhard H. 1944. *The First Lincoln Campaign.* Cambridge: Harvard U. Pr.

McPherson, James M. 1988. *The Battle Cry of Freedom.* New York: Oxford U. Pr.

Maizlish, Stephen E. 1983. *The Triumph of Sectionalism: The Transformation of Ohio Politics, 1844–1856.* Kent, OH: Kent State U. Pr.

Meerse, David E. 1966. "Buchanan, Corruption, and the Election of 1860." 12 *Civil War History* 116.

Mulkern, John R. 1990. *The Know-Nothing Party in Massachusetts: The Rise and Fall of a People's Movement.* Boston: Northeastern U. Pr.

Nevins, Allan. 1947. *Ordeal of the Union*. 2 vols. New York: Scribner's.

————. 1950. *The Emergence of Lincoln*. 2 vols. New York: Scribner's.

Nichols, Roy F. 1948. *The Disruption of American Democracy*. New York: Macmillan.

Niven, John W. 1990. *The Coming of the Civil War, 1837–1861*. Arlington Heights, IL: Harlan Davidson.

Nye, Russel B. 1963. *Fettered Freedom: Civil Liberties and the Slavery Controversy, 1830–1860*. Rev. ed. East Lansing: Michigan State U. Pr.

Potter, David M. 1962. *Lincoln and His Party in the Secession Crisis*. Rev. ed. New Haven: Yale U. Pr.

————. 1976. *The Impending Crisis, 1848–1861*. New York: Harper & Row.

Rawley, James A. 1969. *Race and Politics: "Bleeding Kansas" and the Coming of the Civil War*. Philadelphia: J.P. Lippincott.

Roseboom, Eugene H. 1938. "Salmon P. Chase and the Know-Nothings." 25 *Mississippi Valley Historical Review* 335.

Sewell, Richard H. 1976. *Ballots for Freedom: Antislavery Politics in the United States, 1837–1860*. New York: Oxford U. Pr.

Silbey, Joel H. 1985. *The Partisan Imperative: The Dynamics of American Politics Before the Civil War*. New York: Oxford U. Pr.

————. 1991. *The American Political Nation, 1838–1893*. Stanford, CA: Stanford U. Pr.

Stampp, Kenneth M. 1950. *And the War Came: The North and the Secession Crisis, 1860–1861*. Baton Rouge: Louisiana State U. Pr.

————. 1980. *The Imperiled Union: Essays on the Background of the Civil War*. New York: Oxford U. Pr.

————. 1990. *America in 1857: A Nation on the Brink*. New York: Oxford U. Pr.

Van Deusen, Glydon G. 1965. "Why the Republican Party Came to Power." In George H. Knole, ed., *The Crisis of the Union, 1860–1861*. Baton Rouge: Louisiana State U. Pr.

CHAPTER 4

Party Organization in Nineteenth-Century America

Joel H. Silbey

Political organizations, mostly small scale and relatively undeveloped, appeared in colonial America long before the existence of national political parties. In many of the original colonies, contested popular elections were frequent enough to need some degree of organization. Candidates were often nominated by themselves or their friends, but collective activities to mobilize and persuade voters, and to supervise election day activities all occurred, in however rudimentary a form. In a strictly local society with relatively few voters, elaborate political organization was unnecessary. What structures there were, therefore, did not reach everywhere or last very long.

During the late eighteenth and early nineteenth centuries, particularly in the years 1815–1835, this informality changed, albeit slowly and sporadically. After 1789, a new national political arena established by the Constitution demanded more elaborate mechanisms for nominating major officeholders and for running the business of state and national legislatures fiercely debating alternative public policies. As political parties evolved in the 1790s to meet these responsibilities, organizational development followed. These early political organizations were often dominated by cadres of notables working together in the rarified atmosphere of non-popular politics to secure a political advantage, a nomination or appointment, or a specific public policy. The characteristic organizational element at this time was the legislative caucus, a small self-created group that operated with minimal reference to the larger population of citizens outside of its numbers. Legislative caucuses set agendas, nominated candidates, and took the lead to shape and direct political activity.

While popular election campaign activities remained minor until the 1830s, they too had to be accepted more systematically after 1789 when national elections became part of the regular American political scene. Nominating candidates became a more public act—the first national convention met in 1808 to nominate Federalist candidates for president and vice-president. A few more followed at the state and local levels, but in far different form from later mass political conventions, attuned as they were to the elite-dominated past. And so were other election activities in what remained a nondemocratic political system.

After 1815, however, organizations expanded rapidly in response to a new political environment. The number of voters and their political participation increased at all levels, in response to which party leaders constructed a framework to manage electoral politics—from nominations to campaigns to elections themselves. Voters had to be mobilized and managed in an increasingly contentious republic that featured a range of public policy debate, frequent elections, and a legislative system of constant activity. A new era of vigorous popular politics had dawned, making politics more than the maneuvers of elite factions. Most important, despite the American political culture's lingering hostility to them, political parties and other organizational structures took deep root in the American landscape. Parties articulated political philosophy, offered voters cues to behavior, staffed the government, and fought to advance specific policy objectives and group values which they then promoted and protected against their enemies.

A new organizational imperative accompanied this vast party development, since the structures that the parties built were the mechanisms for accomplishing their many goals. The parties developed from occasional and unusual factions into disciplined, complete, national forms, whose activities were increasingly routinized and repetitive. Given their purpose and function, political organizations unsurprisingly became a major characteristic of the American political experience for the rest of the nineteenth century.

The Chronological Frame

Like the party system itself, individual political organizations did not appear all at once but developed unevenly over several decades. In the decade between the mid-1820s and mid-1830s, many of the characteristic elements of effective political organization came into sporadic being often for some immediate electoral purpose; this decade was thus the incubation period for most of the familiar American political institutions.

Jacksonian Democrats took the lead. Introduced by the great political innovator, Martin Van Buren and his colleagues in New York State, new forms and directions took shape and came to dominate political life. In the 1820s, Van Buren's Albany Regency and New Hampshire Democracy's Concord Cabal were, in the words of Donald Cole, two prototypes "that served as fore-runners of modern political machines." Out of these two also appeared a new breed of professional politician (always male), who applied his managerial skills on an increasingly broad canvas. The emergence of these professional politicians led to the firm establishment of caucuses and conventions, first at the state level and then, in the early 1830s, nationally. Campaign organizations designed to mobilize voters through the activities of networks of party activists followed. American politics now existed as a three-level pyramid: At the top was a policymaking, ambitious leadership; at the base was the increasing number of voters seeking direction and stimulation; and filling the space between was the organizational apparatus.

The presidential election of 1840 established these institutions most thoroughly in the national landscape, where they sank deep and permanent roots. The impetus came from the leaders of the Whig party, who organized a campaign to elect William Henry Harrison to the presidency by dramatizing the dominant issues in colorful and far-reaching ways.

They set up caucuses and called conventions, created correspondence committees to coordinate nationwide activities, and
built up a vigorous party press to spread the word. As a result,
W.N. Chambers maintains that party organization "reached
previously unprecedented levels. If the party was not yet a
machine, it could muster a political drill that matched or over-
matched the uniformed militia of the time. To rally the
faithful, win recruits, and mobilize the voters—such was the
militia style which the Harrison men brought to near
perfection." The Whigs mobilized voters in numbers beyond
anything previously known. Concomitantly, the Democrats
were not far behind in this "hurrah campaign." Their leading
political operative, Amos Kendall, in addition to running the
party's electioneering activities, issued his "Address on
Political Organization" in 1840; it was a handbook for party
workers that was widely distributed, copied, and used.

Now politics could not turn back; organizational commitment became the intellectual and behavioral norm on the
American political scene as the forms and structures built in the
1830s took root and matured, stimulated by close electoral
competition in most areas of the country. Although organizational forms differed from state to state (largely based on the
degree of electoral competition between the parties), many
common themes linked organizations together into a whole;
both parties learned from and copied each other and applied
their joint lessons widely. Even among the Whigs, some of
whom initially expressed hesitation and resistance to the new
partisan imperatives, the commitment to organization became
commonplace in the 1840s.

All of this activity added up to an incomplete but
substantial edifice for carrying out the people's political business. The need to mobilize a mass electorate was clear enough;
what became crucial was the realization that in order to gain
specific policy objectives, each party had to pay attention to
every part of the system, coordinating and managing contests at
every level of politics. Attention to one leader's fortunes at the
top of the ticket every four years had to be replaced by
constant, repeated concern for each office if the party wanted to
accomplish policy objectives and protect its gains.

After the 1840s, existing organizational forms were further elaborated, although little new was added. Each party enjoyed a national reach and carried on its activities with an eye to all local, state, and national electoral prizes. Neither the style nor the structure of party organizations changed very much. The roots planted in the late 1830s which grew over the next decade provided strong underpinnings for subsequent party campaign activities. The partisan age had established its characteristic way of doing business, a style that was maintained even when disruptive forces emerged to affect the political scene in the 1850s. The 1860s and 1870s continued this pattern. They were not innovative years; rather they were the decades of the political organization's most mature phase, when they ran at maximum effectiveness. In the era immediately after the Civil War, the great state and national party bosses, leading massive political organizations, thoroughly dominated the playing fields of American politics.

Shape, Structure, and Function

The purposes of political organizations were clear enough to nineteenth-century Americans: to impose order on the political system; to discipline its constituent elements; and to prepare, direct, and promote all electoral, legislative, and administrative activities. The recruitment of candidates, the mobilization of voters, and the management of activities at every level had to be implemented. It was generally recognized that spontaneity in politics was no longer enough. As George Luetscher wrote, "[W]hen large bodies of men are drawn out to act [for some common purpose], their action cannot be effectual without organization and discipline. Ten men may perform a common work without formal regulations, but ten thousand cannot act without regular leaders and subordination." Therefore, another wrote, "party organization is as necessary to the success of principles as truth is to their usefulness and vitality."

Organizations of this kind were tripartite in location (local, state, and national), pyramidical in structure (consisting of hundreds of committees and conventions from the grassroots through the state level to the national convention), and bivariate in approach (expressive and public on the one hand, introspective and hidden on the other). Participatory partisanship stimulated particular kinds of organizations that were deeply imbedded in local communities throughout the country. Political life originated in thousands of towns, rural crossroads, and big-city wards, where the polls were located, where the candidates appeared, and where the citizenry's original attitudes toward public life and policies were formed and expressed. Here, as elsewhere, politics was carried on and managed by political organizations. Local structures of similar shape and purpose grew up to handle the party affairs of even a few hundred voters or less.

The centers of gravity of party organization have been at the state level for most of our history, certainly until quite recent times. Although national in name and reach, both parties were decentralized, made up of blocs of state organizations, largely self-sufficient and administratively disunified no matter how hard they worked in a common cause. National campaign structures were established for each presidential and congressional election. A Democratic National Committee (first chaired by Benjamin Hallett of Massachusetts) appeared in 1848; the Whigs followed in 1852; the Republicans, under Edwin D. Morgan of New York, in 1856. These national committees were supported by small staffs and a number of campaign and finance committees. But, as Robert Marcus concludes in his study of the Republican organization after the Civil War, "decentralization was fundamental to American political life." State and local parties were "scarcely disturbed from outside" by the national party organizations, which were "the servant of the state parties."

Wherever they were, all political organizations looked the same; all adopted similar structures and behaved in similar ways. At every level of political activity, another pyramidical organizational structure developed. At the point of the apex was each organization's leadership. In the early days, newspaper editors—such as Isaac Hill, Amos Kendall, and Thurlow Weed—were often the leaders of the organization, sharing power with an emerging class of professional politicians who had become "paid workers like everyone else" in nineteenth-century America. Later in the century these professional politicians, often holding high government offices, ruled the party structures alone.

These full-time professionals became adept operators of the system through long experience. Their role late in the nineteenth century has been well described by Richard L. McCormick. New York's boss Thomas Platt

> was a master at managing the hierarchy of party committees and at calling and running harmonious conventions. When the nominations were made, Platt knew how to mold the hundreds of party newspapers into an efficient propaganda machine to send the right speakers to the right places, and to rouse voters' enthusiasm. On election day his organization spread the campaign fund judiciously, got the Republicans to the polls, and frustrated Democratic attempts at fraud. When Republicans won office, Platt made the most of the patronage their positions brought and strengthened the party for the next election.

State party leaders usually rose through the ranks of the multitiered political organizations they came to head. Platt of New York held in turn practically every position in the committee hierarchy of his own party: chairman of his county committee, national congressional campaign committeeman, chairman of the executive committee of the state committee, chairman of the state committee, and national committeeman. During his years of training, he carefully refined the techniques of political management. Their effective application required Platt's years of actual experience. In Harold Gosnell's words, he and his colleagues in other states were "the general manager[s] of the organization."

Below Platt and his colleagues in the other states were the local "bosses"—county chairmen usually—who presided over affairs at the local level and who ran their venues with the same attention to detail as the state leaders did. The ballot boxes of American politics were placed in thousands of localities where county, town, ward, and precinct leaders kept close tabs on them. Precinct captains at the base of the pyramid established and maintained the regular face-to-face contacts with the voters and were considered vital to party success. New York State had 4,600 such local organizations, for example, in the late nineteenth century.

What these men ran were networks of committees and conventions, usually elected and guided by some form of the representative principle. American political parties tended to be "cadre" institutions, lacking masses of official members, and dependent on volunteers called together by the small group of local and state chairmen and secretaries. Yet, as suggested, the organizations were elaborate and encompassing. In 1840, Abraham Lincoln, one of the Whig party's organizational mainstays in Illinois, laid out for his colleagues a meticulous plan of party activity from the county down to more local jurisdictions for that year's election. He wrote the following:

> The Whig county committees should,
>
> 1st.   Appoint one person in each county as county captain, and take his pledge to perform promptly all the duties assigned him.
>
> Duties of the County Captain
>
> 1st.   To procure from the poll-books a separate list for each Precinct of all the names of all those persons who voted the Whig ticket in August.
> 2nd.   To appoint one person in each Precinct as Precinct Captain, and, by a personal interview with him, procure his pledge, to perform promptly all the duties assigned him.
> 3rd.   To deliver to each Precinct Captain the list of names as above, belonging to his Precinct, and also a written list of his duties.
>
> Duties of the Precinct Captain
>
> 1st.   To divide the list of names delivered him by the county Captain, into Sections of ten who reside most convenient to each other.
> 2nd.   To appoint one person of each Section as Section Captain, and by a personal interview with him, procure his pledge to perform promptly all the duties assigned him.
> 3rd.   To deliver to each Section Captain the list of names belonging to his Section and also a written list of his duties.

Duties of the Section Captain

1st.   To see each man of his Section face to face, and procure his pledge that he will for no consideration (impossibilities excepted) stray from the polls on the first Monday in November; and that he will record his vote as early on the day as possible.

2nd.   To add to his Section the name of every person in his vicinity who did not vote with us in August, but who will vote with us in the fall, and take the same pledge of him, as from the others.

3rd.   To *task* himself to procure at least such additional names to his Section.

The convention system was the centerpiece of political organization in nineteenth-century America, according to Richard P. McCormick, defining and reflecting the party system and its structural contrivances. The convention was "the key device of the new party organization," the organization's "crowning achievement." At first, conventions were little more than ad hoc mass meetings, called in unsystematic and highly informal ways and attended by anyone so inclined. Like everything else in the organizational sphere, only slowly did they become regular and powerful, reflect clearly defined rules of representation, and gain the ultimate power to direct and flesh out party organizations. Conventions became working meetings of party managers and political activists called together to nominate candidates and establish the organizational framework for each year's campaign.

Conventions were called for every election and held at every level of electoral politics: district, county, state, and national. The local meetings at the town, ward, or precinct level, usually called the primary meetings, began the process that was elaborated at each subsequent level. Held at a convenient community center—a hotel, saloon, or church—they had three purposes. First, they nominated candidates, passed statements of policy, and drafted platforms. Second, they elected delegates to the higher level conventions still to meet. Third, they established the local committee apparatus that ran the campaigns and that also had the responsibility for running the parties' affairs between conventions. Conventions at each succeeding level—county, legislative district, congressional district, and state—repeated the same functions, each in turn. Every four years the whole was capped by the meeting of the national convention where all this political maneuvering came together. The national candidates, McCormick writes, were named and "a sense of unity" and "enthusiasm for a common cause" advanced strikingly.

Conventions came to be understood as having the party's sovereign powers. Their word was the party's law. No other institution of the organizational structure better reflected the theory of party operations or better illustrated the organizational imperatives underlying party activities. The convention system, like the partisan networks themselves, reflected nineteenth-century America's commitment to the norms of delegated democracy: the notion that in each increasingly wide arena of politics, delegates, "fresh from the people," in Andrew Jackson's words, represented the views and acted on behalf of the hundreds and then thousands of party members whom they had been selected to represent. Pyramidical structures—delegated in principle and resting on local primary meetings—expressed the American notion of party organization. Conventions more accurately characterized that notion than did anything else in nineteenth-century American political life.

Of course, the democratic features of a convention were never unalloyed. Party leaders and partisan officeholders, sharing similar values and loyalties to the party organization, dominated the meetings. Convention rules, such as the unit vote that bound everyone rather than allowing for individual expression, gave party leaders a great deal of clout while relegating dissenters to the status of outvoted minorities. Still, democratic regulators did exist. Party leaders in conventions, as elsewhere, were bound by some limits; they did have to consider what the rank and file wanted or would accept and were never entirely free of some degree of supervision. As one experienced and prominent officeholder put it in 1852, party leaders paid constant "unacknowledged deference to public opinion." Public attitudes directly affected their behavior. They shaped platforms as they selected candidates: to represent the party's claims and reflect the desires of the party's constituent elements.

The point of the nominating and platform-writing phase of the campaign sequence was to provide for the general expression of preference by party members. Then, however, the convention moved into a second, reflective stage; party leaders shaped that expression according to the dictates of the need to solidify their coalition and maximize the party's electoral chances. Conventions first heard, the theory went, the expression of opinion based on interests, personal commitments, or prejudices; and then moved to another level, at which experience, shrewdness, and wisdom tamed the variety of expressions heard. (It is this later, reflective stage that has been extensively weakened in the late twentieth century.) The interaction between expression and reflection, in theory, and to a great extent in practice, gave conventions their central standing, role, and meaning within the parties' organizational structure and the partisan political culture.

Central to all of the convention's activity was the notion of collective discipline. Party leaders sought to impose order and obedience on the collective in pursuit of their common aim. One purpose of organization was to rationalize the procedures for selection of candidates and reduce the effect of internal party factionalism on the outcome of the election. Contentious individualism and group rivalries had to give way to the party's greater claims. As historian James Kehl sums it up, "state bosses were masters of enforcement. They recognized that disagreements must end when the nominee was chosen or [else] the party would face possible defeat at the polls." A common aphorism of mid-nineteenth-century politicians stated their aim well: "Union, harmony, self-sacrifice, everything for the cause, nothing for men."

The party committees appointed at these delegated meetings executed the will of the convention. The New York State Central Committee in the late nineteenth century, for example, was made up of one representative from each congressional district, elected by the state convention delegates from that district. The State Committee oversaw the day-to-day activities of the party in the campaign and its purpose was

voter mobilization. Each party's major goal was to construct
those campaign structures that could manage the electoral
process most efficiently. Exuberant ratification meetings,
frequent rallies, parades, spectacular displays, and heavily
attended public meetings were all norms of the campaign
months. Behind all of this apparently spontaneous enthusiasm
was a wide-ranging panoply of organization and management.
Networks of speakers' bureaus and publicity and finance
committees appeared. Often elaborate polling of individual
voters went on as did constant supervision of all events.
Nothing was left to chance.

All of these schemes required people, money, and
instruments of expression and direction. State committees raised
money in their own states. Often they asked the national
committee to supplement local funds and raised money from
both officeholders and well-endowed party supporters. As the
century passed, the public arena and government patronage
provided an increasing share of party resources through the
assessments of each partisan officeholder. Finance committees
organized part of this fundraising; local committeemen, as well
as the very top leaders, also participated.

Partisan clubs, ethnic and otherwise, from the
Tippecanoe Clubs of 1840 to the Republican Wide Awakes to
Irish volunteer fire companies, engaged in electioneering
activity at every level. Federal and state officeholders—
postmasters, census takers, land agents, and others—served as
particularly valuable foot soldiers for party organizations,
largely because of their ability to distribute newspapers and
pamphlets and to seek out and compile lists of voters. Their
activities brought the mechanism of party organization
directly onto the local scene everywhere in the country.
Whereas conventions at every level set the policies and the
boundaries of a party's activities, the local agents of the
political organization provided the main instrument for directly carrying on party actions. Each campaign season always
gave the locals a great deal to do.

Party organization also worked to insure victory. Election
day organizational activity capped the whole sequence of
events that had been initiated months before by the calls to

local conventions. Parties, not the government, largely controlled the electoral apparatus. Each organization provided individual ballots or tickets to voters, got everyone out to the polls, and kept close watch on all matters dealing with the process. A story in the *New Hampshire Statesman*, appearing just before the state elections in 1839, sums up this aspect of organizational activity very well. The election was the following week and the editor wrote:

> "ARE YOU READY?"
> Is every town properly, thoroughly organized?
> How are the committees of vigilance? Are they on the alert?
> Are the Whig lists completed, that every town knows its strength?
> Are the names of the Whig voters on the check lists?
> Are the names of those Tories [i.e., Democrats] who are not entitled to vote, stricken off?
> Have arrangements been made to secure the attendance of every man at the polls? Carriages and attendants provided for the aged and infirm?
> And, lastly, have the printed votes been received—the Whig votes—in every town?

At the polls, party workers supervised and guided (some said intimidated) eligible citizens to vote the right way. Finally, they saw to the counting of votes after the polls had closed. Like everything else in the extraordinarily competitive partisan environment of American politics in the nineteenth century, all of these election day activities became even more elaborate and complex as the years passed. They capped each year's efforts and insured a hard won victory (at least for one party).

Linkage among all of these activities was always essential—and carefully overseen. Stump speakers and candidates, editors and legislators, all stayed in constant touch through an extraordinary communications network. Party platforms, drafted in conventions, provided the instructions and cues subsequently disseminated largely by newspapers, the main agency for transmitting party outlooks and strategies. The press transmitted information and exhortation in widening circles to the party committed through exchanges and correspondence between different areas. Before the Civil War, each party maintained a major national publication, situated in Washington, that published a partisan worldview and issued directions to officials elsewhere. The Democrats' Washington *Globe* and then the *Union* exemplified these party organs of the 1830s, 1840s, and 1850s. Every state capital also saw the publication of a major newspaper for each party. Weed's Albany *Evening Journal* spread the Whig party's word in New York State as did the Democratic Richmond *Enquirer* in Virginia. In both the state capitals and in the national capital, party newspapers benefited from the governments' printing patronage, a boon that allowed them to concentrate on their main (partisan) purpose. Local newspapers in county seats repeating the word, exhorting the faithful, and detailing activities filled out the system. In every election special campaign newspapers appeared, filled with a single-minded devotion to the party's electoral fortunes.

Conditions in the newspaper world changed just before the Civil War, and the creation of the Government Printing Office in Washington in 1861 ended a very direct relationship between newspapers and government patronage. The press now had to depend less on government resources for survival, but newspapers still served partisan purposes. Such newspapers as the *New York Tribune*, the *New York Times*, the *Chicago Tribune*, and other major regional dailies came to dominate the scene from the Civil War onward; they were still party newspapers, however, espousing a partisan line and feeding it to the faithful in every place they reached. Most editors were not independent of party, nor did they want to be. Some, like Horace Greeley and Whitelaw Reid, ran for office. But their many energies were devoted primarily to communication. They served unstintingly as a major force in the political mobilization of the American voter.

Moreover, organizations issued pamphlets publicizing the party line and compiled campaign handbooks containing a representative sample of speeches, editorials, platforms, and statistics for the political guidance of the faithful. Campaign biographies of presidential candidates appeared early and became routine by mid-century. All of these publications were widely distributed and found their way into stump speeches at every level as well as into local newspapers. Their propaganda gave the faithful a fairly uniform and national picture of the party's outlook and activities. Styles of presentation were exhortative, simplified, vulgarized, and popular. Whatever the guise, the outpouring of printed material performed a major post-convention function in the politically charged atmosphere leading to election day.

All of this mobilization was rarely designed to persuade people to vote for a party that they usually did not support. In this extraordinarily partisan age of American politics, from the 1830s to the 1890s, individual and group party loyalty was deep, intense, powerful, and persistent; strategic options were limited, obvious, and well understood. Party organizations worked primarily to arouse those already committed, unstintingly loyal, intensely partisan members of their own party, most of whom could be counted upon to vote if properly stimulated. Given the closeness of elections, no one could be forgotten. Parties were very unlikely to convert loyalists of either side. The real problem was thus paramountly organizational— insuring unity and harmony, instilling discipline, and mobilizing the maximum turnout of the already committed. When turnout at the polls reached 90 percent of those eligible, as it did, the fruits of such organizational activity were clearly seen.

The final purpose of party organization was to manage the government. Legislative caucuses, as noted, had long been a feature of state and national politics. In the 1820s and 1830s, the widespread introduction of patronage appointments to government offices became another firmly imbedded and characteristic element of the American political scene, bringing the disciplined party outlook directly into every area of government administration. Party leaders determined appointments. The state committeemen in the thirty-four congressional districts in late-nineteenth-century New York State, for example, were the clearinghouse for all federal and state government patronage. Party and government were more than symbolically entwined. The extent of the partisan organization's influence on government is suggested by the fact that several men who made their early reputations largely as soldiers or commanders in various party structures (Martin Van Buren, Abraham Lincoln, Franklin Pierce, Chester Alan Arthur) became presidents. And no one succeeded in government without the organization's imprimatur.

Scope and Assessment

Party organizations sometimes did add additional elements to their structures. Urban political machines took shape in large eastern cities from the 1850s onward. By the 1880s, they had developed their characteristic pattern to become the one new element added to political organization after the innovative period of the 1830s and 1840s. Machines functioned for similar purposes and had structures similar to the other parts of the organizational mechanism. Tammany Hall, after all, was the New York County Democratic Committee. Below it, and other machines like it, was the usual array of precinct and ward committees, with their chairmen, secretaries, and other committeemen. Committee headquarters became less casual, however, as the lease on a few rooms above a tavern or in a storefront during the campaign season was replaced by more permanent arrangements, a base of operations (at every level) that stayed open throughout the year and were manned at least part of every day.

Of course, these urban political machines added new roles to the functions of political organizations. Their basic coin of exchange continued to be elections and patronage. In that, little had changed. Beyond campaign administration and electoral mobilization, however, urban machines played another role as well: They served as ombudsmen and social welfare agencies for their immigrant constituents. As a result, what now existed was a further stage of organizational development but one that was firmly rooted in existing structures and assumptions about parties and organization.

American political organization in its heyday never achieved the ideal model of systematic efficiency, scope, centralization, and permanence. Parties were nowhere near as thorough, systematic, and sustained as many thought necessary. Constant exhortations for some group to get going appeared in state party newspapers and attested to some lack of necessary activity. During campaigns, party organizations took frequent missteps, lacked coordination, and failed to raise enough money, while the various state campaigns did not always fully mesh. On the day after an election, as one student has noted, "virtually the entire organizational edifice . . . entered into a mad race of dissolution." Party machinery largely disappeared or went into suspended animation.

On the other hand, the importance of this dissolution can be exaggerated. Parties in America, Richard P. McCormick correctly remarks, have been "more heavily burdened with electoral tasks than those of any other democracy." Because elections in America were held so frequently, organizational machinery had almost always to be kept in place. State and local elections preceded the presidential election; not everyone voted on the same day. Few months of the year passed without their quota of elections. One set of party meetings and conventions ended, often to be succeeded quickly by another set for another office. This regularity and ubiquity had significant impact. One of the most repeated of historical cliches attests to the decentralized nature of American party organizations. Yet regular, repetitive, and similar decisions made and activities carried out suggest the existence of a powerful national organizational culture whatever the formal decentralization of activities and ultimate decisionmaking power.

Some of these organizational forms were expressive and popular: rallies and conventions, for example; some—like the smoke-filled rooms—were not. All served some purpose in electoral and policy mobilization. As has been noted, all were in theory, and to a degree in actuality, not dictatorially directed from the top, but interactive. The notion of cynical bosses, corrupt activities, issueless and watered-down campaigns distinctive only for drama not for substance, permeates much of our understanding of nineteenth-century party organizations. No discussion of party organization can avoid the presence of charges of partisan and frequent corruption, vote manipulation, bribery, and illicit financial activities for the benefit of individuals and parties. Corruption of this kind was always closely coupled, by unfriendly observers and the losing side, to the existence of party organizations and their activities. Parties were, after all, always looking for an advantage, always in need of money to lubricate their activities.

Some of these charges were true. But the democratic implications of the pyramidical shape of party organizations were not entirely fictitious. Parties, led by elites but dependent upon the mass of voters, had to take into account the outlooks and perspectives of the commoners, a political fact that set boundaries on elite control. Organizational norms dictated a process of movement upward from local meetings to ever more central conclaves in a pattern of reciprocal understandings, exchanges, and ideas. Cadres of local leaders at the precinct, town, and county level contributed as much as the statewide boss to the organizational imperatives and the political wisdom shaping the decisions that dominated partisan politics. At the same time, political parties did stand for and espouse different outlooks and policies, did represent different social groups, and did articulate a powerful battle for the soul of America that was not without substance. Finally, the persistent cries of fraud attested more, perhaps, to the abilities and power of party organizations than to the full truth of the charges made. Political losers cried fraud as soon as the polls closed, always blaming avaricious organizational imperatives for the denial of the people's will—that is, a victory for the losing party.

Still, because America's political culture retained powerful antiparty sentiments that have never fully died, partisan organizations were often viewed suspiciously even after parties had been firmly established as the basic centerpieces of American political life. A severe critique of parties, partisanship, and the activities of party organizations intensified with the growth of independence and mugwumpery (as well as appearances of increased corruption) from the 1870s onward. This negativism eventually took hold and took its toll. Major economic and social changes such as industrialization and urbanization also affected attitudes toward parties and their ability to function as they had. Nationwide economic interest groups found parties less responsive to their needs than they wished; urban reformers saw in Tammany Hall and other political machines unacceptable levels of corruption. These perceptions had political impact. The late nineteenth century marked the dawn of a new political era, with significant consequences for the practices of partisan politics. Party organizations came increasingly under state regulation. With the rise of a new kind of political boss (first personified by Ohio Republican Mark Hanna), the full realization of the socioeconomic changes by the 1890s, and the weakening of the era's characteristic electoral competitiveness owing to the voter realignment of 1896, the central thrust of party organization began to change. Political bosses and conventions lost their power, parties were no longer the mainstays of American politics. The golden age of American partisan political organization passed.

References

Allen, Howard W., and Kay Warren Allen. 1981. "Vote Fraud and Data Validity." In Jerome M. Clubb, William H. Flanigan, and Nancy H. Zingale, eds. *Analyzing Electoral History: A Guide to the Study of American Voting Behavior*. Beverly Hills, CA: Sage.

Basler, Roy P., ed. 1953. *Collected Works of Abraham Lincoln*. New Brunswick, NJ: Rutgers U. Pr.

Benson, Lee. 1961. *The Concept of Jacksonian Democracy: New York as a Test Case*. Princeton: Princeton U. Pr.

Bland, Richard A. 1975. "Politics, Propaganda, and the Public Printing: The Administration Organs, 1829–1849." Ph.D. diss., U. of Kentucky.

Burnham, Walter Dean. 1965. "The Changing Shape of the American Political Universe." 59 *American Political Science Review* 7.

Chambers, William N. 1963. *Political Parties in a New Nation*. New York: Oxford U. Pr.

———. 1971. "The Election of 1840." In Arthur M. Schlesinger, Jr., ed. *The History of American Presidential Elections*. Chatham, NJ: Chelsea House.

Chase, James S. 1973. *Emergence of the Presidential Nominating Convention, 1789–1832*. Urbana: U. of Illinois Pr.

Cole, Donald B. 1984. *Martin Van Buren and the American Political System*. Princeton: Princeton U. Pr.

Duncan, Bingham. 1975. *Whitelaw Reid: Journalist, Politician, Diplomat*. Athens: U. of Georgia Pr.

Formisano, Ronald P. 1983. *The Transformation of Political Culture: Massachusetts Parties, 1790s–1840s*. New York: Oxford U. Pr.

Gosnell, Harold F. 1924. *Boss Platt and His New York Machine*. Chicago: U. of Chicago Pr.

Hays, Samuel P. 1957. *The Response to Industrialism: 1885–1914*. Chicago: U. of Chicago Pr.

Hofstadter, Richard. 1969. *The Idea of a Party System: The Rise of Legitimate Opposition in the United States, 1780–1840*. Berkeley: U. of California Pr.

Holt, Michael F. 1978. *The Political Crisis of the 1850s*. New York: Wiley.

Howe, Daniel W. 1979. *The Political Culture of the 1850s*. New York: Wiley.

Jensen, Richard. 1971. *The Winning of the Midwest: Social and Political Conflict, 1888–1896*. Chicago: U. of Chicago Pr.

Josephson, Matthew. 1938. *The Politicos, 1865–1896*. New York: Harcourt, Brace.

Kehl, James A. 1981. *Boss Rule in the Gilded Age: Matt Quay of Pennsylvania*. Pittsburgh: U. of Pittsburgh Pr.

Keller, Morton. 1977. *Affairs of State: Public Life in Late Nineteenth-Century America*. Cambridge: Harvard U. Pr.

King, Preston. 1852. "To Jabez D. Hammon, August 11th." Miscellaneous Papers, New York Historical Society.

Kleppner, Paul. 1979. *The Third Electoral System, 1853–1892: Parties, Voters, and Political Cultures*. Chapel Hill: U. of North Carolina Pr.

Kruman, Marc A. 1983. *Parties and Politics in North Carolina, 1836–1865*. Baton Rouge: Louisiana State U. Pr.

Leonard, Thomas. 1986. *The Power of the Press: The Birth of American Political Reporting*. New York: Oxford U. Pr.

Luetscher, George. 1903. *Early Political Machinery in the United States*. Philadelphia: U. of Pennsylvania Pr.

McCormick, Richard L. 1981. *From Realignment to Reform: Political Change in New York State, 1893–1910*. Ithaca: Cornell U. Pr.

McCormick, Richard P. 1966. *The Second American Party System: Party Formation in the Jacksonian Era.* Chapel Hill: U. of North Carolina Pr.

———. 1982. *The Presidential Game: The Origins of American Presidential Politics.* New York: Oxford U. Pr.

McGerr, Michael. 1986. *The Decline of Popular Politics: The American North, 1865–1928.* New York: Oxford U. Pr.

McSeveney, Samuel T. 1972. *The Politics of Depression: Political Behavior in the Northeast, 1893–1896.* New York: Oxford U. Pr.

Mandelbaum, Seymour. 1965. *Boss Tweed's New York.* New York: Wiley.

Marcus, Robert D. 1971. *Grand Old Party: Political Structure in the Gilded Age.* New York: Oxford U. Pr.

Mushkat, Jerome. 1971. *Tammany: The Evolution of a Political Machine.* Syracuse: Syracuse U. Pr.

Nichols, Roy P. 1967. *The Invention of the American Political Parties: A Study of Political Improvisation.* New York: Macmillan.

Ranney, Austin. 1975. *Curing the Mischief of Faction: Party Reform in America.* Berkeley: U. of California Pr.

Silbey, Joel H. 1985. *The Partisan Imperative: The Dynamics of American Politics Before the Civil War.* New York: Oxford U. Pr.

Smoger, Gerson Henry. 1982. "Organizing Political Campaigns: A Survey of 19th and 20th Century Trends." Ph.D. diss., U. of Pennsylvania.

Stave, Bruce. 1984. *Urban Bosses, Machines and Progressive Reformers.* Malabar, FL: Krieger.

Summers, Mark. 1987. *The Plundering Generation: Corruption and the Crisis of the Union, 1849–1861.* New York: Oxford U. Pr.

Sydnor, Charles S. 1952. *Gentlemen Freeholders: Political Practices in Washington's Virginia.* Chapel Hill: U. of North Carolina Pr.

Thornton, J. Mills. 1978. *Politics and Power in a Slave Society: Alabama, 1800–1860.* Baton Rouge: Louisiana State U. Pr.

Wattenberg, Martin. 1990. *The Decline of American Political Parties, 1952–1988.* Cambridge: Harvard U. Pr.

Wiebe, Robert. 1967. *The Search for Order, 1877–1920.* New York: Hill and Wang.

Wood, Gordon. 1987. "Ideology and the Origins of Liberal America." 44 *William and Mary Quarterly* 628.

CHAPTER 5

Legislative Government in the United States Congress, 1800–1900

Allan G. Bogue

Conceptual Theories

Most efforts to build or to apply theories of legislative behavior and institutional process in the United States Congress focus on the years since 1950. Older institutional studies are useful primarily for their descriptive content. In recent years increased interest in diachronic (changes over time) analysis has been evident, and scholars have suggested a variety of theoretical approaches and analytic techniques. Particularly they have explored the usefulness of modernization theory. In 1968 Nelson W. Polsby hypothesized that the differentiation of the institution from its environment, the degree of internal complexity in the legislative process, and the tendency to move from particularistic and discretionary practices to universalistic and automatic decisionmaking were measures of institutionalization. His time series suggested that significant changes in these respects occurred during the late nineteenth and early twentieth centuries. A major breakthrough, Polsby's article was admittedly oversimplified. It did not treat the environmental factors that are increasingly viewed as the generative forces in congressional operations and performance, particularly the party system. Scholars interested in developing conceptual frameworks for

understanding congressional government during the nineteenth
century now posit a constituency-driven congressional system,
draw upon organization analysis (subject to the constraints on its
application implied in a system of separated powers, geographic
constituencies, and plurality electoral processes), and turn to
rational choice theory in explanations of individual behavior. As
yet such theory-based treatments of the nineteenth-century
Congress are too few to serve as the foundation for a comprehensive discussion of legislative government there.

Periodization

We can identify successive eras of congressional development, although the exact points in time at which boundary lines
should be drawn are arguable. A period of initial development
extends into the late 1820s or early 1830s. These years were
characterized by an expanding agrarian-mercantile economy,
efforts to legitimize a national identity abroad, a diminution of
habits of deference in politics, and the growth and decay of the
first national party structure. Era 2, subsuming some fifty years,
coincided with significant transformation toward an industrial
economy, intense sectional or center-periphery conflict, and unbridled two-party patronage politics. In Era 3 the Union and
the federal government stood reaffirmed, finance capitalism
emerged, Congress enunciated formulas of industrial control,
and changes appeared in the Congress that have been defined as
institutionalization. Era 1 began in the late eighteenth century
and Era 3 continued into the twentieth century. Although such
periodization is useful, it can also be argued that the Civil War
marks a significant break point in congressional development.

The Lawmakers

United States representatives and senators have typically
been members of the country's elite. Some 40 percent of the
representatives entering during the 1790s had attended college.

By the end of the next century more than 60 percent fell in that group, although David Crockett's frontier education clearly shocked de Tocqueville. Occupationally, legislators have been predominantly lawyers; some 40 percent during the first twenty years and more than 60 percent after 1830. Agriculturists represented more than 15 percent of the members in the first decade of the nineteenth century, but only 5 to 10 percent after 1830. Southern planters predominated in the group until the postbellum period. Ten to 15 percent of the representatives had business backgrounds until the 1850s; that figure remained slightly above 20 percent for the most part after 1860, with northerners always predominant in this category. Other professionals always fell in the 5 to 10 percent range, and a small fringe of miscellaneous or unknown backgrounds appear consistently in the data. Military service, usually at the commissioned rank, has always been common, although veterans were only a majority during the 1790s. Individuals related to other congressmen— earlier, current, or later—made up a third of the House during the 1790s, almost 20 percent during the 1840s, and some 12 percent during the 1880s and 1890s. Southern representatives included larger proportions of veterans and had more congressional relatives.

During the early national period more than 70 percent of the representatives had experience in state office. The proportion was still above 50 percent during the 1890s. Some 30 percent of early national congressmen had held local-level office, the figure increasing to about one-half by 1900. Of the representatives, some 8 to 15 percent had occupied federal or judicial posts. But during the nineteenth century, fewer than half of the representatives had served at more than one level of service; experience in three was uncommon. Occasionally, local conditions or fortuitous occurrences enabled men with little political experience to win election.

The median length of public service among the cohort of congressmen entering the House during the 1801–1810 period was four years—identical to that of the entrants of the 1890s. Between these dates, however, the median term fell to two years among the entering cohorts of the 1850s and 1860s—the contraction attributable, it is believed, to the fierce party competition of the antebellum years, the practice of rotation among office-holders in various regions, and the disruptive impact of the Civil War. Although some representatives extended their service in Washington by moving to the Senate, the number of truly seasoned representatives in the House was always small during the nineteenth century. A marked trend toward longer service became apparent only when the entering cohort of the 1890s marked the emergence of a growing number of one-party districts. Through the Seventh Congress (1801–1803) to the Fifty-fifth (1897–1899) a majority of the representatives in thirty-three Congresses had not held seats in the previous House. Thus the membership of the House of Representatives was composed during the nineteenth century of a shifting mix of short-term representatives with a relatively small core of longer-serving veterans. If the House was to be an effective legislative body, then it had to develop a structure of detailed rules and an institutional framework within which inexperienced legislators could work productively. As one author wrote, "this large, unwieldy, changing body holds its own with the smaller, longer-lived, more experienced Senate and Executive by centralizing its power remarkably in its older members—in the Speaker and the committee chairmen."

Early National Period

An apportionment of 106 seats was in effect in the House of Representatives when the members of the Seventh Congress assembled in December 1801, and the supporters of Thomas Jefferson assumed control of the federal government. Their basic charter of powers, rights, privileges—and to some degree, practice—lay in Article 1 of the Constitution. Although providing the time and frequency of meetings and restricting the length of adjournments within sessions, that document specified as to organization only that the "Representatives shall choose their Speaker and other officers," be judge of "the elections, returns and qualifications" of their colleagues, accept a majority of members as a quorum, determine the rules of proceedings, punish members for disorderly conduct, and expel members, provided that a two-thirds majority assented. The Speaker could look for guidance to British and colonial parliamentary practice, a growing body of House rules and precedents, and the remembered example of four predecessors. Congress by Congress the representatives also chose a clerk, a sergeant-at-arms, and a doorkeeper. These officers plus a few minor clerks and pages constituted the staff cadre of the Jeffersonian House.

A Standing Committee on Elections appeared in 1789 and Claims, Commerce, and Revisal and Unfinished Business committees followed in the 1790s. As the initial practice of using large numbers of ad hoc select committees proved unsatisfactory in areas of continuing interest, six more standing committees appeared between 1800 and 1810, including Ways and Means in 1802. But select committees were still used.

Committees, both standing and select, might be assigned portions of the president's message for consideration and for the possible reporting of bills. In this era the typical method of initiating legislative activity was a resolution from a member that initiated committee activity and bill drafting. Measures of particular interest to executive departments were drafted there and brought into the House by appropriate committees or friends of the administration.

What were the sources of authority to which representatives looked in this era? The isolation of the early national lawmakers in the raw village of Washington has been exaggerated. They arrived with a deep understanding of their constituents' desires and needs, generally assumed that they were the delegates of their districts, received letters from their constituents, and presented and nurtured the petitions or requests of interests or groups at home. Discussion or caucusing within state delegations clarified understanding and provided moral reinforcement. They might expect to be requested (if representatives) and instructed (if senators) by their state legislatures to take particular positions on legislation.

Then, as later, the representative prospered in his designs if he stood well with sources of authority in the House. Preeminent among them was the Speaker. Although those of the 1790s have sometimes been dismissed as mere moderators of debate, they recognized party preference at an early date in exercising the power to make the committee appointments that the House bestowed upon the office in 1790. Nathaniel Macon (1801–1807) followed suit, although considerations of state and regional balance, native ability, and prior experience at the state or federal level were all involved. The originator of the seed resolution was generally considered to be the appropriate choice for chairman of a select committee. Jeffersonian Speakers were not, however, aggressive in using the appointive power, giving strict heed to President Jefferson's wishes. The representatives' rejection in 1806 of a proposal to elect committee members by ballot was fateful in the institutional development of the House.

The Federalist and Democratic-Republican parties of the early national years lacked the national conventions, platforms, and organizational forms of later eras, but their members subscribed to common ideologies and legislative agendas. Party was a meaningful distinction under Jefferson, and he sought more actively than either of his predecessors to organize support for his policies in the Congress. During the Seventh and Eighth Congresses (1801–1805), Jefferson was notably successful; less success marked his second term because of disagreement over foreign policy issues.

Although William B. Giles initially exerted major influence on the floor, John Randolph, the chairman of Ways and Means, emerged as leader of the administration party in the House. But Randolph opposed the administration's request for funds with which to purchase West Florida. The incident highlighted congressional concern with enunciating standards for executive request, administration, and report of finances—a concern that continued through the initial era of institutional structuring. Randolph and a little band of Old Republicans were banished from party councils. But, given the importance of the fiscal measures under the control of Ways and Means, the logic of its chairman serving as floor leader remained. The arrangement held (with varying degrees of commitment to administrative policy on the part of its chairman) until the Appropriations Committee was created during the Thirty-eighth Congress (1865). Randolph's bitter harangues, criticizing the majority position in 1811, inspired his colleagues to accept a rule authorizing one-fifth of the members present to demand the previous question—a major step in developing the House's most effective device for limiting debate.

During the last generation scholars have conducted systematic scaling analyses of the roll calls in many of the nineteenth-century Congresses. The research shows that a congressman's voting could usually be categorized as reflecting the influence of party, section, individual constituency, or personal idiosyncrasy. Party voting was usually dominant, but sectional deviation was intermittently important, and other types of deviation were of minor importance, although occasionally of prophetic or symbolic significance. The student of the nineteenth-century Congress must show how party agendas were translated into policy and law and the ways in which the institutional structure of the Congress was adapted to facilitate these processes.

During his presidency, Thomas Jefferson provided much of the vital force in these matters but by the early 1820s a state of highly factionalized nonpartisanship had been attained. Although the party caucus emerged during this era as a means of designating presidential candidates and focusing policy objectives, it was not a well-drilled force in the planning of legislative strategy and mobilization of voting majorities. But informally at least, party and subparty groups, including state delegations, caucused for these purposes. Although the boardinghouse or hotel mess facilitated communication among its residents up to and beyond the Civil War, such groups were almost invariably composed of kindred party spirits with a common regional affiliation. Shared party and regional values and objectives brought the messmates together and served as referents in subsequent behavior.

The unsettled authority structure in the House during the Jefferson years underwent significant change during the James Madison and James Monroe administrations. Henry Clay strongly influenced legislative proceedings and practice. A brilliant speaker of the Kentucky legislative assembly and twice briefly United States Senator, Henry Clay arrived in the Twelfth Congress as part of a cohort of aggressive young Democratic-Republicans who favored a more aggressive foreign policy toward the belligerents of the Napoleonic Wars than that of previous years. Elected Speaker, Clay asserted the dominance of the legislative branch; he and his colleagues forced Madison to lead the country into the War of 1812. Clay was reelected Speaker five more times before becoming Secretary of State, interrupting his service to be a peace commissioner subsequent to the War of 1812 and by resignation in 1820. Clay greatly increased the parliamentary power of the Speaker, strengthened the informal or personal influence wielded by that officer, and asserted his claim to be a major legislative leader. During his years, Congress assumed the initiative in developing the legislative agenda, and Clay controlled the legislative majorities more successfully than any other congressional leader to that time. The 1812 war agenda, the elements of the American system, the Missouri Compromise legislation, and policies supportive of the emergent republics of Latin America bore his stamp. Unlike earlier leaders, he participated actively in the shaping of legislation in the Committee of the Whole; he asserted his right to vote on measures, irrespective of whether that vote would change the outcome; and his tactical and partisan use of the House rules of procedure far surpassed that of his predecessors.

During the Clay years, the structure of standing committees took shape. Between 1813 and 1825, seventeen more joined the ten thus far created. Five of these were charged with reviewing the expenditures in executive departments, thus institutionalizing the supervisory authority that had been a source of contention. Although Clay found Monroe to be much less compliant than Madison, the precedents for a vigorous exercise of power by the Speaker and independent agenda formulation and realization in the Congress were now established. Clay is ranked among the greatest of innovative Speakers; his leadership style combined forensic skills, personal charm, imagination, and a talent for compromise. None of his antebellum successors matched him and none served for a comparable period of time.

Era of Major Sectional Stress

Although politicians labored throughout the period 1800–1860 to create national political parties, differing regional economies and institutions (notably slavery), and changing cultural values imparted sectional tilts to the party cohorts and leadership structures in the Congress. In the period of Federalist dominance, the 1790s, all four Speakers were from northern states; during the next sixty years thirteen of nineteen Speakers came from southern constituencies. Eight of ten presiding officers selected between 1860 and 1900 came from northern states. Between 1800 and 1860 northerners presided over the House in approximately one year in four. That ratio was exactly reversed during the next forty years. The same regional disparity marked the selection of the chairmen of the Ways and Means Committee in antebellum America. Although eight northerners and fourteen southerners held the office, southerners actually chaired this committee for forty-four years, northerners for sixteen.

Some have suggested that the chairmanship of Ways and Means was a common stepping stone to the Speakership. Yet for only four of the forty-five men who were chairmen of either the Ways and Means or the Appropriations (subsequent to 1865) committees during the nineteenth century was this true: Langdon Cheves (1812), James K. Polk (1833), Samuel J. Randall (1875), and Joseph C. Cannon, who did not become Speaker until 1903. No Speaker of the nineteenth century matched Clay's record of six elections and ten years of service. The unremarkable Virginian, Andrew Stevenson, came closest, serving for seven years (1827–1834), while the second American party system emerged. The modal service among other Speakers before the Civil War was but one term. Although none thereafter equaled John Randolph's six years of service as chairman of Ways and Means, double terms in that post were common. But frequent turnover in the two most important offices was the rule, and although some incumbents moved to the Senate or accepted diplomatic posts, the usual explanation of turnover between 1830 and 1860 was the defeat of the incumbent's party.

Speakers in this era varied greatly in the vigor and skill with which they selected committees for partisan ends. It remained unclear as to whether the Speaker was to make common cause with his leading party colleagues in the House or to take his cues mainly from the executive branch. Factional allegiances, splinter group activity, recurrent realignment, and ineffective party discipline usually made authority structures ineffective during the twenty years before the Civil War. Although party caucuses sought to solidify support behind particular candidates for the position of Speaker, eleven multiple-ballot Speaker elections took place during the period 1809–1861; those of 1839, 1849, 1855, and 1859 required 11, 63, 133, and 44 ballots. Once elected, Speakers differed in the degree to which they reconciled partisan commitments with fair treatment of all members. Some invited opposition members to preside over sittings of the Committee of the Whole and occasionally asked distinguished members of the opposition to chair committees. However, Speakers began to list all majority party members on committees before any minority party members—a change from the practice in the early national period when the names of members of the majority and minority parties were alternated.

His biographer maintains that James K. Polk was the "first Speaker to be regarded frankly as a party leader, responsible for pushing a party program through the House." Presiding over the Twenty-fourth and Twenty-fifth Houses (1835–1839), Polk "passed through severer trials than any previous Speaker" as militant Whigs challenged his rulings and even called him "*a tool of tools.*" The presentation of abolitionist petitions demanding the extirpation of slavery in the District of Columbia provoked fierce debate, and Polk concluded that the House could refuse to receive a petition. A select committee based its report on this foundation, proposing the famous gag rule: petitions and other papers relating to slavery or its abolition "shall, without ever being printed or referred, be laid upon the table, and that no further action . . . be had thereon." Against this position the ex-President, now Congressman John Quincy Adams, marshalled all his eloquence and parliamentary knowledge. Fierce challenges to the Speaker's rulings and floor behavior, intemperate to the point of fisticuffs, canings or subsequent invitations to the dueling ground occurred sporadically during this period.

While the southern wing of the democracy controlled the Congress during 1854, the adoption of the Kansas-Nebraska Act appeared to surrender Kansas Territory to the incursions of slavery. Bleeding Kansas revitalized the slavery controversy and catalyzed party realignment. So mixed in their allegiances were the representatives of the Thirty-sixth House (1859–1861) among Republicans, Whigs, American or Know-Nothing party adherents, and various Democratic factions that protracted balloting resulted in the selection of a first-term member as Speaker. A fair-minded Whig, William Pennington, had little impact upon the office except that he was the first Speaker to serve on the Rules Committee, at that point a select committee.

Governance within the House of Representatives changed little in terms of structure or major precedent during the years between the election of Polk to the Speakership and the outbreak of the Civil War. Party voting was strong, but sectional issues related to southern expansion and the place of slavery in the Union recurrently shocked the system. Sectional and ideological commitments worked against the institutional development that might have accompanied longer-serving Speakers and a more stable alignment of opposing parties. The standing committee structure changed little; between 1837 and 1860 only the Standing Committee on Engraving was established with expenditures in the interior department added in the latter year.

Many of the items of the issue agenda in the thirty years before the Civil War were developmental in nature. Should the federal government subsidize internal improvements, impose protective tariffs, provide strong central banking, and use federal lands for purposes other than fostering a class of virtuous freehold farmers? On these issues Whigs and Democrats differed, the former being the most developmentally inclined. Representatives tried to shape national party policy in ways most favorable to their constituencies; they were also most apt to break party lines on issues of regional significance. The moral questions related to the institution of slavery increasingly complicated the developmental agendas; congressmen evaluated legislative measures in terms of their impact upon slavery. The

Speakers' selections of members for the committees on territories, the District of Columbia, public lands, and the judiciary were viewed as vital in efforts to protect, limit, or to destroy that institution.

Although party caucuses were used during this period and sometimes to good effect, their power to aggregate, plan, and enforce party strategy does not appear to have grown perceptibly. After Jackson, and excepting only James K. Polk (1845–1849), a succession of weak presidents provided little legislative leadership, in part because party control was common to the executive branch and both houses in only four of the ten Congresses between 1841 and 1861. During the Civil War, the Republican party controlled the House, Senate, and presidency and the magnitude of the crisis opened opportunities for the executive branch to provide leadership that might establish new patterns of governance.

Unhampered by representatives from eleven southern states, the Republican majorities in House and Senate compiled one of the most impressive legislative records in congressional history during the Thirty-seventh Congress. A strongly protective tariff, the Homestead Law of 1862, provision of a national banking system, incorporation of a Pacific Railroad, and the Land Grant College Act were notable legislative achievements, among others. However, Republicans had strong differences of opinion over the methods by which slavery was to be ended, the war prosecuted, and the Union reconstructed. The moderate Abraham Lincoln encountered strong opposition from radical elements of his party in the Congress.

National mobilization of material and human resources greatly increased congressional work loads; the numbers of resolutions and bills considered rose sharply. Both select and standing committees exercised investigative or oversight functions to a greater degree than during the previous decade. The unprecedented Joint Committee on the Conduct of the War vigorously investigated unsuccessful campaigns, military defeats, and atrocities. The House immediately (with the Senate ultimately following suit) elected to use a quorum based on the representatives of states present, rather than the total in the Union. The houses adopted Joint Rule 22, allowing immediate and secret consideration of matters relating to the suppression of the rebellion on the request of the president. But the president never asked that the procedure be used. The Speakers of the Civil War—Galusha A. Grow and Schuyler Colfax—have been characterized as figureheads in style of leadership and conservative in their use of the powers of their office. Neither worked vigorously to advance the policies of the executive branch nor, with minor exceptions, to expedite particular legislative programs. Grow, a Pennsylvanian, was criticized for favoritism to the Middle States in making committee assignments and was defeated for reelection to the House because of a Democratic resurgence in his state. His successor, Colfax, twice won reelection before becoming vice-president, but he was suspected at the White House of being allied with the president's radical opponents.

Grow appointed his fellow Pennsylvanian, Thaddeus Stevens, as chairman of Ways and Means. Elderly and irascible, this radical Republican has been described as one of the great House floor leaders. During his tenure the House successfully developed the fiscal and monetary policies that allowed successful prosecution of the war. Stevens also actively supported radical policies in relation to war and reconstruction. Still, his motions on the floor were often defeated, and there were said to be considerable differences of opinion within his committee. He forthrightly espoused the prerogatives of the Congress relative to the executive branch and caustically denounced the president and cabinet in caucus. The conflict between the executive and legislative branches to which Stevens contributed under Lincoln culminated when he became chairman of the House managers seeking impeachment of Lincoln's successor, Andrew Johnson. At his death in 1868, Stevens had served seven years as floor leader, longer than any predecessor.

Speaker Grow named chairmen of 37 nine-, five-, and three-man standing committees. Twenty-one members had not served on their committee during the previous Congress. The mean prior congressional service of the chairmen of Grow's large committees was 3.2 years and that of the smaller only 1.7 years. Just under 15 percent of the committee members of the next Congress, the Thirty-eighth, had served on the same committee in the preceding House. Such records of service were not wartime phenomena but symptomatic of the era. Like most senior leaders before them, Grow and Stevens had considerable congressional experience—ten and six years respectively—but the ranks of such veterans were always thin.

The Republicans enjoyed a substantial majority in the House during the Thirty-seventh Congress and a reduced but effective predominance in the Thirty-eighth. The radical Republicans rejected Lincoln's leadership on matters relating to slavery and southern reconstruction, but the presence of more moderate Republicans and Border State members provided the potential for the defeat of radical proposals. On southern issues, legislation failed to satisfy either the various congressional factions or the president. In both houses the party caucus developed legislative strategy and party positions on pending legislation. For all that, caucusing was not completely successful, although apparently more effective in the Senate than in the House. Senators carried caucus activity to the point of agreeing to request a reorganization of the cabinet, but Lincoln astutely foiled them. House Republicans discussed the same subject in caucus, only to hear the chairman of a caucus committee charged with devising ways of instilling vigor into the administration ask to be excused from a hopeless task. Attendance at the caucuses was often sparse, and Stevens once declared that he would not be bound by majority opinion within any caucus.

Governmental power in Washington was quite diffused during the Civil War years. Immediately thereafter, however, the impeachment of Andrew Johnson suggested that Thaddeus Stevens and other radical Republican congressional leaders exercised unparalleled influence. On the other hand, impeachment failed, and the Democratic party regained strength in the House until it won control in the Forty-fourth Congress. Slower-paced institutionalizing processes would have more impact upon House governance than the coup directed at the Johnson administration.

Era of National Consolidation and Institutionalizing Processes

The federal census takers of 1860 counted some 31 million Americans; their successors of 1900 recorded the presence of almost 76 million. During this period great areas of western America passed through the territorial stages of government; the 33 states of 1850 had become 45 by 1900. The average number of bills per Congress during the first decade of the nineteenth century had been some 200; the figure was pressing 2,000 by the 1860s; it stood at more than 15,000 during the 1890s. James A. Garfield (1877) noted a great increase in the congressional business in the postbellum years, most of which he attributed to the Civil War. Much of the increase, as in the case of veteran's affairs, was indeed directly attributable to that conflict. But the rise also stemmed from positions endorsed by the Republican party during the war relating to banking and monetary policy, railroads, the tariff, and land policy. The unbridled patronage of the 1850s and 1860s, moreover, spurred interest in civil service reform.

Increasing size, greater and more complex workloads, and the greater subdivision of functions suggested the need for the exercise of greater authority by some agency. Ultimately control derived from both the national party infrastructure and from party leaders in the Congress. The discipline displayed within the political parties of the late nineteenth century was unmatched in either earlier or later eras. Party leaders likened electoral contests to military campaigns and party workers to loyal soldiers. Given the prominent place of the Grand Army of the Republic and the empty sleeve in postbellum politics, the analogy was an obvious one. House leaders thought in the same terms, and members cooperated. Perhaps true as well, the issue agendas after the early years of Reconstruction were less value-laden and stressful than was true in antebellum America.

Although some alternation of party control took place in the House, a good deal of continuity remained. Beginning with the Thirty-sixth Congress, the Republican or Union party controlled eight successive Houses. Starting with the Forty-fourth, the rejuvenated Democrats held a majority in eight of the next ten Houses; then with the convening of the Fifty-fourth, the Republicans gained the ascendancy for the next eight. Considerable continuity in party control thus enhanced the possibility that individual leaders might try to simplify the exercise of authority and reduce the uncertainties of members by introducing impersonal criteria in decisionmaking and standardizing legislative routines. Change in length of service on the part of the House leaders, however, was modest. After Clay's first election and prior to 1861, Speakers on the average had served 6.3 prior years in Congress and occupied the office some 2.7 years. From Grow through David B. Henderson (1899–1903), mean previous experience was nine years and the Speaker's mean term was 4.2 years. The day when House veterans with more than twenty years of prior service grasped the Speaker's gavel began with Joseph G. Cannon in 1903; the next six Speakers as well had served for more than twenty years.

Although the era of the wily veteran as Speaker did not come until the twentieth century, late-nineteenth-century officers were impressive. Scholars of those years compared the Speaker to the prime minister in the British system of legislative government. Michael C. Kerr (1874–1875) died shortly after taking office and J. Warren Keifer (1881–1883) is regarded as retrogressive. But five of the seven Speakers (1869–1899) are considered to have been innovative in their use of powers and effective in their leadership. James G. Blaine, Samuel J. Randall, John G. Carlisle, Thomas B. Reed, and Charles F. Crisp raised the power of the Speakership to its highest level in American political history.

All five men used the office to further the objectives of their party. The first, James G. Blaine, was a highly skilled parliamentarian who used the right of recognition to control business, reviewed and suggested changes in bill content, and framed resolutions for introduction on the floor. His committee selections reflected the legislative directions of which he approved. Ambitious for the presidency, Blaine sought, as Speaker, to bolster his personal popularity and, as a result, was less arbitrary in his behavior than some of his successors.

Samuel J. Randall (1876–1881) was the first of three strong Democratic Speakers during the late nineteenth century and the "first Speaker who aimed directly at power through alteration of the rules." During the Hayes-Tilden election controversy, he ruled that obstructive motions need not be recognized. John G. Carlisle (1883–1889) assumed that the Speaker should develop his own legislative program and use the powers of his office to get it accomplished. He also realized the potential of the House Rules Committee to serve as a de facto steering committee. Accordingly, he named the chairmen of the Appropriations Committee and of Ways and Means to serve with him as its majority members.

Despite his extraordinary action in controlling dilatory motions, Randall was unwilling to place meaningful curbs on such activity within the House rules. In 1880 he headed a talented Rules Committee that conducted a complete review of the rules, but Randall vetoed suggestions that would have impeded the minority's power to obstruct. Still a possibility was the opportunity to make repetitive dilatory procedural motions, resulting in successive time-consuming roll calls. Nor was Randall willing to change the definition of the quorum as a majority of all members of the House. This interpretation allowed members to refuse to answer their names even though present, thus allowing issues to be lost for lack of a quorum when party majorities were narrow (as was frequently the case during the late 1870s and the 1880s). Randall defended these positions forcefully as a member of the Rules Committee during Carlisle's service as Speaker.

Carlisle's attitude on such matters was similar to Randall's. In thus endorsing potentially obstructive practices the two men mirrored the Democrats' negative legislative agenda of the time, emphasizing frugality in government and opposition to the use of the tariff to foster industrial development. The two were also very solicitous of the desires of southern members that federal powers should be curtailed and state prerogatives protected. Serving as a minority representative on the Rules Committee in these years, Thomas B. Reed unsuccessfully offered proposals to expedite business. Critics complained by 1885 that only three types of general measures could win approval—minor bills for which unanimous consent could be obtained to consider them out of calendar order, legislation so important that a two-thirds majority voted to suspend the rules, and measures that the Appropriations Committee allowed as riders to appropriation bills.

When the Republicans returned to power in the House in 1889, Reed became Speaker. His impact upon the office was the greatest since Henry Clay's. Determined to remedy the legislative impotence of the House of Representatives and to allow the Republicans to compile a significant legislative record despite a thin majority, Reed moved on two fronts. Before the Speaker's Rules Committee reported, he counted House members who were present but not voting in order to achieve a quorum. The report of the Rules Committee of the Fifty-first Congress in 1890 constituted his second line of attack.

The "Reed Rules" involved changes in eighteen of the forty-seven House rules of the previous Congress. The basic changes involved four categories of practice. Reed sought to eliminate dilatory behavior by eliminating the provision providing that privileged motions to fix the day of adjournment, to adjourn, and to take a recess should always be in order. A blanket clause provided that "No dilatory motion shall be entertained by the Speaker." Secondly, those present but not voting were to be counted in the determination of quorums. The quorum for decisionmaking in the Committee of the Whole was reduced to 100, and that new body was now allowed to close debate on sections or paragraphs of bills under discussion. The fourth category of innovative changes in the Reed Rules simplified the processes by which bills, memorials, and resolutions were placed in legislature train. Substituting action by the Speaker for the Monday call of the states and territories, the Speaker now referred a wide variety of material to appropriate committees without debate. The handling of "unfinished business" was accelerated. A sixty-minute period (extendable if required) was introduced after the handling of unfinished business, a period allowing committees to supervise consideration of "bills of a public character which do not appropriate money." Now committee reports would be delivered to the clerk of the House for printing and calendar entry, rather than formally being reported to the House.

Amid the Democratic denunciation that greeted the report of the Reed Rules, William S. Holman predicted that the "Speaker, instead of being as for the past one hundred years, the servant of the House, shall be its master; that the Speaker and the chairmen of committees shall be a petty oligarchy, with absolute control of the business of the House." When the Democrats regained control of the House in the next election, Speaker Charles F. Crisp abandoned the Reed Rules. But he strengthened his powers of control by ruling that reports from the Rules Committee that he headed should be free of consideration. When the Fifty-third Congress assembled with a reduced Democratic majority, Crisp returned to the Reed Rules in somewhat revised form. After Reed assumed the Speaker's chair in the Fifty-fourth and Fifty-fifth Houses, he enforced a discipline on colleagues and proceedings unmatched in previous Congresses. But even Reed admitted that the powers of the president exceeded those of the Speaker, and he retired to the private practice of the law after becoming disenchanted with William McKinley's foreign policy. In general, the behavior of the House leaders of the late nineteenth century reflected the fact that the power of the House remained high in relation to the executive branch. But as the monetary stakes of lobbying increased beyond that of previous eras, the authority and esteem of the House was threatened from another quarter. Opponents accused both Blaine and Randall of succumbing to the enticements of lobbyists.

The committee system also developed considerably during the postbellum years. The process of enlarging the standing committee roster began during the Thirty-eighth Congress (1863–1865), reflecting the strains that the war placed upon old structures and also the Republican developmental agenda that reflected the structural changes occurring within the national economy. The decisions of 1865 to place the appropriations business of the Committee of Ways and Means in the hands of a new Committee on Appropriations and to create a committee on Banking and Currency were in part of the first type. The new committees on Coinage, Weights, and Measures (1864), Pacific Railroads (1865), and Mines and Mining (1865, but in the Thirty-ninth Congress), reflected the changing nature of the American economy. Pressing toward forty by 1860, the number of standing committees had neared sixty by the turn of the century.

Certain standing committees dealt with private legislation. Others supervised executive expenditures. Some dealt with the specific processes of lawmaking. Still others framed public legislation—this sphere subdivided by a historian of the late nineteenth century into finance, industry, public property, war, law, social affairs, and international relations. The size of membership and the relative importance of the committees in House affairs varied. Three, five, or nine members was the practice during the Civil War; by 1900 as many as seventeen served on some. Charged with raising and dispensing revenues, and authorized to report at will, Ways and Means was the most powerful of all House committees until the end of the Civil War. Its chairman ruled the floor, with the cooperation of the Speaker. Even by the time of the war, the committees charged with oversight of executive expenditures were moribund, the committee clerk primarily a secretary to the chairman. Despite some revitalization of these oversight committees during the Civil War, and the organization of an additional one later, their status as "slumbering watchdogs" was well recognized.

The committee power structure in the House changed significantly when the Appropriations Committee appeared in 1865. That committee's duties included the preparation and submission of the various appropriations bills; when the former chairman of Ways and Means, Thaddeus Stevens, became chairman, floor leadership moved with him. It is unclear that the Ways and Means Committee was thereafter always regarded as subordinate to Appropriations, but the vital source of power— control of the expenditures—now rested in that group. All other committees were dependent upon Appropriations, and the expanding practice of allowing substantive riders from other committees to be attached to appropriations bills enhanced its power. A decade later the position of the Appropriations Committee was strengthened still more when the House accepted an amendment of Congressman Charles S. Holman. Endorsed by the members of the Appropriations Committee, this rule stated that additions to appropriations bills must be "germane to the subject matter of the bill" and "shall retrench expenditures."

In 1877 a forceful chairman of the Commerce Committee played upon the avarice of his fellow representatives by winning a suspension of the rules under which the House acted upon his committee's bill appropriating funds for rivers and harbors improvement, repeating this coup in the following years. In 1880 the Commerce and Agriculture committees won the right to bring their appropriation bills directly to the floor. The Rules Committee of 1885 proposed that the committees on foreign, military, naval, and Indian affairs, as well as post offices and post roads, should be given the right to report appropriations measures and the Appropriations Committee thereafter retained charge of but six such bills. (The responsibilities for appropriations remained decentralized until 1920.) In part this decentralization reflected efforts to speed up House business, and in part it was an outgrowth of a contest for power between the chairman of Appropriations, Samuel J. Randall and rivals, some of whom opposed his Pennsylvania-tinged views on tariff legislation. The liberalized procedures also mirrored constituency pressures and a general sense that the prosperity and growth of the country could support higher levels of expenditure than members of the Appropriations Committee favored.

Although several notable joint select committees labored during the Civil War and Reconstruction years, the number of select committees in a Congress had become insignificant by the end of the 1870s. Conversely the use of subcommittees of standing committees greatly increased, their chairmen serving typically as floor managers for business emanating from them. Although well-endowed chairmen sometimes performed the functions of party Whip during the nineteenth century, that officer did not formally emerge until 1899.

The Senate as Contrast

This article has focused on the House because the House was the locus of many of the political struggles and much of the partisan and institutional development in the nineteenth century. But contrasts with the Senate are instructive. Lacking power under the Constitution to initiate appropriations bills, the Senate was initially believed to be a less-important body than the House, despite its advisory powers relative to treaties and presidential nominees. Meeting at first behind closed doors, senators attracted less public attention than did representatives. But when major congressional figures of the early national period—particularly Clay, Webster, and Calhoun—moved into the Senate, it became the great national forum where the most eminent sectional and party leaders elaborated the problems of the era of sectional stress. And the senator looked forward to longer service than the representative. In the early 1830s, de Tocqueville found the quality of the men and proceedings in the Senate impressive in contrast to the House.

Institutional differences in both performance and function were apparent in the two houses during the nineteenth century. Neither the presiding vice-presidents, nor the presidents *pro tempore* elected to serve in their absence, wielded power comparable to that of the Speakers. As with the representatives, the senators initially placed most of the detail of legislative activity in the hands of special committees. They moved more slowly from this practice than did the representatives, but by 1816 four standing committees had emerged and a substantial number of others were added in that year. Committee assignment did not become the continuing prerogative of the presiding officer. Until 1823 senators elected their committee members by ballot, and for the next twenty-three years they experimented with various methods, in most of which the presiding officer named some or all of the committee. But in 1846 Senators adopted the practice of having a spokesman of the majority party present a list previously approved by the party caucus. Some years later the minority party was allowed to designate its representatives for the minority slots on committees, although this practice was not followed during the Civil War. These lists came to be prepared by a party caucus committee on committees.

Although the chairman of the Senate Finance Committee had emerged by the time of the Civil War as the most powerful figure in Senate legislative proceedings, he was much less so than the chairman of Ways and Means. Nor at that time had the chairman of the caucus emerged as a preeminent leader in the Senate. The Republican senators used a caucus steering committee during the Civil War, but it put few restrictions on self-willed Solons.

Senate rules were fewer and less complex than those in the House. Whereas representatives developed restraints on debate—the previous question and the hour rule—and three calendars and two Committees of the Whole for the classification of business, Senate curbs on debate remained minimal and procedures for the handling of the various types of business and obtaining votes were much simpler.

By 1900 the United States had ninety senators who faced problems of national growth and increased workload after the Civil War similar to those in the House. As a result significant consolidation of power in the hands of the party caucus chairman and steering committees occurred after 1880, culminating in William B. Allison's service as Republican caucus chairman. Beginning in 1897 Allison served both as chairman of the Republican caucus and of that group's committee on the order of business (steering committee) and sat unofficially on the caucus committee on committees. Allison and his trusted colleagues controlled these caucus committees completely and through them selected the membership of the Senate committees and managed floor business. Allison himself served as chairman of the Senate Appropriations Committee.

References

Alexander, DeAlva S. 1916. *History and Procedure of the House of Representatives*. Boston: Houghton Mifflin.

Benton, Thomas H. 1968. *Thirty Years View: Or, A History of the Workings of the American Government for Thirty Years, from 1820 to 1850*. 2 vols. Westport, CT: Greenwood Pr. Orig. pub. 1854–1856.

Blaine, James G. 1884. *Twenty Years of Congress*. 2 vols. Norwich, CT: Henry Bill Publishing.

Bogue, Allan G. 1989. *The Congressman's Civil War*. New York: Cambridge U. Pr.

————, Jerome M. Clubb, Caroll R. McKibbin, and Santa A. Traugott. 1976. "Members of the House of Representatives and the Processes of Modernization, 1789–1960." 63 *Journal of American History* 275.

Brady, David W. 1988. *Critical Elections and Congressional Policy Making.* Stanford, CA: Stanford U. Pr.

————, and Joseph Cooper. 1981. "Toward a Diachronic Analysis of Congress." 75 *American Political Science Review* 988.

Cooper, Joseph. 1971. *The Origins of the Standing Committees and the Development of the Modern House.* Houston: Rice U. Pr.

Cunningham, Noble E., Jr. 1963. *The Jeffersonian Republicans in Power, 1801–1809.* Chapel Hill: U. of North Carolina Pr.

————. 1978. *The Process of Government Under Jefferson.* Princeton: Princeton U. Pr.

Dodd, Lawrence C. 1981. "Congress, the Constitution, and the Crisis of Legitimation." In Lawrence C. Dodd and Bruce I. Oppenheimer, eds. *Congress Reconsidered.* Washington, DC: Congressional Quarterly.

————. 1985. "A Theory of Congressional Cycles: Solving the Puzzle of Change." *Working Papers in Political Science No. P–85–3.* Stanford, CA: Hoover Institution.

Fiorina, Morris P., David W. Rohde, and Peter Wissel. 1975. "Historical Change in House Turnover." In Norman J. Ornstein, ed. *Congress in Change.* New York: Praeger.

Follett, Mary P. 1902. *The Speaker of the House of Representatives.* New York: Longmans, Green.

Galloway, George B. 1976. *History of the House of Representatives.* Revised by Sidney Wise. New York: Crowell.

Garfield, James A. 1877. "A Century of Congress." 40 *Atlantic Monthly* 49.

Haynes, George H. 1938. *The Senate of the United States: Its History and Practice.* 2 vols. New York: Houghton Mifflin.

McConachie, Lauros G. 1898. *Congressional Committees: A Study of the Origins and Development of Our National and Local Legislative Methods.* New York: Crowell.

Polsby, Nelson W. 1968. "The Institutionalization of the U.S. House of Representatives." 62 *American Political Science Review* 144.

Price, H. Douglas. 1975. "Congress and the Evolution of Legislative Professionalism." In Norman J. Ornstein, ed. *Congress in Change.* New York: Praeger.

Robinson, William A. 1930. *Thomas B. Reed: Parliamentarian.* New York: Dodd, Mead.

Rothman, David J. 1966. *Politics and Power: The United States Senate, 1869–1901.* Cambridge: Harvard U. Pr.

Silbey, Joel H. 1981. "Congressional and State Legislative Roll Call Studies by U.S. Historians." 6 *Legislative Studies Quarterly* 597.

Thompson, Margaret S. 1985. *The 'Spider Webb': Congress and Lobbying in the Age of Grant.* Ithaca, NY: Cornell U. Pr.

CHAPTER 6

Urban Political Machines

William Crotty

Representing one of the most colorful chapters in the history of American politics, the machine, as it was usually referred to, epitomizes the best and worst of the political parties. The urban political machine was best in the sense that it provided the flexibility and adaptability for the nation's political system to adjust to fundamental economic and demographic changes during the nineteenth century (industrialization, immigration, urbanization) that radically transformed the American nation; and it provided the basis for a minority party—normally the Democrats during this era—to build its base and eventually to compete effectively with the dominant party, the Republicans. The inclusiveness, adjustment to mass suffrage, and the mobilization of new and competing electorates provided alternative choices and helped serve the democratic ends of a more representative and accountable party and political system.

When the localized politics of the urban machines were eventually tied to national-level party concerns and candidates— manifested in the presidential bid of machine-product Governor Alfred E. Smith of New York in 1928, which forged a nationwide coalition of the cities, the South, labor unions and working-class people, and the small farmer—the consequence was a critical realignment of American politics that resulted in the New Deal Party System and the dominance of the Democrats nationally from the 1930s to the present. Curiously, the New Deal itself and the social programs it spawned, along with the enmity of political figures like Franklin Roosevelt, Fiorello La Guardia, and

131

reform governors at the state level, contributed to the end of the machine's glory days.

The machine performed a service in acculturating and assimilating immigrants, located most prominently in the major industrial cities of the Northeast and Midwest, into the American mainstream. These newcomers were the Irish, Poles, Jews, Germans, Czechs, Italians, Swedes, and, in the machine's later stages and with less certainty or success, African-Americans. This group migrated from the South in the post-Depression years to work in the steel plants and automobile assembly plants of the North.

Less admirable, and the object of constant attack from critics, was the corruption, favoritism, patronage, and other abuses of public office associated with the machine and its leaders. The antimachine reformers—themselves mostly middle- to upper-middle-class professionals and earlier immigrants well removed from the entry-level social status of the ethnics who formed the machine's base—constantly railed against the thievery and lax moral and ethical standards that it associated with the machine and those who supported it. The reformers called for a basic change in government structure and in the operations of city government, including the introduction of "good government" principles of economy and efficiency of operation combined with an emphasis on minimal governmental activity and responsibility. The Progressive era reformers wanted to apply their conception of business-like assumptions to local politics, and they were to prove largely successful.

In fact, the machine may have fulfilled its functions all too well. As the ethnic groups that provided the base of the machine's support progressed economically, they became less dependent on the political largesse of the local boss. The waves of immigration that fed the nineteenth-century's need for cheap and unskilled industrial labor abated; the government began to supply on a general basis the social benefits once given on a personalized and particularistic basis by the machine; and the poor who had lived in the slums and ethnic ghettoes, those most dependent on machine help, moved up the social ladder and, in the process, relocated to the suburbs. As these events took place, the days of the machine drew to a close.

The machine era is not as far in the past as some Americans might assume. The period laid the basis for the modern party system, and it is worth remembering that many machines persisted well into the post-World War II years. Some machines—or their remnants—continue to operate in urban areas (most notably in Chicago) to this day. As late as 1950, the Committee on Political Parties of the American Political Science Association reported in *Toward a More Responsible Two-Party System* that the United States still suffered from a parochial, localized, and issueless machine politics, even in the postwar years. The call in the report for a "responsible" party system based on the presentation in campaigns and implementation once in office of policy positions of national relevance was offered as contrast to the limited, shortsighted, and corrupt approaches identified with the machine.

The era of the machine was then both an unusually boisterous one in American politics and one of the most significant for understanding the operations, the contributions, and most importantly, the adaptability of the party system in the United States to the political and social demands that shape its being.

This article offers a definition of the machine and a fundamental analysis of its contributions; it traces in broad strokes the history of the political machine and identifies the distinguishing characteristics of its operations and then provides a discussion of the major reasons for its decline.

The machine aspect of American politics is the most written about, the best recorded, and the most romanticized in U.S. political history. Not to be ignored is the fact that the machine rose to fulfill social and political needs that were inadequately handled by other governmental or private agencies. The machines' long-run contributions were as real as their readily apparent venality and corruption. The costs of machine government were high, but the services provided were essential to the development of the contemporary party system and, even more significantly, to the assimilation, or socialization, if you will, of new groups into an expanding national culture and consciousness.

Defining a Political Machine

A political machine was a party organization led by a political leader or boss, with a reasonable cohesive and unified (for American parties) organizational structure. It controlled nominations for public office within its areas of jurisdiction, usually on the local level (city, county, or rural area, although a statewide political machine, while rare, was not unknown), and it controlled the operations of local government, including the awarding of patronage jobs, city services, contracts, and preferential treatment for favored groups and individuals.

The machine's operations were often extralegal and at times corrupt. Its aim was to wield political power and then to use this power for personal and group profit. An exchange theory analogy can be used to explain the machine's approach. The voter's support was given in exchange for rewards (i.e., services, jobs, symbolic gratifications) provided by the machine. To be able to give the rewards, the machine had to control the local government. The machine was built on the support of groups in the city's electorate that it represented. These groups were usually ethnic groups living in the major urban areas of, in particular (but not exclusively), the Northeast and the industrial cities of the Midwest and Great Lakes states.

The machine offered symbolic rewards and recognitions as well as jobs and other tangible benefits and assisted in the acculturation to American society for newly arrived immigrant groups. The machine and its local ward leaders and precinct workers often acted as brokers, or intermediaries, between the immigrants and the government, the courts, the police, and other official agencies such as naturalization officers, tax collectors, and city inspectors. In return the machine received the votes of the people it represented. The consistent, unquestioning electoral support of these groups allowed the machine to operate city governments with relative impunity, often unchecked and unaccountable to any public agency or constituency. This extraordinary power eventually led to the abuses of office that finally contributed to the machine's decline.

The calculus was simple enough. The machine and its leaders wanted political power. Political power led to personal wealth. To gain power, the machine needed to control public office by determining who the candidates were and by assuring them a loyal and predictable vote in elections. In return, the quid pro quo was that the machine provided services and tangible, material rewards on a personal basis to those who supported it.

The reward system was particularistic and personal, and it emphasized material gains. For this reason, machine politics has been called conservative, nonideological, and nonprogrammatic. This lack of any purposive political program is one of the major criticisms directed at the machine in the previously mentioned report of the American Political Science Association, and is largely true.

The machine did not directly challenge the class or social divisions or the economic system or government forms found in American society. It accepted the basic political and economic principles underlying a liberal democratic structure within a capitalist economic system. The machine contented itself with trying to get for itself, its leaders, and its clientele groups a share of the action—a piece of the American dream.

Still, in a way often overlooked and basically unanticipated and unacknowledged by its leaders, the machine was an innovative and even revolutionary force in American politics. It contributed, for practical rather than ideological reasons, to a concept of positive government, one that weighed in on the side of the least advantaged in American society. The fruition of the machine ethos in this regard was the New Deal of Franklin Roosevelt and its commitment of political resources to assist those most in need. The degree of commitment and the level of support for redistributive policies has varied in successive administrations and by political party since the inception of the New Deal, but the basic conception of the positive role of government while challenged has not been reversed.

The machine was a personalized, service-oriented political institution that was ripe for much of the romanticizing and myth making found in novels and films (for example, Edwin O'Connor's *The Last Hurrah*, 1956) as well as for sympathetic depictions in social science literature. The system was almost feudal in its operation, depending on kinship ties (Irish helping Irish, Poles helping Poles, and so on), an informal but clearly understood reciprocal reward structure (votes equal power equal services), and a personal web of obligations that served to tie subject to master in a never-ending series of mutual exchanges.

In many respects also, the machine was a self-contained, well-bounded ecopolitical system. It operated most effectively in a concentrated geographical area among people with shared views, backgrounds, and political expectations (the political "ethos" that Edward Banfield and James Wilson and others refer to). As times changed and the boundaries of the system expanded, it failed to adapt effectively. The geographical dispersion of populations, the changing social status of its core supporters, and a redefined role for the national government all had their impact, as did changes in technology and in the increasing availability of information through a more depersonalized and accessible media. All these developments were to contribute to the machine's difficulties. Its inability to accommodate itself to a changing political climate led to its decline in all areas and to its demise in most.

Key phrases to use in describing the machine then would include power-oriented; profit-motivated; service-based; clientelistic; patronage- and job-oriented; particularistic and parochial in its concerns; pragmatic and nonideological in policy matters; materialistic; personalized; and, in many if not most cases, corrupt.

The Social Role of the Machine

The political machine operated at many different levels. At one level was its role within and contributions to the broader society of which it was a part. In this context, the sociologist Robert Merton has identified the functions served by the machine for the broader social and political system. These functions can be "manifest," obvious, easily identified, and recognized by all who participate in or observe them. Or they can be, and often are, "latent," unintended, and usually unrecognized consequences of activities in which the machine engaged. Employing this concept then, the functions performed by the machine for the American system are virtually uncountable.

The political machine helped acculturate generations of immigrants into American society. It figuratively and literally met people at their boats, helped them settle in ethnic neighborhoods, provided them with gift baskets of food or clothing or coal for heating at Christmas and Thanksgiving (a tradition still practiced in some ward organizations in the city of Chicago), occasionally got them jobs, and acted as an intermediary with government agencies. The political machine gave these newcomers a political voice and, over time, a helping hand in moving up in American society.

In the process, the form of acculturation that the machine emphasized clearly provided benefits to the governing system. The machine never questioned the underlying assumptions of American society. Indeed, the machine provided an outlet for social frustrations and a way to adapt to an unfamiliar and often threatening environment, thus providing a legitimating force on behalf of the government and a strong alternative to potential violence and to radical political movements. In effect, the machine, with all its faults, helped manage and direct conflict and change within the accepted political arena. It deemphasized class conflict and helped raise its supporters to middle-class status. The machine fostered support for the governing system among the poor and the recently arrived by presenting a benign and supportive face to government bureaucracy.

The political machine helped overcome the factionalization of government and the decentralization of power and authority inherent in American political structures. The government of the United States uses a system emphasizing separation of powers and a federal alignment of authorities with shared power. This arrangement is reflected at successively lower levels of government, from national to state, county, and local jurisdictions and including even special election and tax districts (school, parks, judicial, legislative, recreational, water, conservation, land regulatory, among others). Coherent political action can be difficult to achieve. The machine, at one level, provided a sense of direction and a decisionmaking structure that helped government to work.

It expanded the conception of the role of government, involving it more broadly on a social welfare basis in the affairs of individuals and in using government as a lever on behalf of society's less fortunate. It helped the nation adjust to a number of transformations that took place during the extraordinary growth experienced in the nineteenth century: the implementation of mass suffrage and the other by-products of the radical democratic movement of the Andrew Jackson years and its aftermath, the expansion of the nation westward, the influx of large numbers of immigrants, and the changeover from a rural country with an agrarian base to an urban one with an industrial one.

The political machine was selective in those it chose to help, and the cost was often high. But it played a significant role in the political development of the American nation, one not fully appreciated until its declining days.

The Machine as Service Agency

Theorizing about the machine and its impact is one thing; describing its operations is quite another. Operationally, the activities engaged in by the machine and those who worked on its behalf were specific, people-related, and primarily materialistic, tied to immediate needs and involving personal rewards. The machine was the major social service agency for the poor in the urban areas before the introduction of the welfare state with the New Deal. Its only competition came from limited and privately financed charitable organizations and from early social work experiments such as Jane Addams's Hull House in Chicago. Local government had always restricted itself basically to limited management activities and to police and safety functions. Yet the contest between machine and private agency was hardly equal; the social engineering efforts of the day had severely limited outreach. The machine, on the other hand, could reach into any ward in the city, providing the services needed to meet the challenges of living in the primitive conditions present in many cities during the nineteenth century.

In addition to the assimilation and social and economic adjustment functions provided for its ethnic base, the machine met the needs of many in the business community for a quick and sympathetic response to their problems. The implementation or enforcement of zoning codes could be adjusted; public services (electric power, transit lines, sewage disposal, water delivery) could be franchised; construction permits, building code exemptions, and the licensing of professional and business concerns could be expedited; city contracts awarded; ordinances selectively enforced or ignored; roads paved or upgraded; and civic services (water, sewerage, police, and fire protection) provided—all, of course, for a price— to meet a businessman's need to compete. In some cities, just about everything was for sale. In Chicago, during the 1890s, certain aldermen (the "Grey Wolves" as they were called) were accused of selling the very streets of the city at minimal prices to a private developer to build transit lines. Another example from the same city, approximately three-quarters of a century later, shows how the machine can use its governing powers, in this case powers of eminent domain and condemnation, to close a street in the downtown area and then sell it to a private corporation for development. In this case, the corporation was Sears Roebuck, and the result was the construction of the Sears Tower, the world's tallest office building.

This second instance was considered good business in that it induced a major company to remain in the city, providing jobs and creating wealth (although Sears, with new tax breaks, relocated to the suburbs two decades later). The enormous building programs that preceded and followed the Sears project—superhighways; public buildings; colleges and universities; water filtration plants and drainage canals; harbor developments and river improvements; construction of the world's largest airport; new libraries, fire, and police stations; public parks and forest preserves; the construction of massive public housing complexes, exposition halls, and trade centers, cultural and sports complexes—illustrate how the modern machine of Chicago's Richard Daley worked to provide access to money, patronage jobs, and kickbacks as well as business and popular support that formed the core of the machine's existence.

The difference between the Daley machine and others that preceded it was that its actions in these areas were generally acclaimed by the business community, builders, civic leaders, the media, and many social scientists as a model of what a machine—or any forward-looking, business-oriented administration—could do within the context of contemporary politics.

The machine could also benefit small- and medium-sized businesses through such awards of insurance, road service, and building contracts; legal fees; and the placement of public funds in banks or through bonding agencies. In Chicago, as an example, it is a rare alderman or ward leader who does not maintain a law office, own an insurance firm, run a security service, or operate some other small business positioned to benefit from public largesse.

Also noteworthy in this context was the need of criminal elements for machine cooperation to shield their activities— extortion, bookmaking, prostitution, drug running, racke- teering—from official sanctions. Organized crime became associated in varying degrees with the machines in many urban areas; racketeers could pay handsomely for the services they wanted, and many machine leaders were more than willing to comply.

The Machine as Vote Mobilizer

A third activity of the machine, directly related to the services that it supplied to its constituents, was the mobilization of votes to win elections. The businesses provided the money, the machine and its allies—the trade and, especially, city workers' unions and organized crime in some cities—provided the manpower. The ward and precinct leaders—that is, the ones who wished to hold onto their jobs—turned out the machine vote on election days. Machine control of election activities may not have been as difficult as it might seem. As indicated, many people depended on the machine for jobs and selective benefits. In Chicago, the Daley machine was estimated to have between 30,000 and 50,000 patronage jobs at its disposal at any given time in city and county government and through access to friends in private enterprise. If numbers of this magnitude are subdivided by the fifty wards in the city, the incentives for individuals and the families dependent on these incomes to see the machine succeed in elections is formidable. It has been shown, not surprisingly, that in another machine city (Gary, Indiana), the areas with the greatest patronage concentrations vote more heavily for machine candidates.

Turning out the vote did not end the machine's activities. The machine controlled every aspect of the electoral process, from writing the laws governing the elections, certifying who could vote, registering voters, and counting the ballots to deciding—through electoral commissions it appointed or judges it nominated and elected to office—any disputes that might arise over procedures or outcomes. The election judges, the police who maintained order at the polling places, the printers who supplied the ballots, the election boards and court officials who ruled on disputed ballots and election fraud practices, all were directly controlled by the machine. Add to the sympathetic election officials such practices as repeat voting, ballot stuffing, voting by inhabitants of graveyards, the registration of voters from empty lots or abandoned buildings, vote buying, padded registration rolls, and the voting of those who had moved from the area, then no one could be surprised that the machine seldom if ever lost an election of consequence (this means primarily local elections; statewide, congressional, and presidential elections were often of secondary importance).

Perhaps the most marked illustration of a machine's power to deliver the vote in modern times came in an election of national consequence—the presidential election of 1960. A belief (encouraged by both the machine itself and the losing candidate, Richard M. Nixon) has it that the Daley machine held out its vote count until the downstate Illinois Republican totals were in. The machine then delivered just enough votes in Cook County to give Illinois and the presidential victory to John Kennedy in one of the closest contests in American history. The role the machine played received extra credibility when the new President invited the Daley family to be his first overnight guests in the White House.

Working for the Machine

In this regard, taking a look at machine operations from the perspective of the local precinct worker might prove worthwhile. Chicago under the Daley machine can serve as an example. Often a "payroller's" (that is, someone paid for a job on the public payroll for which he/she seldom if ever showed up) real assignment as a party worker was to keep in close touch with the voters in his area. This liaison often meant door-to-door canvassing between elections as well as during campaigns, serving as an intermediary in such matters as getting trees pruned, sidewalks and streets paved, free trash cans delivered (a tradition in Chicago), or in acquiring other public services and in resolving disputes with city agencies. In addition, the party worker was expected to spend several nights a month in the ward headquarters and to attend all ward-level candidate rallies. In return, the machine took care of the worker, providing a job and an income—the more indispensable the worker, the better the job—as a city roof, water, safety, or electrical inspector; a sanitation worker; a policeman; a janitor; a security guard; an insurance adjustor; a clerk in the assessor's or recorder's office or their equivalents; and, for the more successful, a smooth path to public office. The party work expected of the precinct captain in some machines such as Chicago's was demanding; the rewards, however, were substantial.

Overall, the system functioned reasonably well. Most people associated with the machine benefited directly in some manner, many quite tangibly. Few personally or directly lost anything; the cost was picked up by the public treasury.

The Rise of the Urban Machine

The rise of the machine was in direct response to fundamental changes in the development of the nation. Many of these have been mentioned, but they deserve brief review.

The election of Andrew Jackson as President in 1828 ushered in a new era of mass democracy, one that in its provisions for an expanded mass suffrage helped establish the political climate that made the machine possible. Before this period, politics had been elitist with the vote restricted by property and wealth as well as by race and sex.

The second contribution to machine politics was economic. The increasing industrialization of the country created the need for cheap labor to work in the factories and to lay the tracks for the railroads during the nation's westward expansion. A constant demand for large quantities of unskilled immigrant labor resulted. As much as they were disliked by the Americans who had preceded them and their culture, language, and even morality stereotyped and ridiculed, the nineteenth century's rapid economic expansion depended on immigrants.

Third, then, are the social changes brought on by mass immigration between the 1830s and 1921, when it was effectively curtailed through new immigration laws. The Irish, Germans, Scandinavians, Italians, and other southern Europeans came to the United States in successive waves. The Irish, Italians, and Jews from various Eastern European countries and, more selectively, the Germans and the English settled in the developing cities of the Northeast and, as the nineteenth century evolved, the industrial cities of the Midwest.

Not all groups took with equal facility to politics. The Irish, possibly because they had immigrated early in heavy numbers, spoke the language, had a general familiarity with the system, enjoyed a strong sense of ethnic identity and a solid community base built around the Catholic church, and had an immediate and lasting effect on the development of the machine. Many of the early machine leaders were Irish, and well into the twentieth century, despite changing ethnic constituencies, the Irish remained firmly in political control of many cities.

Fourth, and directly related to both industrialization and mass immigration, was the rise of the city. At the time the Constitution was adopted, the United States was 95 percent rural; the nation's five largest cities had estimated populations between 16,000 and 40,000. The cities began to grow in the decades immediately preceding the Civil War. In the last half of the nineteenth century, urban populations outgrew rural areas by a three-to-one ratio. By 1920 and the close of mass immigration, the United States had completed the shift from a dominantly rural nation to one with a majority of the population living in urban areas. The city, of course, provided the social, geographical, and political base for the machine.

Finally, as indicated earlier, a need emerged for a centralized and positive governing authority in a political system that before the advent of the machine had emphasized decentralized, localized, and fractionalized decisionmaking and public agencies with limited responsibilities. The demand for a more responsive government, one more attuned to the concerns of ethnics and business interests in a period of rapid economic expansion, provided an opening that the machine was quick to fill.

A particular configuration of economic, social, and political forces then created the unique historical conditions that gave rise to a new conception of government. The new political demands created the environment that gave birth to the machine. Seen in this context, the machine was a creature of its time and a particular stage in the political evolution of the nation.

Types of Machines

As indicated, most of the major political machines were located in the urban areas of the Northeast and upper Midwest. The Progressive movement that dominated much of the political thinking at the turn of the century was particularly antimachine and, more broadly, antipolitical party and antipolitics. Many of the Midwest, Plains, Mountain, and Far West states that were settled in the heyday of the Progressive era enacted stringent limitations on both party activities and on organizations that made normal political party operations, much less machine practices, difficult. The extremes may be found in states like California and Wisconsin that effectively crippled formal party development.

Machine operations and characteristics varied widely. Cities with major political machines included New York City and Albany; Chicago; Gary, Indiana; Jersey City, Hoboken, and

Newark in New Jersey; Pittsburgh and Philadelphia; Boston; Cleveland, Toledo, and Cincinnati in Ohio; Memphis; and on the West Coast, San Francisco. The complete list is, of course, much longer. These machines were often identified with their leaders and their political styles, ranging from the vengeful and petty "Boss" Crump of Memphis to the respected Republican Boss Cox of Cincinnati; from the genial and charismatic James Michael Curley of Boston to the dour, meticulously organized, and efficient Richard J. Daley in Chicago; and from the generally ethical Charles F. Murphy of New York's Tammany Hall and Martin Lomasney of Boston to the corrupt and mob-dominated operations of Frank Hague in Jersey City. The diversity in operations and leadership styles belies any simple description as to how they operated.

Possibly the most famous of machines is that of Tammany Hall in New York City, and a brief sketch of its life cycle provides one model of machine operations. Tammany Hall was originally founded as a fraternal organization at about the same time that George Washington was being sworn in for his first term as President. Initially a social club, Tammany became more political as the years passed, eventually emerging as the dominant party organization in Manhattan. Its fortunes and its reputation fluctuated with those of its leaders: "Boss" (William Marcy) Tweed, Charles Murphy, and Richard Croker were among the more prominent. Tammany Hall flourished from the 1870s to the 1930s when it began to experience a series of reversals that were to eventually destroy it.

Tammany Hall's corruption in the latter half of the nineteenth century was legendary. As examples, the Tweed Ring is estimated to have skimmed off some $100 million in graft in one three-year period alone. Up to 90 percent of the cost of some public buildings was attributed to corruption. Some Tammany leaders became millionaires. One (Croker) eventually went to jail, a rare occurrence for a boss. Still, the organization remained powerful, controlling political offices in New York City and constituting a force in state and national elections. Tammany— and Murphy—protégé Alfred E. Smith served a distinguished term as governor of New York and ran as the Democratic candidate for president in 1928. Tammany also supported (although reluctantly) Smith's successor as governor and a later Democratic presidential nominee, Franklin D. Roosevelt.

Roosevelt, while elected with machine support nationwide, really did not depend on an urban ethnic base; he was not sympathetic to the corruption and abuses of machine operations. FDR eventually assisted in the formation in New York City of a labor-based, antimachine political group in the mid-1930s, the Liberal party, to support New Deal policies and to contest with Tammany for political control. Roosevelt's antipathy coincided with the election of a Fusion candidate running on an antimachine platform, Fiorello La Guardia, to the mayor's office. La Guardia served from 1933 to 1945 and spent much of his considerable political power undermining the machine and destroying its patronage base. Along with other opponents, he helped start local reform clubs as an alternative to the machine's ward organizations. These reform clubs endorsed and ran their own candidates for political office. Yet Tammany lingered on under leaders such as Carmine DeSapio until the 1960s when its own corruption and continuing ties to organized crime (in addition to a changing political environment) combined to deprive it of whatever influence it still retained.

Tammany Hall is not representative of all of the urban machines. Each had its own political history, and each responded to a different mix of social and economic forces. Taken together, however, the political machine dominated the politics of the latter nineteenth century and many lasted well into the twentieth century, some operating in one form or another up to recent times. The post-New Deal era, however, has been notably unsympathetic to machine operations.

The Decline of the Machine

Most political machines were corrupt to some degree. As time and public attitudes changed, toleration for machine graft diminished. "We saw our chances and we took them," according to Tammany leader William Plunkitt, who made a distinction between "honest" graft and "dishonest" graft. "Honest" graft included selective awarding of contracts, jobs, legal fees, and the like, and profiteering from insider information (as for example in land acquisitions and contract bidding). "Dishonest" graft would be the bid rigging, kickbacks, bribes, and the payoffs from criminal activities that were patently illegal. According to Plunkitt, "honest" graft was acceptable; "dishonest" graft was not.

It is unlikely that most machines made such a fine distinction. These categories of kinds of graft were clearly spurious. On the other hand, all machines were corrupt to varying degrees. They were in business for profit, and they all stole in one manner or another from the public treasury. As their corrupt practices received more attention—through the cartoons of Thomas Nast in the nineteenth century and later through the angry and sensationalistic exposés of "muckraking" journalists like Lincoln Steffens (*The Shame of the Cities*, 1960) around the turn of the century—and as public tolerance for both the machine and its corrupt practices decreased, the beginning of the end had set in.

The Progressive movement of the early twentieth century was a response to machine abuses. It advanced measures intended to cripple the machine and destroy the power of the boss. While progressivism did not accomplish such ends immediately, it did hurt the machine and, not incidentally, political parties more generally, and it did permanently reshape the environment in which the machine operated and the context in which local politics in the future would be conducted.

Progressive era reforms were advocated by middle-class and upper-middle-class business, professional, intellectual, and publishing interests not directly benefited by machine operations. These groups advocated standards of official behavior distinctly different from those of the machine, stressing objective professional competence and public service motivations for those who served in government. Decisionmaking was to be based on business-like principles of efficiency and economy in government.

To achieve such ends, the Progressives advocated a series of structural reforms in political institutions, preferring not to deal with the social conditions and social reforms needed to address the problems that gave rise to the machine. The

Progressives advocated the direct primary to break the machine's hold on political nominations. They endorsed the short ballot, both to centralize authority and accountability and to lessen the information burden for the prospective voter. They lobbied for civil service exams and procedures and merit appointments to eliminate patronage. Progressives espoused stringent campaign law and restrictive party statutes to control political receipts and expenditures and to limit party organization and activities. At-large (rather than district or ward) elections, which were supposed to dilute the power of ethnic groups, combined with nonpartisan electoral systems that actually prohibited political party activity, are standard now in the majority of American cities (three-fourths of those over 25,000 in population have nonpartisan elections). Progressives championed proportional representation, the city manager and city council forms of government, initiative, referendum, and recall provisions, the Australian (secret) ballot, and the reorganization of urban and state governments to increase service delivery and decrease political control. The broad public administration movement and good government groups such as the National Municipal League (established in 1894) intended to professionalize public service grew out of this movement.

Another factor leading to the decline of the machine was the limits put on immigration. By 1921 the last of the great waves of immigration, bringing millions of southern and eastern Europeans to the United States, had virtually ended, depriving the machine of its traditional base of support. The new immigrants—African-Americans, who came north seeking jobs in the automobile and steel factories during the Depression and after World War II, Hispanics, and, to a lesser degree, Asians— did not integrate well into machine operations. In fact, these newcomers were often perceived of as a threat to the machine and its leaders. In effect, the machine stopped growing and adapting. Steven Erie has recently argued that the machine never served other groups as well as it did its original Irish constituents. As its client groups moved up to middle-class status and out to the suburbs, the machine's base contracted, and it died.

The rewards that the machine could offer began to pale in comparison with what the welfare state could supply nationally and apolitically on the basis of demonstrated need. The machine had always had a limited appeal to an emerging middle class. The postindustrial period, accordingly, has not been hospitable to a continued machine presence.

All of these ingredients combined to decrease the influence of the machine. Basically, time had run out. The machine was a product of a particular historical era and set of social conditions. When the nation changed, the machine was not able to operate effectively in an environment in which its political base had eroded and the rewards it could offer were less significant. Public attitudes and political structures changed; the machine could not compete effectively in the new political environment. With its operations curtailed by law, economics, and social change, the machine became something of a historical curiosity.

The Pros and Cons of the Machine

Americans' general perception of the machine, perhaps understandably, has been negative. Assessing the machine and its operations, Alex Gottfried has written:

The political, social, economic, and financial costs of corrupt machines are incalculable but enormous, whatever their inevitability or functional utility. The cost in terms of the "degradation of the democratic dogma" cannot be measured. Tens of millions of Americans have developed cynical attitudes toward the myths of our political system. . . . The low prestige of politics and politicians is another result, since it has served to keep many potentially able people away from the public arena. The civil service has been degraded. The United States lagged fifty years behind European countries in adopting public welfare and social insurance programs. The physical city and the quality of life therein have deteriorated. Few cities have been specifically planned, and thus lack parks, beaches, and other public amenities. Inadequate schools, inadequate fire protection, inadequate and/or brutal police service, the development of slums, lack of minimum standards for housing, neglect of tenements, rent gouging, lack of consumer protection, wholly inadequate hospital and public health services, almost total lack of protective labor legislation, and long delays in legislation for the protection of women and children—all have been caused by rapacious machines.

Political analysts find an element of truth in each of these indictments, although some wonder if other, broader social forces in the United States did not contribute significantly to the conditions attributed to the machine.

Other observers argue that in the post-machine era, government may become more fragmented, aloof, and inaccessible than ever before. These critics maintain that the reforms advocated by the Progressives have a decided bias toward upper-middle-class interests and values and that cities adopting Progressive reforms may be less responsive to minority interests and less likely to engage in public spending. The research on these questions to date has been inconclusive. Certainly, nonpartisan elections have resulted in low turnouts, poorly mobilized and informed electorates, insulated officeholders, and, more arguably, a political upper-middle class and Republican party bias in the vote.

The relevance of debating the achievements or costs of machine politics may be limited. Yet an understanding of the machine and its operations does help in understanding contemporary politics, where we are and how we arrived at what we have. But for Americans with a limited historical perspective, it may also be sufficient to remember that the machine was a product of an era and its evolution. Its rise and demise, strengths and weaknesses, formed an integral part of the social and economic drama that have combined to produce the American experience.

References

Adrian, Charles, and Oliver Williams. 1959. "The Insulation of Local Politics Under the Nonpartisan Ballot." 53 *American Political Science Review* 1052.

Allswang, John M. 1971. *A House for All Peoples*. Lexington: U. Pr. of Kentucky.

———. 1978. *The New Deal and American Politics: A Study in Political Change*. New York: Wiley.

———. 1986. *Bosses, Machines, and Urban Voters*. Baltimore: Johns Hopkins U. Pr.

American Political Science Association. 1950. *Toward a More Responsible Two-Party System*. Washington, DC: American Political Science Association.

Andersen, Kristi. 1979. *The Creation of a Democratic Majority 1928–1936*. Chicago: U. of Chicago Pr.

Banfield, Edward C. 1961. *Political Influence*. New York: Free Press.

———, and James Q. Wilson. 1963. *City Politics*. New York: Vintage.

Beatty, Jack. 1992. *The Rascal King: The Life and Times of James Michael Curley (1874–1958)*. Reading, MA: Addison-Wesley.

Binkley, Wilfred E. 1971. *American Political Parties: Their Natural History*. New York: Knopf.

Bridges, Amy. 1984. *A City in the Republic*. Cambridge: Harvard U. Pr.

Browning, Rufus, Dale Rogers Marshall, and David Tabb. 1984. *Protest Is Not Enough*. Berkeley: U. of California Pr.

Buenker, John D. 1973. *Urban Liberalism and Progressive Reform*. New York: Scribner's.

Callow, Alexander B., Jr. 1970. *The Tweed Ring*. New York: Oxford U. Pr.

———, ed. 1976. *The City Boss in America*. New York: Oxford U. Pr.

Connors, Richard J. 1971. *A Cycle of Power: The Career of Jersey City Mayor Frank Hague*. Metuchen, NJ: Scarecrow Press.

Costikyan, Edward N. 1966. *Behind Closed Doors*. New York: Harcourt, Brace & World.

Crotty, William J. 1986. "Local Parties in Chicago: The Machine in Transition." In William Crotty, ed. *Political Parties in Local Areas*. Knoxville: U. of Tennessee Pr.

Curley, James Michael. 1957. *I'd Do It Again*. Englewood Cliffs, NJ: Prentice-Hall.

Cutright, Phillips. 1963. "Measuring the Impact of Local Party Activity on General Election Vote." 27 *Public Opinion Quarterly* 372.

Dorsett, Lyle W. 1968. *The Pendergast Machine*. New York: Oxford U. Pr.

———. 1977. *Franklin D. Roosevelt and the City Bosses*. Port Washington, NY: Kennikat.

Ebner, Michael H., and Eugene M. Tobin, eds. 1977. *The Age of Urban Reform*. Port Washington, NY: Kennikat.

Erie, Steven P. 1988. *Rainbow's End: Irish-Americans and the Dilemmas of Urban Machine Politics, 1840–1985*. Berkeley: U. of California Pr.

Eulau, Heinz, and Kenneth Prewitt. 1973. *Labyrinths of Democracy: Adaptations, Linkages, Representation, and Policies in Urban Politics*. Indianapolis: Bobbs-Merrill.

Flynn, Edward J. 1947. *You're the Boss*. New York: Viking.

Fuchs, Ester R. 1992. *Mayors and Money: Fiscal Policy in New York and Chicago*. Chicago: U. of Chicago Pr.

Gardiner, John A., and David J. Olson, eds. 1974. *Theft of the City*. Bloomington: Indiana U. Pr.

Glazer, Nathan, and Daniel P. Moynihan. 1970. *Beyond the Melting Pot*. Cambridge: Harvard U. Pr.

Gosnell, Harold F. 1937. *Machine Politics: Chicago Model*. Chicago: U. of Chicago Pr.

Gottfried, Alex. 1962. *Boss Cermak of Chicago*. Seattle: U. of Washington Pr.

Gove, Samuel K., and Louis H. Masotti, eds. 1982. *After Daley: Chicago Politics in Transition*. Urbana: U. of Illinois Pr.

Green, Paul M., and Melvin G. Holli, eds. 1987. *The Mayors: The Chicago Political Tradition*. Carbondale: Southern Illinois U. Pr.

———, and ———, eds. 1990. *Restoration 1989: Chicago Elects a New Daley*. Chicago: Lyceum Books.

Grimshaw, William J. 1992. *Bitter Fruit: Black Politics and the Chicago Machine, 1931-1991*. Chicago: U. of Chicago Pr.

Guterbock, Thomas M. 1980. *Machine Politics in Transition: Party and Community in Chicago*. Chicago: U. of Chicago Pr.

Handlin, Oscar. 1951. *The Uprooted*. New York: Grosset & Dunlap.

———. 1958. *Al Smith and His America*. Boston: Little, Brown.

Hawley, Willis D. 1973. *Nonpartisan Elections and the Case for Party Politics*. New York: Wiley.

Heidenheimer, Arnold J., ed. 1970. *Political Corruption: Readings in Comparative Analysis*. New York: Holt, Rinehart & Winston.

Hershkowitz, Leo. 1978. *Tweed's New York: Another Look*. Garden City, NY: Anchor Books.

Hicks, John D. 1960. *Republican Ascendancy 1921–1933*. New York: Harper & Row.

Higham, John. 1972. *Strangers in the Land*. New York: Atheneum.

Hofstadter, Richard. 1959. *The Age of Reform*. New York: Knopf.

Holli, Melvin G. 1969. *Reform in Detroit: Hazen S. Pingree and Urban Politics*. New York: Oxford U. Pr.

———, and Paul M. Green, eds. 1984. *The Making of the Mayor: Chicago 1983*. Grand Rapids, MI: Eerdmans.

———, and ———, eds. *Bashing Chicago Traditions: Harold Washington's Last Campaign*. Grand Rapids, MI: Eerdmans.

Jones, Bryan D. 1985. *Governing Buildings and Building Government*. University: U. of Alabama Pr.

Key, V.O. 1959. "Secular Realignment and the Party System." 21 *Journal of Politics* 198.

Kleppner, Paul. 1985. *Chicago Divided: The Making of a Black Mayor*. DeKalb: Northern Illinois U. Pr.

Ladd, Everett C., Jr. 1970. *American Political Parties: Social Change and Political Response*. New York: Norton.

———, and Charles Hadley. 1975. *Transformations of the American Party System*. New York: Norton.

La Guardia, Fiorello H. 1948. *The Making of an Insurgent: An Autobiography 1882–1919*. New York: Capricorn Books.

Lee, Eugene. 1960. *The Politics of Nonpartisanship*. Berkeley: U. of California Pr.

Lowi, Theodore J. 1964. *At the Pleasure of the Mayor*. Glencoe, IL: Free Press.

Lubell, Samuel. 1951. *The Future of American Politics*. New York: Harper.

Mandelbaum, Seymour J. 1965. *Boss Tweed's New York*. New York: Wiley.

Mann, Arthur. 1965. *La Guardia Comes to Power. 1933*. Philadelphia: Lippincott.

Merton, Robert K. 1957. *Social Theory and Social Structure*. Glencoe, IL: Free Press.

Meyers, Gustavus. 1937. *The History of Tammany Hall*. New York: Modern Library.

Miller, William D. 1964. *Mr. Crump of Memphis*. Baton Rouge: Louisiana State U. Pr.

Miller, Zane L. 1968. *Cox's Cincinnati*. New York: Oxford U. Pr.

Morgan, David, and John Pelissero. 1980. "Urban Policy: Does Political Structure Matter?" 75 *American Political Science Review* 722.

Mushkat, Jerome. 1971. *Tammany: The Evolution of a Machine, 1789–1865.* Syracuse, NY: Syracuse U. Pr.

Nixon, Richard M. 1962. *Six Crises.* Garden City, NY: Doubleday.

O'Connor, Edwin. 1956. *The Last Hurrah.* New York: Bantam Books.

O'Connor, Len. 1975. *Clout: Mayor Daley and His City.* Chicago: Henry Regnery.

———. 1977. *Requiem: The Decline and Demise of Mayor Daley and His Era.* Chicago: Contemporary Books.

Ostrogorski, M. 1921. *Democracy and the American Party System.* New York: Macmillan.

Parenti, Michael. 1967. "Ethnic Politics and the Persistence of Ethnic Identification." 61 *American Political Science Review* 717.

Peel, Roy V. 1935. *The Political Clubs of New York City.* New York: Putnam's.

Pinderhughes, Dianne. 1987. *Race and Ethnicity in Chicago Politics: A Reexamination of Pluralist Theory.* Urbana: U. of Illinois Pr.

Rakove, Milton. 1975. *Don't Make No Waves . . . Don't Back No Losers.* Bloomington: Indiana U. Pr.

———. 1979. *We Don't Want Nobody Sent.* Bloomington: Indiana U. Pr.

Riordan, William L. 1963. *Plunkitt of Tammany Hall.* New York: Dutton.

Robinson, Frank S. 1977. *Machine Politics: A Study of Albany's O'Connells.* New Brunswick, NJ: Transaction Books.

Rossi, Peter H., and Philips Cutright. 1961. "The Impact of Party Organization in an Industrial Setting." In Morris Janowitz, ed. *Community Political Systems.* Glencoe, IL: Free Press.

Royko, Mike. 1971. *Boss: Richard J. Daley of Chicago.* New York: Signet.

Salter, J. T. 1935. *Boss Rule: Portraits in City Politics.* New York: McGraw-Hill.

Scott, James C. 1972. *Comparative Political Corruption.* Englewood Cliffs, NJ: Prentice-Hall.

Shannon, William V. 1963. *The American Irish.* New York: Macmillan.

Shefter, Martin. 1976. "The Emergence of the Machine: An Alternative View." In Willis D. Hawley and Michael Lipsky, eds. *Theoretical Perspectives on Urban Politics.* Englewood Cliffs, NJ: Prentice-Hall.

———. 1978. "The Electoral Foundations of the Political Machine: New York City, 1884–1897." In Joel H. Silbey, Allan G. Bogue, and William H. Flanigan, eds. *The History of American Electoral Behavior.* Princeton: Princeton U. Pr.

Steffens, Lincoln. 1960. *The Shame of the Cities*. New York: Hill and Wang.

Sundquist, James. 1973. *Dynamics of the Party System*. Washington: Brookings.

Tarr, Joel Arthur. 1971. *A Study in Boss Politics: William Lorimer of Chicago*. Urbana: U. of Illinois Pr.

Tolchin, Martin, and Susan Tolchin. 1972. *To the Victor*. New York: Vintage.

Tucker, David M. 1981. *Memphis Since Crump: Bossism, Blacks, and Civic Reformers, 1948–1968*. Knoxville: U. of Tennessee Pr.

Walton, Hanes, Jr. 1972. *Black Politics: A Theoretical and Structural Analysis*. Philadelphia: Lippincott.

Welch, Susan, and Timothy Bledsoe. 1986. "The Partisan Consequences of Nonpartisan Elections and the Changing Nature of Urban Politics." 30 *American Journal of Political Science* 128.

––––––– and –––––––. 1988. *Urban Reform and Its Consequences*. Chicago: U. of Chicago Pr.

Wendt, Lloyd, and Herman Kogan. 1971. *Bosses of Lusty Chicago*. Bloomington: Indiana U. Pr.

Wilson, James Q. 1960. *Negro Politics: The Search for Political Leadership*. Glencoe, IL: Free Press.

Wolfinger, Raymond E. 1972. "Why Political Machines Have Not Withered Away and Other Revisionist Thoughts." 34 *Journal of Politics* 365.

Zink, Harold. 1930. *City Bosses in the United States*. Durham, NC: Duke U. Pr.

CHAPTER 7

The Fourth Party System and Progressive Politics

Samuel T. McSeveney

The Fourth Party System can be said to have run from the electoral-political realignment of the 1890s until that of the 1930s, each triggered by a severe economic depression and an attendant social crisis. For the purposes of analyzing change and continuity in many basic partisan political characteristics of successive party systems, the aforementioned chronology has much to commend it, but for understanding other vital aspects of the political order one should also appreciate that a range of economic, social, and political developments, sometimes related to, but even then not synonymous with, the electoral-political realignment of the 1890s, contributed to a new political order in the early twentieth century. The new structures of the Progressive era not only differed significantly from those before it, but also remained influential beyond the passing of the Fourth Party System itself.

The emerging political order was characterized by a marked nationwide decline in voter turnout, which has been only episodically and partially reversed since the mid-1920s. To be sure, the realignment of the 1890s played a role in that significant decline, seriously weakening electoral-political competitiveness across much of the nation, with negative consequences for voter motivation and party organizations as agents of voter mobilization. But other factors figured in the portentous erosion of voter participation. To begin with, the introduction (1889) and rapid spread of the Australian ballot,

which was prepared and distributed by the state and listed all
certified candidates, supplanted party tickets, which were
prepared by party organizations and distributed by local party
workers and which identified only the candidates of each party.
The new ballot made it more difficult for ill-educated and
marginal eligibles to vote, while rendering it easier for informed
voters to kick the addictive party habit by balloting for
candidates regardless of party affiliation. ("Split the ticket"
echoes down the years, but it was more easily accomplished with
Australian *ballots* than with party *tickets*.) Reformers sought this
substitution to curb corruption and the parties' influence on the
casting of votes: Election day and the act of voting were to be
transformed from a partisan occasion and ritual to a civic
occasion and duty. (This wish also underlaid the placement of
polling places in respectable locations such as public schools,
instead of neighborhood businesses, tobacco stores, barber
shops, and the like, and the restriction of rowdiness, e.g.,
drinking and bonfires, on election day.) Many party leaders
favored or accepted ballot reform because it reduced the ability
of local organization workers to trade votes or otherwise betray
candidates for whom they were ostensibly working. Socializing
election day costs reduced the parties' financial burdens, but
substituting public officials (even if patronage appointees) for
party workers also frayed ties between parties and voters.

    With ballot reform went the possibility of other state
actions to influence electoral politics. Access to the ballot could
be controlled: e.g., minor parties might be required to secure
prescribed percentages of the vote to remain on the ballot in
subsequent elections; winning a place on the ballot by petition
could be made difficult by stipulating the number and/or
distribution of signatures necessary for such placement; third
parties—and the weaker major party in particular jurisdictions—
could be handicapped by prohibiting fusion (or the running of
joint tickets). Such measures strengthened the hand of the major
parties, but especially that of the dominant party in affected
locales. By so doing they further reduced the potential for
interparty competition and with it the value of the vote. The
spread of state direct primary and personal registration laws
during the early twentieth century further affected the political

order. The former had many significances, among them the legitimizing of party nominations and, although it hardly overturned party influence on nominations, the strengthening of the hand of popular officeholders. The latter reform, supposedly intended to reduce fraudulent voting, often initially targeted urban areas (more likely to contain immigrant concentrations) and presented a further hurdle to would-be voters.

Taken together, the erosion of electoral-political competition and the passage of a range of laws affecting voters, political parties, and linkages between the two contributed to a decline of voter turnout at and especially after the turn of the twentieth century. But it bears emphasizing that while interparty competitiveness sharply fell in the short run, turnout continued to decline for years afterward; that turnout sank in jurisdictions unaffected by personal registration, as well as in those in the same states covered by the requirement; and that the Australian ballot facilitated, but did not require, split-ticket voting (as the lag between reform and changed behavior was to make clear). The foregoing has led to the plausible conclusion that the decline in voter participation was an interactive and cumulative phenomenon, i.e., that diverse developments and innovations reduced voter turnout and so affected political parties that they largely lost the ability to maintain turnout and party loyalty at formerly high levels; and that the erosion in voter turnout was a consequence of the inevitable replacement of cohorts that had been politically socialized during the intensely partisan late nineteenth century by others formally entering, but not comparably participating in, the early twentieth century electorate—persons coming of voting age, immigrants acquiring citizenship, and women upon their enfranchisement. To this one may add that particular national campaigns and candidacies appear to have accelerated or decelerated the demobilization of the electorate. If from 1896 through 1916, nonsouthern turnout in presidential elections fell by 17.1 percentage points, the declines were greatest in 1904 (–6.1), when Democrats were cross-pressured, and 1912 (– 8.4), when Republicans were, and less marked in 1900 and 1908 (–3.6, –0.4). The two-horse race between incumbent Democrat Woodrow Wilson, and ex-

Progressive Republican Charles Evans Hughes actually produced a small increase in turnout (+1.4) in 1916.

Outside the South election reforms were espoused by very different groups for widely dissimilar reasons. If many consequences of rule changes were intended, others were unforeseen (at least by some of their advocates). In the eleven ex-Confederate states, however, these "reforms" were highly successful in achieving the reactionary purposes for which they were designed—restricting the suffrage, especially of blacks, but of poorer whites as well, and crippling opponents of the Democratic party. Black Belt elites dominant in the democracy pressed for the revision of state constitutions and/or the passage of laws to cement their power at home and to neutralize any renewed national supervision of federal elections. They were most active during 1889–93 and 1898–1902. In the earlier period, the Republicans' capture of the presidency and both houses of Congress in 1888 and their subsequent introduction of the Lodge federal elections bill spurred Democratic efforts. In the later period the Democrats acted to prevent any resurrection of Republican-Populist fusion, such as had temporarily succeeded in North Carolina during the turbulent 1890s. The Democrats' means included the poll tax, complex voter registration laws, the Australian ballot, and literacy and property tests; the granting of extensive authority to local voter registrars and the institutionalization of the white Democratic primary (to contain conflict within the party) riveted the new political order in place. The northern suffrage reform movement included nativists, but they were not as numerous, strident, or successful as their racist and antidemocratic counterparts in the South. According to the definitive study of southern suffrage restriction, outside the South voter turnout in presidential elections fell from 73 percent of adult males in 1888 to 65 percent in 1908, within the South from 62 percent to 30 percent. Suffrage restriction, de jure subordination of blacks, and (in all but enclaves) one-party politics from top to bottom continued to characterize the South until the 1960s.

The emerging Progressive era political order was also marked by significant and enduring developments in governance. Again, distrust of political parties as traditionally organized was evident. Also manifest were the concerns that legislative bodies no longer adequately met public needs and the belief that the executive and an enhanced governmental administrative capacity were essential to dealing with myriad and complex political issues. The cities, directly transformed by urbanization, industrialization, and immigration, home to a disproportionate share of the expanding corporate and professional leadership that sought to bring their perspectives and expertise to bear on governmental, economic, and social problems, witnessed the most fundamental changes. It should be borne in mind that from the very emergence of urban political "machines" and "bosses" during the third quarter of the nineteenth century, the cities' older commercial elites and their allies had railed against the alleged corruption and parochialism of city governments so dominated and had proposed reforms, some of which anticipated those of the Progressive period. Further, given the limitations of municipal home rule, urban reform frequently depended on state action, which sometimes was imposed on cities opposed to the very innovations in question.

Urban governmental reform agendas differed among cities, and reform did not carry the day everywhere, but numerous small and mid-sized cities adopted commission or manager-commission forms of government. Nonpartisan municipal elections gained in popularity, as did the desynchronization of city elections, putatively dealing with administration, from state and national contests, that were obviously partisan. Mayoral powers were enlarged, and at-large representation on city councils replaced ward-based representation. (In some locales, at-large elections were instituted to deny representation to black neighborhoods, but whatever their intent they favored candidates able to mobilize city-wide support, rather than those dependent on their own neighborhood communities.)

No directly comparable elective governmental reorganizations occurred on the state or federal level, but strong governors and presidents provided executive leadership, sometimes by appealing to the public over the heads of legislators and politicos, at least regarding popular issues.

Further, on the state level, the initiative, referendum, and recall measures of "direct democracy," adopted most frequently in the West, where party-voter linkages had been comparatively weak for some time, strengthened the hand of the electorate, but even more that of groups well enough organized to win support from voters lacking information and cues in elections marked by reduced turnout. The direct election of United States senators, provided for in the Seventeenth Amendment to the Constitution, was a democratic reform and one that severed the link between senators and state legislatures, which formerly had chosen them. With the decline of electoral competition, partisan turnover in the House of Representatives also declined. So, too, did the turnover of congressmen. As careers lengthened, seniority came to play the determining role in the attainment of committee chairmanships. With the growing autonomy of veteran congressmen and the weakening of the House party leadership went a long-term decline in party as an influence on congressional voting.

Although older private elites and traditional politicians played essential roles in the transformation of the American political order, newer business and professional organizations gave it crucial distinguishing characteristics. Business groups involved in the rapidly changing national economy, in production, distribution, transportation, and finance, increasingly aware of their self-interest, often functionally organized, came to find nineteenth-century party- and legislative-based government on all levels inadequate to their needs. Government could and did allocate rewards and resources (franchises, charters, land grants), but it fell short when it came to effective regulation of various aspects of economic life, this during a period when increasing numbers of businessmen came to question the consequences of either cutthroat competition or unrestrained economic power. Meanwhile, the rapid expansion of professions—law, medicine, sciences, engineering, social sciences, and academics; and architecture, city planning, public health, and social work—and the growth of professional schools introduced important elements—expertise and (supposedly) disinterestedness—into the political equation.

The influence of businessmen and professionals rested in part on the resources at their command, in part on their organization, which enabled them to bring effective pressure to bear on the political system. In a brief essay one can but highlight private organizational developments as they affected the early twentieth-century political order. Insofar as economic interests were concerned, the National Association of Manufacturers, the United States Chamber of Commerce and state and local chambers of commerce, the American Bankers Association, and the Farm Bureau Federation (formed only in 1919) were umbrella organizations. Specialized organizations represented businessmen or farmers in particular fields or with common problems, e.g., transportation needs. Thus the national Rivers and Harbors Congress advocated federal improvement of inland waterways, while Iowa's Corn Belt Meat Producers Association sought revision of railroad rates. In the professional world, the American Medical Association and the American Bar Association (and their state and local affiliates) were long prominent, but other organizations sprang up, e.g., the National Municipal League, the National Conference on City Planning, and the American City Planning Institute; also the National Conference of Charities and Corrections, which became the National Conference of Social Work, and the American Public Health Association (these involving "public-service professionals"). Meanwhile, some businessmen funded the first generation of private institutions designed to bring professional expertise to bear on public policy questions, e.g., the Russell Sage Foundation (1907) and the Institute for Government Research (1916), the latter of which, with two other institutes, became the Brookings Institution (1927).

It was against this backdrop that the Progressive era witnessed extended debate regarding major economic issues, many of them affected by the depression of the 1890s, and the passage of federal legislation dealing with reorganization and concentration in key sectors of the economy; the monetary and banking systems; and tariff policy. Thus railroad rate regulatory or related measures were passed in 1906, 1910, and 1913; a Republican tariff in 1909, divisive to the party, and a Democratic one in 1913, incorporating a federal income tax; the Federal

Reserve Act (1913); and creation of a Bureau of Corporations (1903) and the Clayton Antitrust and Federal Trade Commission acts (1914). The emphasis on appointive bodies and expertise was obvious from the Interstate Commerce Commission (1887) through (especially) the Federal Trade Commission and the Tariff Commission created in 1916.

Indeed, the expansion of administrative agencies and regulatory activity was striking on all levels of government. Building on precedents in other cities, New York City adopted the first comprehensive municipal zoning law to govern land use and buildings (1916). Hundreds of cities followed suit. States provided for the regulation of the life insurance and banking industries, and of public transportation and utilities. State railroad regulatory commissions were revitalized to deal with intrastate issues and to represent state interests before the Interstate Commerce Commission. States legislated to regulate working conditions, hours, even minimum wages, for women and/or children; they also provided for workers' compensation, substituting administrative action for court litigation to compensate job-related injury victims.

Social-medical problems were also addressed by the emerging administrative-regulatory state, above all alcohol, prostitution, venereal disease, and tuberculosis. Organizations that comprised professionals and lay persons, sometimes backed financially by businessmen, investigated these problems and propagandized to win public and political support for their agendas. Even as the Anti-Saloon League campaigned for nationwide prohibition, Congress outlawed the shipping of alcoholic beverages into dry states. Urban vice commissions and a number of organizations spearheaded campaigns that resulted in local measures to curb prostitution, censor films, and regulate movie theaters, dance halls, and other suspect enterprises; state laws to require medical interviews and (in some cases) examination of prospective bridegrooms (but not brides); and state and local requirements that physicians include venereal diseases among communicable diseases to be reported. (Meanwhile, Congress with the Mann Act outlawed the interstate transportation of women for immoral purposes.) The National Tuberculosis Association focused on "the white plague": States mandated the testing of cattle for TB and the pasteurization of milk; cities enacted antispitting ordinances. Eugenicists' and others' concerns over the "quality" of the population led to two drastic public policies: the numerical and discriminatory restriction of immigration (1921, 1924, 1929) and, earlier, various state laws requiring the sterilization of persons defined as not fit to reproduce.

It bears iteration that during the early twentieth century, government on all levels continued to deal with many public issues in much the same way it had during earlier eras: "Politics as usual" did not magically disappear. Still, the shift toward administrative-regulatory government was pronounced and of lasting significance. Congress's grant of discretionary administrative authority to the Federal Trade Commission was far more sweeping than its initial legislative delegation to the Interstate Commerce Commission twenty-seven years earlier. At the same time, struggles with (and within) the courts over administrative regulation and broad exercises of national power (e.g., a federal child-labor law) still had a long course to run. The new state had yet to take on major redistributive functions; not all state and city governments were transformed to the same degree; and not all agencies (e.g., those dealing with workers' concerns) were adequately funded and staffed. Even so, the political economy of modern America was beginning to take shape during the Progressive era, the first decades of the Fourth Party System.

Insofar as party politics are concerned, the new party system arose out of an electoral-political realignment during which from 1893 through 1896 the Republican party triumphed first over the traditional Democracy of Grover Cleveland and then the Democratic-Populist coalition of William Jennings Bryan. In the initial stage of the realignment (1893–95) the Republicans won clear-cut victories in congressional, gubernatorial, and state legislative elections in the politically decisive Northeast and Midwest. They exploited voter discontent arising out of the hard times that had arisen in 1893 by emphasizing economic issues, especially the protective tariff as a means by which government could create and maintain conditions conducive to the flourishing of the private economy, and by playing down cultural issues (e.g., statewide prohibition or drastic restrictions on the sale of alcoholic beverages, state Sunday closing laws, and state statutes that required common school instruction in English), which had divided their party's coalition and worked to the advantage of the Democrats in elections from 1889 through 1892.

Shifts in strength between the parties in the Northeast and Midwest affected both, in strengthening the hand of GOP leaders who favored the gold standard in their party's 1896 national campaign and undermining the position of Democrats who felt likewise. In the end, the Republicans supported the gold standard, alienating politicians from the Rocky Mountain states, where free silver had become an article of faith across party lines, while the Democrats declared for free silver, angering adherents of the gold standard, primarily from the Northeast. The positions taken by the national parties in 1896 led or well-nigh compelled dissenting factions and lesser parties to reconsider their positions in the ensuing presidential campaign. Gold Democrats formed their own party; many of them supported the Republicans. For many Democratic politicians in the Northeast, it was *sauve qui peut*: Only nominally supporting their party's national ticket (if at all), they concentrated on retaining influence in their party organizations and saving lesser Democratic candidates. Silver Republicans backed the Democrats, as did the People's (Populist) party and one wing of the Prohibition party.

The contest between William McKinley (Republican) and William Jennings Bryan (Democrat-Populist) influenced politically decisive shares of the electorate. The Democrats retained the South, but every Border State save Missouri fell to the Republicans. Bryan swept the Mountain States, but he carried only Washington on the Pacific Coast and lost North Dakota on the Plains. Even had Bryan swept the aforementioned "colonial" regions, he would have had to carry one state in the Midwest to win in the electoral college. This he also failed to do, coming close only in Indiana and Ohio. In the Northeast, "the Enemy's Country," as Bryan had aptly put it, the Democratic ticket was routed. Within the Midwest and Northeast, Bryan rallied Populists (less numerous than elsewhere) and many

Prohibitionists, but few Republicans. Some Democrats voted Republican or Gold Democratic; many contributed to Bryan's debacle in the Northeast by abstaining. Thus although the election produced high voter turnout levels elsewhere and overall, such levels were not matched in the Northeast, where nonvoting reflected the cross-pressuring of normally Democratic voters, rather than indifference on the part of voters. Of earlier nonvoters and newly eligible voters who voted, most went Republican.

The ensuing presidential election of 1900 again pitted McKinley against Bryan, this time against a backdrop of America's victory over Spain in a "Splendid Little War," restored prosperity, and reduced social tension. Nationwide, party strengths were virtually unchanged from 1896, but far larger gross shifts revealed the temporary, exaggerated nature of dramatic movements four years earlier. Bryan's partial recovery in the Northeast and Border gained him only Kentucky; his losses from the Midwest westward cost him one Pacific, two Mountain, and three Plains states. Voter turnout declined between the two elections.

In 1904, McKinley was three years dead and Bryan was not a candidate for nomination. The death of Senator Marcus A. Hanna (Ohio) removed the only possible challenger to President Theodore Roosevelt, who was then nominated for a presidential term in his own right at a celebratory Republican national convention. Bryan attended the Democratic national convention, where he met with indifferent success in credentials and platform fights and shied away from endorsing William Randolph Hearst, the primary challenger to conservative domination of the gathering. For president, the Democrats nominated Judge Alton Parker of New York, a staunch conservative and advocate of the gold standard and Henry Davis, a former senator from West Virginia, for vice-president. Davis was wealthy, but at eighty he was also the oldest man ever nominated for national office by a major party—tip-offs, perhaps, to the Democrats' estimation of their party's chances.

Running against a popular incumbent, the candidate of the dominant party, during prosperous times, would likely have doomed any Democrat in 1904, but Parker's dismal showing suggested that a conservative Democrat could not do as well as Bryan in a losing cause. Roosevelt's 56.4 percent of the nationwide popular vote set a new record that would not be surpassed until 1920. Parker added seven of Maryland's eight electoral votes to the Democratic column, but he lost five states won by Bryan in 1900 and carried no northern state. Various measures—sectional differences in the decline of Democratic strength and of turnout, ticket-splitting, and increased support for the Socialist, Prohibition, and People's parties—suggested continued Bryanite-conservative Democratic tensions ran along geographic lines.

William Jennings Bryan lost his third and final presidential race in 1908, this time to William Howard Taft (Ohio), Theodore Roosevelt's anointee. Bryan ran a marginally stronger race than Parker, though his own weakest, receiving 43.1 percent of the popular vote to Taft's 51.6 percent and carrying three states that had voted Republican in 1904. Unlike the case in 1900 and 1904, the Democrats gained a few congressional seats in 1908, this after beginning a comeback two years earlier, rather than lose ground as their national ticket again went down to defeat. They also won some gubernatorial elections and two senate seats. Such gains, however modest, revealed the growing separation between the parties' strength in national contests and in state and local ones, most evident in midterm and off-year canvasses, but now even in a presidential election year. The development reflected (and contributed to) the weakening of political parties as agents of electoral mobilization. State and local parties out of step with their national party—as were Democrats in the Northeast— emphasized their own candidates and issues of state and/or local appeal, rather than the (nonexistent) unity of party tickets from top to bottom. Major candidates campaigned in person, further reducing the role of party; they were advertised in newspapers, whose increasing independence ended their role as party organs.

Democratic gains during 1905–1908 recouped ground lost in the debacle of 1904, but growing conflicts (over policies, power, and personalities) within the Republican party during the presidency of Taft (1909–1913) provided the Democrats with opportunities to score more significant successes. In 1910 the

Democrats recaptured control of the House of Representatives, gained ground in the Senate, and won gubernatorial contests in Ohio (their third straight there), New Jersey, New York, and Massachusetts. Victories brought new men to the fore: At the Democratic National Convention of 1912, one of them, Governor Woodrow Wilson (New Jersey), won the presidential nomination on the forty-sixth roll call over Congressman Champ Clark (Missouri), Speaker of the House. (The Democrats' two-thirds rule may have delayed Wilson's eventual victory, but it had earlier saved him when Clark enjoyed majority support on a number of tallies).

Within the troubled Republican camp, Roosevelt challenged President Taft for the nomination and revealed his popularity among GOP rank-and-file by winning nine of twelve state Republican presidential primary elections to one for Taft and two for Senator Robert M. LaFollette (Wisconsin). But presidential primaries were an innovation, far from a decisive influence. Taft's forces controlled the party and convention machinery and with them the nomination. Southern state delegations, dominated by politicians dependent on federal patronage, contributed to Taft's victory. (By this time southern Republicans were essentially irrelevant to the outcome of national elections; they played their major political role in party conventions.) Roosevelt and his followers, who had already been thinking of an independent presidential race, immediately began to plan their own national political convention. There the Progressive or Bull-Moose party nominated Roosevelt for president. At the risk of oversimplification, one can argue that Roosevelt and important (though by no means all) supporters advocated a statist approach to economic developments and their consequences, one emphasizing the regulation of corporations and the provision of social welfare services, while Wilsonian Democrats initially sought to maintain or enhance competition and to let organized labor fight workers' battles.

Wilson easily won the presidential election of 1912, but not because of any Democratic surge. His popular vote *and* percentage (41.8) trailed Bryan's weakest showing; only in southern states did he receive majority support. Roosevelt (27.4 percent) and Taft (23.2 percent) divided a *majority* Republican vote. TR carried six states, Taft two, Wilson the rest. Although lesser Progressive party candidates ran behind the popular Roosevelt, their diversion of GOP votes, together with abstentions by cross-pressured Republicans, further increased the Democrats' strength in Congress and at the state level. Indeed, the Democrats' capture of state legislatures resulted in their gaining control of the United State Senate.

The national election of 1912 was further noteworthy in that it proved the highwater mark of the Socialist party. Bringing together in 1901 the new Social Democratic party and a faction of the older Socialist Labor party, the Socialist party stood committed to public ownership and supported a range of nonsocialist reforms. With Eugene V. Debs as their perennial candidate, the socialists had contested for the presidency in 1900 (as Social Democrats) and 1904 and 1908 (as Socialists), polling less than 3.0 percent of the national vote. Now, in 1912, Debs won 6.0 percent nationwide, finishing second in Florida and third in four states with four-way races. In fifteen southwestern and far western states, his mean support exceeded 10 percent. Although never as strong as European social democratic and labor parties, the socialists ran well in numerous lesser races during the era, capturing two congressional seats (in Milwaukee and New York City), a handful of state legislative contests, and numerous mayoral elections (in small and middle-size cities).

During 1913–1914 the Wilson administration secured congressional enactment of an impressive legislative program, but these successes, however important to government's changing role in the economy, did not translate into Democratic victories in the midterm elections of 1914. The year was marked by economic recession. Earlier Democratic successes had depended on Republican factionalism. There was no TR on a Progressive ticket in 1914; Republican wounds were beginning to heal. The Democrats' midterm reversals at least contributed to the administration's legislative program of 1916, which reached out to a range of groups with measures that Wilson had earlier ignored or opposed—a child-labor law; workmen's compensation for federal employees; a measure reducing the workday of operating railway workers from ten to eight hours with no diminution in wages; and bills of interest to agricultural interests, including one creating federal farm loan banks. A military preparedness program divided advocates and foes of increased spending on the armed forces, but its funding by increasingly progressive federal taxation made possible by the Sixteenth Amendment placated many otherwise critical of the program.

Meanwhile, America's role during the Mexican Revolution and especially the Great War added new dimensions to political debate. Republicans such as Theodore Roosevelt castigated Wilson for his policy of neutrality, but others in the GOP feared that TR's stridency would alienate antiwar Republicans. (Wilson's foreign policy served him well politically: Not only could Democrats claim that the president was preserving "peace with honor," but neutrality was also proving highly profitable for the nation.) Roosevelt so aspired to the Republican nomination that he employed the threat of another run as a Progressive to pressure the GOP into choosing him. In the end the Republicans turned to Charles Evans Hughes, whose investigation of insurance-utilities-political scandals and reform governorship of New York had earlier won him a national reputation, and whose subsequent service on the United States Supreme Court had removed him from the Republican factional crossfire.

In the election, Wilson barely defeated Hughes winning 49.2 percent of the popular vote and an edge of 277–254 in the electoral college. Hughes ran 22.9 points ahead of Taft. But Wilson won over sufficient Progressive Republicans, Socialists, and new voters to eke out victory. In sectional terms, he put together the coalition that had eluded Bryan in 1896, one based on the South, Border, Pacific Coast, Mountains, and Plains, together with Ohio in the Midwest (and New Hampshire in the Northeast). Examinations of election returns over time in various settings understandably have led some scholars to view Wilson's 1916 vote as anticipatory of the Democrats' later New Deal coalition, but it should be borne in mind that Wilson's victory was both narrow and personal. His party lost ground in lesser races; 1916 hardly presaged Democratic successes to come.

Five months after Wilson's reelection, the United States entered the First World War. America's war effort involved unprecedented activity by government and private economic and other organizations to coordinate and maximize the production of war material, assure broad support for the war, and stifle opposition thereto. The immediate postwar period (1918–1920) was to experience a retreat from wartime government's expanded economic role, but it witnessed continued interest in private organizational efforts to achieve a stable, prosperous economy, encouraged, though not dominated, by government. Meanwhile, ethno-religious, racial, ideological, and cultural conflicts racked wartime and postwar America.

Divisions—over entering the war and peacemaking afterward; wartime economic policies; prohibition, women's suffrage, renewed large-scale immigration, and race; radicalism and the suppression of civil liberties; labor militancy and the frustration of workers; and inflation, followed by agricultural depression—provided the setting for a repudiation of the Democratic party that not only reversed its important, if limited, successes of 1910–1916, but essentially submerged it nationally and outside the South for the remainder of the Fourth Party System.

The Democratic disaster initially revealed itself in the midterm congressional and state elections of 1918, which gave the Republicans control of Congress. During the Fourth Party System, midterm election turnout fell off more markedly from presidential election turnout than in the Third Party System, whose electorate had been so effectively and lastingly mobilized. Now, in the wartime elections of 1918, it fairly plummeted. Almost one hundred congressional districts, mostly Democratic and southern, experienced uncontested elections or ones with nominal opposition. (As the Republican party atrophied across much of the South in the wake of suffrage restriction, it contested fewer congressional races, especially in midterm years, but 1918 marked a low point in this regard.) Meanwhile, in a small number of northern congressional districts, Socialists provided the primary opposition, in a few cases to Republican-Democratic coalitions.

In 1920, the vulnerable Democrats nominated Governor James M. Cox of Ohio for president (on the forty-fourth roll call), and the confident Republicans gave the nod to the affable

Senator Warren G. Harding (Ohio) on the tenth round. For vice-president, the respective parties chose Franklin D. Roosevelt, assistant secretary of the navy, and Calvin Coolidge, governor of Massachusetts. The Republican national ticket swept to a record-breaking popular victory: its 60.3 percent of the total vote has since been narrowly surpassed only three times since then (1936, 1964, 1972). For the first time since 1876, the Republicans carried an ex-Confederate state (Tennessee); outside the South, the Democrats salvaged only Kentucky. Across the North, where Wilson had carried 784 counties in 1916, Cox won only forty-two. Lesser Democratic candidates generally ran stronger races, but most were buried in the Republican landslide. Again running for the Socialists, this time from a federal prison for having violated the wartime Espionage Act, Eugene Debs polled his largest popular vote, but only 3.4 percent of the total vote. He showed better in the Upper Midwest, where antiwar ethnic support was strong, than in earlier strongholds in the Southwest and West. Repression and internal divisions over the Bolshevik Revolution had sharply weakened the Socialist party. Nationwide, voter turnout collapsed; it fell dramatically from 61.8 percent (1916) to 49.3 percent.

With ratification of the Nineteenth Amendment earlier in the year, the elections of 1920 became the first in which women voted on fully equal terms with men in all states. From 1910 through 1918, women won full voting rights in eleven states after having done so in four during the nineteenth century. The campaign of the National American Woman Suffrage Association to win full suffrage for women in all states by amending the federal Constitution was aided by the organization's support for the war effort, as well as by women's gaining the vote in New York (1917) and Michigan (1918). Most women thus entered the electorate during a period of limited voter mobilization, so it comes as no surprise that their turnout was initially lower than that of men, especially in recent immigrant and working-class communities.

Republican dominance was fairly assured during the 1920s. Although the Harding administration was beset by scandal, four key cabinet secretaries (state, treasury, agriculture, and commerce) were distinguished. Indeed, Secretary of

Commerce Herbert Hoover was central to the defining of government's appropriate peacetime role in fostering constructive activities among economic interest groups the better to serve public, as well as private, purposes. Despite depressed economic conditions in staple-crop agriculture and a number of industries, prosperity was widespread. Meanwhile, the Democrats offered no persuasive alternative economic program. Moreover, cultural conflicts of the 1920s, over immigration restriction, the Ku Klux Klan, and Prohibition, divided Democrats more than they did Republicans.

So it was at the Democratic National Convention of 1924, with delegates narrowly divided between denouncing the KKK by name (542 $7/20$) or ignoring it (543 $3/20$) in the platform (as the Republicans did), that they deadlocked over the nomination until settling on John W. Davis (West Virginia) on the 103rd roll call. Two frustrated aspirants to the nomination—Governor Alfred E. Smith (New York) and Wilson's son-in-law, William Gibbs McAdoo (California)—personified the Democrats' inner divisions, with Smith strongest in the Northeast and among Catholics, immigrants, foes of Prohibition (wets), and urbanites; and McAdoo dominant in the South and West and among Protestants, the old stock, supporters of Prohibition (drys), and ruralites. The Republicans chose Calvin Coolidge, who had become president when Harding died in 1923. A new Progressive party nominated Senator Robert M. LaFollette (Wisconsin) for president and the Socialist party endorsed his candidacy as well. Coolidge easily won the presidential election, polling 54.1 percent of the popular vote to 28.8 percent for Davis and 16.6 percent for LaFollette. Davis carried the South and Oklahoma; LaFollette his home state. The Progressive ran second in eleven other midwestern and western states. Voter turnout declined fractionally, a modest drop in the South outweighed a trifling gain elsewhere. Democratic losses in Congress partially undid the party's limited recovery in the previous midterm elections. Democratic successes in gubernatorial and/or senatorial elections in the Rocky Mountain states, as well as in a few industrial states, especially in 1922 and 1926, but even in 1924, could not conceal the overall weakness of the divided minority party outside of the South during the 1920s.

The presidential campaign and election of 1928 painfully revealed the depth of cultural conflict in the United States and proved to be the climax of the Fourth Party System. Declining to seek another term and offering no encouragement to a draft, Coolidge gave way to his Secretary of Commerce Herbert Hoover (Iowa) as the Republicans' presidential nominee. The Democrats turned to Alfred E. Smith, four-term governor of New York (whose only defeat had come during the party's debacle of 1920). A Roman Catholic of Irish descent, a foe of Prohibition, and a politician schooled in New York City's Tammany Hall, Smith was the very antithesis of Hoover who had been raised as a Quaker in Iowa and was a mining engineer. The Democrats sought to avoid any repetition of 1924's fratricidal conflict: McAdoo declined to seek nomination; the party met in a southern city, Houston (for the first time since 1860); Smith was nominated after only one roll call; the convention adopted a conciliatory platform (though Smith's subsequent call for "fundamental changes" in Prohibition upset dry delegates) and nominated Senator Joseph Robinson of Arkansas, a dry southerner, for vice-president.

After a bitter campaign that focused on Smith, Hoover convincingly won the election, by 444 to 87 in the electoral college and 58.2 percent of the popular vote. Given the political and economic contexts, any Democrat was all but certain to lose in 1928, but Smith's candidacy powerfully influenced the pattern of that defeat. The heated contest increased voter turnout by 3.5 points in the South, 9.2 points elsewhere, and 8.0 points nationwide. But Smith was ill-suited to capitalize on agricultural discontent in the Midwest and West. His candidacy cost the Democrats five overwhelming Protestant southern states, all but one for the first time since Reconstruction. On the other hand, Smith narrowly carried Massachusetts and Rhode Island, states with large Catholic populations, neither ever before lost by a Republican in a two-way presidential race. (New York State voters rejected Smith for president, even as they elected another Democrat, Franklin D. Roosevelt, as governor.)

Al Smith's urban strength was formerly emphasized in accounts of 1928; his showing in defeat was deemed a harbinger of the New Deal coalition. But Smith's election performance in cities was mixed; voters drawn to Smith no more necessarily became committed Democrats than those rejecting him thereby identified themselves as Republicans. The election of 1928 reflected the issues of the 1920s much more than it anticipated those of the 1930s.

During 1929, a Democrat, writing in a national magazine, asked: "Will the Democrats Follow the Whigs?" But that same year the stock market crashed. The Great Depression that followed and the partisan clash over governmental responses to unparalleled economic crisis would result not in the disappearance of the party that traced its origins to Jefferson, but in the breakup of the Fourth Party System and the emergence of the New Deal system dominated by the Democrats. The new party system was marked by at least a partial revitalization of electoral politics, but even in this groups outside the Democratic party—lesser parties in a few states and expanding organized labor in many—played major roles in the New Deal "revolution." The New Deal expanded the role of the federal government in many ways, some of them unprecedented, but it generally did so in ways characteristic of the Progressive political order, e.g., through executive leadership, the administrative-regulatory state, professional expertise, and governmental interaction with myriad organized interest groups.

References

Burnham, Walter Dean. 1982. *The Current Crisis in American Politics.* New York: Oxford U. Pr.

———. 1987. "The Turnout Problem." In A. James Reichley, ed. *Elections American Style.* Washington, DC: Brookings Institution.

David, Paul T. 1972. *Party Strength in the United States, 1872–1970.* Charlottesville: U. Pr. of Virginia.

Diamond, Robert A., ed. 1975. *Congressional Quarterly's Guide to U.S. Elections.* Washington, DC: Congressional Quarterly.

Gould, Lewis L. 1986. *Reform and Regulation: American Politics from Roosevelt to Wilson.* New York: Knopf.

Hawley, Ellis W. 1979. *The Great War and the Search for a Modern Order, A History of the American People and Their Institutions, 1917–1933.* New York: St. Martin's Pr.

Horwitz, Morton J. 1992. *The Transformation of American Law, 1870–1960: The Crisis of Legal Orthodoxy.* New York: Oxford U. Pr.

Kleppner, Paul. 1982. *Who Voted?: The Dynamics of Electoral Turnout, 1870–1980.* New York: Praeger.

————. 1987. *Continuity and Change in Electoral Politics, 1893–1928.* Westport, CT: Greenwood Pr.

Kornbluh, Mark L. 1988. "From Participatory to Administrative Politics: A Social History of American Political Behavior, 1880–1918." Ph.D. diss., Johns Hopkins U.

Kousser, J. Morgan. 1974. *The Shaping of Southern Politics: Suffrage Restriction and the Establishment of the One-Party South, 1890–1920.* New Haven, CT: Yale U. Pr.

Link, Arthur S. and Richard L. McCormick. 1983. *Progressivism.* Arlington Heights, IL: Harlan Davidson.

McSeveney, Samuel T. 1972. *The Politics of Depression: Voting Behavior in the Northeast, 1893–1896.* New York: Oxford U. Pr.

Reynolds, John F. 1988. *Testing Democracy: Electoral Behavior and Progressive Reform in New Jersey, 1880–1920.* Chapel Hill: U. of North Carolina Pr.

CHAPTER 8

The Party System in the United States House of Representatives

David W. Brady

John Ettling

In the twentieth century, national politics has increasingly become the foremost arena in which most American expectations, interests, and issues sooner or later contend. This is not to say that they have always been resolved or accommodated by political means, only that they have been articulated in the language of politics and refracted through the political process. Such has not always been the case, especially in the United States in the nineteenth century, yet no one would argue that nineteenth-century concerns were any less divisive or compelling. Americans in the last century, however, did not as frequently turn to the federal government to arbitrate or reconcile their differences. In this century, the United States has undergone a profound change in popular expectations of government. In the same period, America's rise to world power has brought in its wake a host of consequent demands.

The framers of the Constitution clearly intended the House of Representatives to be the most democratic institution in the federal government. The House has always been preternaturally sensitive to change, and a major consequence has been an increasingly complicated division of labor. Students of the House can chart its response over time to changes in the wider society by tracing the proliferation of its committees and subcommittees.

Complex divisions of labor, however, generate centrifugal forces that tend to pull organizations apart. Lost in the welter of constituent units—each pursuing its own immediate end—are the general interests of the organization as a whole. To counter this process of Balkanization, strong integrative mechanisms must be developed to hold together what the division of labor would otherwise pull apart. In the House of Representatives, the party system traditionally has served this cohesive purpose. Although neither the Constitution nor the rules of the House mentions them, political parties have acted from the beginning as devices to integrate and rationalize the separate activities of congressmen.

One of the most striking differences between the nineteenth- and twentieth-century Houses of Representatives is the decline in the importance of party strength, which a brief glance at the history of party voting will underscore. Likewise, an analysis of the importance of party in the apportioning of committee assignments will reveal a part of what Nelson Polsby has called the "institutionalism of the House of Representatives" (Polsby 1968, Figure 2).

The decline of party strength in the House of Representatives can be documented by focusing on the components of party strength—interparty divisiveness and intraparty cohesion, and can be treated by summarizing issue dimensions over time. The causes of such decline in the House of Representatives are related to both the exogenous political system (e.g., electoral changes) and to structural changes in the House itself, affecting House coalitions, party voting, and the sanctions available to the leadership to bring dissenting members into line. The consequences of party decline are, of course, multiple and complex, but two major results deserve analysis; i.e., its effect on party leadership and on public policymaking.

Any analysis that purports to clarify differences between nineteenth- and twentieth-century Congresses must first decide when the nineteenth century ended and the twentieth began. Different historians have marked the turn of the century differently. McKinley's first election, his assassination, the beginning of World War I, even the opening of the New York

Armory Show all have been advanced as the real point of transition. About the only year that has almost no advocates is 1900. Here, the most meaningful contention is that the new century began in 1910–1911, with the Sixty-first Congress, which redefined the role of the Speaker.

The Importance of Party in the House

The emergence of well-articulated party divisions within the House occurred in the Jacksonian era, at about the same time that real parties emerged in the electorate. As Ronald Formisano has shown, the earlier organized battles between the Alexander Hamilton and Thomas Jefferson factions in Congress, elite in nature, bore many of the features of later party disputes and clearly foreshadowed the appearance of full-fledged political parties in the next generation. By Jackson's second term, the party system had assumed its characteristic dimensions—party in the electorate, party as organization, and party as government. By the early 1830s, both the Whigs and Democrats had acquired party identifiers throughout all regions of the country. They had established separate and competing local and state organizations. And, Joel Silbey (1967) argues, in the House of Representatives both voting patterns and internal organization revealed clearly defined party divisions. Moreover, as McCormick (1966) has shown, the parties were intensively competitive across all states. No region was either solidly Democratic or Whig.

The party system has endured despite the periodic disappearance of major parties, despite sectional cleavages, and despite disruptive changes in the nominating mechanism. The American party system is the oldest in the (Western) world. Voting in the U.S. House of Representatives had a pronounced party component long before party was a factor in other national legislatures. Despite the early development of partisan voting in the House, other Western legislative bodies soon surpassed the House in levels of party voting (Lawrence Lowell, 1901). Thus comparatively low levels of party solidarity distinguish the House from other democratic systems in the modern era. When we argue, consequently, that party strength in the House has declined in the twentieth century, the original point of declension is lower than those typical of European legislatures.

In order to analyze the causes of this decline in the House of Representatives, party strength needs to be defined more carefully. Table 1 shows the decline in party voting in the House as measured by the percentage of all roll calls in which 50 percent of one party opposed 50 percent of the other. The trend from the heyday of party voting in the 1800–1910 period is definitely downward, with the lowest scores registered in the 1966–1980 period. The 1982 to 1988 scores show an upward movement in the levels of party voting. What remains unclear, however, is what is being measured when votes are aggregated in this manner. Aage Clausen (1973) has shown that votes in the House can be broken down into policy dimensions in any given Congress and that some of the issues consequently exposed have historical continuity. Clausen's work, along with that of Barbara Sinclair, demonstrates the abiding nature of certain issue dimensions at least since the New Deal. They can be arranged under headings that would include civil liberties, government management, social welfare, agricultural assistance, and international involvement. In each of these areas, different coalitions have been at work. Party affiliation, for example, determined voting behavior much more strongly on matters pertaining to government management than either international involvement or social welfare.

Similar work on nineteenth-century Congresses has shown that the periods from 1850–1876 and 1884–1900 also reveal issues of continuous legislative interest. Party membership does appear to have influenced voting behavior in these earlier periods more profoundly than in the post-New Deal era. Still, some issues of lasting interest clearly were not structured by party. By using rough measures of party cohesion on roll-call votes, analysts can trace a decline in party strength; it is by no means clear, however, how the mix of issue dimensions affected these percentages over time. A more subtle analysis would have to confront the relationship between aggregate voting patterns and issue dimensions. Unfortunately, practical as well as methodological problems impede such an analysis. For the

Table 1: Party Voting in the House of Representatives—50th (1887) to 99th (1986) Houses

Year Elected	Congress	50% vs. 50%	Year Elected	Congress	50% vs. 50%
1886	50	51.1	1936	75	63.9
1888	51	78.9	1938	76	71.4
1890	52	45.4	1940	77	41.5
1892	53	44.8	1942	78	49.4
1894	54	68.5	1944	79	48.1
1896	55	79.8	1946	80	44.8
1898	56	77.2	1948	81	50.9
1900	57	67.0	1950	82	64.1
1902	58	89.7	1952	83	44.9
1904	59	73.5	1954	84	42.3
1906	60	57.1	1956	85	49.2
1908	61	79.2	1958	86	52.8
1910	62	59.5	1960	87	48.8
1912	63	61.4	1962	88	51.7
1914	64	58.6	1964	89	47.1
1916	65	42.7	1966	90	35.8
1918	66	44.9	1968	91	29.2
1920	67	59.9	1970	92	33.0
1922	68	58.7	1972	93	35.7
1924	69	43.7	1974	94	42.3
1926	70	48.6	1976	95	38.8
1928	71	58.2	1978	96	43.5
1930	72	57.7	1980	97	35.9
1932	73	70.6	1982	98	51.8
1934	74	59.9	1984	99	58.6

purpose of this article, the imprecise measures presented in Table 1 must serve to annotate the decline of party strength in the House. Although useful as blunt indicators of general trends, these figures mask a complicated pattern of underlying issue dimensions, ones that were confronted year in and year out by shifting congressional coalitions, not always congruent with party lines.

On the other hand, party affiliation did have some bearing on issue dimension voting, especially in periods of extreme party voting. In periods of weak party voting, it clearly did not. Probably the aggregate measure of party voting roughly reflects the extent to which the parties structured issue dimension voting at a particular point in time, although the data cannot be broken down more specifically by issue dimension over the entire time series. Two related but distinct components of party voting in Congress—intraparty unity and interparty divisiveness— constitute a second aspect of party strength that should be considered. If, in a given Congress, unity within each party and divisiveness between the two were high, votes tended to follow party lines in a comprehensive fashion. But in another Congress, when unity and divisiveness happened to be low, party affiliation clearly did not structure voting. Two additional combinations of unity and divisiveness are shown in Figure 1.

Figure 1

DIVISIVENESS

		High	Low
U N I T Y	High	Party Structures Voting Comprehensively (A)	Partial Structuring of Voting Consensual (C)
	Low	Partial Structuring of Voting Factional (B)	Party Does Not Structure Voting (D)

When party divisiveness is high but party unity low, party will structure voting on some issues yet not on others. In fact, this is the pattern found by Clausen in the post-New Deal era. If divisiveness is low and party unity high, then party will structure some voting, but also existing will be either a cross-party conflict or a cross-party consensus, such as the conservative coalition of recent years. If we were to rate the combinations by the extent to which party structures voting, the ordering would be *A, B, C,* and *D*—from most to least partisan. In the case of the *AD* diagonal, analysis is relatively straightforward. Party either structures all or most of the voting or none or very little of the voting. Analysis becomes more difficult when one turns to *B* and *C*. Here party structuring of the vote falls somewhere between the two extremes. In one case, party structures voting because the parties disagree on some significant subset of issues, while in the other case divisiveness or conflict between parties is low, but intraparty cohesion is high. Thus, in the first case, party divisiveness structures voting even though intraparty cohesion is low; in the second case, however, intraparty cohesiveness structures voting.

Superimposing a Clausen-type dimensional analysis onto the party voting scores shown in Table 1 results in a decline of party strength in the House from cohesive, opposed parties to less cohesive, nondivisive parties. Until the period 1910–1911, party structured voting across a wide spectrum of issue dimensions. Table 2 shows the extent of party structuring of voting patterns on a range of issue dimensions for selected years from 1852 to 1900. Table 3 shows the extent of party structuring of the vote on a range of issue dimensions from selected Congresses since the 1910–1911 period. In Table 1, the results indicate that party correlated with a wider range of issues than is the case for those dimensions shown in Table 2. Even though party never completely structured voting in any period, the extent of structuring was greater in the nineteenth century. This evidence corresponds to the decline of party voting shown in Table 1. Thus the partial mapping of issue-dimensional analysis onto the overtime party voting series corroborates the decline of party strength in the U.S. House in the twentieth century. The decline of party strength in the House accelerated after 1938 (see

Table 2: Average Correlations Between Party and Voting on Known
Issue Dimensions for Selected Years in the 19th Century

1853–1871	Lowest Correlation	Average Correlation	Highest Correlation
ISSUES			
Slavery, Secession, Civil Rights	.41	.83	.98
Public Works	.59	.76	.91
Railroad/Telegraph Construction	.14	.43	.89
Housekeeping	.27	.78	.96
Money and Banking	.41	.80	.94
Tariff	.02	.67	.92

1890–1900	Lowest Correlation	Average Correlation	Highest Correlation
ISSUES			
Currency	.21	.78	.96
Military Appropriations	.19	.67	.94
Tariff	.20	.81	.98
Business	.40	.87	.98
Public Works	.26	.39	.70
Housekeeping	.73	.91	.99
Immigration	.26	.52	.81
Taxation	.85	.89	.92

Taken from D. Brady (1982).

Table 3: Average Correlations Between Party and Selected
Issue Dimensions for Some 20th Century Houses

1925–1938	*Lowest Correlation*	*Average Correlation*	*Highest Correlation*
ISSUES			
Government Management	.90	.93	.96
Agricultural Policy	.09	.52	.93
Social Welfare	.78	.84	.92
Civil Liberties	.17	.21	.46

1953–1964	*Lowest Correlation*	*Average Correlation*	*Highest Correlation*
ISSUES			
Government Management	.88	.90	.96
Agricultural Assistance	.74	.80	.92
Social Welfare	.51	.63	.83
International Involvement	.05	.38	.78
Civil Liberties	.12	.14	.22

Taken from Barbara Sinclair (1977) and Aage Clausen (1973).

Table 1). This statistical phenomenon reflects the rise of the Conservative coalition in the Congress. This bloc of southern
Democrats and Republicans voting against liberal legislation is
by definition antiparty, since elements of one party cross party
lines to vote with the opposition. From 1938 until at least the
Ronald Reagan era, the Conservative coalition has been a prominent voting alliance in the U.S. House; however, as David Rohde
has shown, southern Democrats increasingly have begun to vote
like northern Democrats. Rohde argues that the rise in levels of
party voting in the 1982–1988 period results from the increased
demographic similarity of the southern Democratic districts to
the northern Democratic districts.

In sum, party strength in the U.S. House of Representatives in general has declined, although the Reagan presidency
generated a rise in the level of party voting. This decline can be
characterized as the movement from highly cohesive and opposed parties to only fairly cohesive and less divisive parties. It
means that the extent to which party-structured voting on issue
dimensions has dropped over time. The decline in party strength
from its nineteenth-century highs began with the revolt against
the Speaker in the 1910–1911 period and continued with the rise
of cross-party coalitional government in the House. It is important to recognize the existence of low points in party voting.

Causes of the Decline of Party

The federal arrangement of the American system has
produced a fragmented party system. Each of the fifty states has
a separate party system, and underlying that system is a pattern
of local interests, issues, and voting patterns. At the national
level, the American party system is an amalgam of overlapping
state, local, and regional interests. The nineteenth-century party
system was certainly affected by the federal nature of the
American government. Unlike the modern party system,
however, partisanship in the last century was stronger in the
electorate. Historians' accounts of party strength in the
nineteenth century show partisan voting to be important.
McCormick on the Second Party System, Hays (1975) and

McKitrick (1975) on the Third Party System, and the electoral work of Jones (1964) and Jensen (1971) clearly demonstrate the importance of party as the major variable accounting for electoral results. The reasons put forward to account for the high levels of partisanship in the last century's elections are numerous. They include the use of list voting rather than the Australian ballot, the role of elections as entertainment, and a technological inability to communicate the personal character-istics of candidates to large numbers of voters.

Within the formal party organization, however, elected politicians were able to control the nominating process at every level—local, state, and national—thus providing for a greater degree of party control. The general practice of rotation in office, particularly in the House of Representatives, kept congressmen from building local sources of support independent of the party organization. The fact that there were no primaries in which members of the same party competed with one another also strengthened the party organization. In sum, a considerable body of evidence suggests that both party in the electorate and party organization were stronger in the nineteenth than in the twentieth century. Whether this stronger partisanship was the result of structural factors or of psychological, behavioral differences is beyond the scope of this analysis (see Rusk and Converse, 1974). Suffice it to say that for whatever reasons, party was stronger in the nineteenth than in the twentieth century. If both the electorate and the party organization were strong, a student would expect to find party strength greater in the House. However, the electoral connection between member and constituent has clearly changed.

The most immediate and direct relationship exists between a congressman and his electorate, since without a plurality of votes, a candidate does not become a congressman. Thus, if partisan voting has declined over time, some corresponding changes must have taken place in the electoral process. The major change is that in the twentieth century congressmen are able to control their own fates more easily than their forebears in the last century. The process of nominating candidates has shifted from the party to the individual. In the first half of the nineteenth century, candidates were rotated by local parties. The famous example of Abraham Lincoln waiting for his turn to run for the House and then serving only one term is a good example of rotation. Until the latter part of the nineteenth century, voting in elections was by party lists rather than by Australian ballot. Both of these mechanisms and what appears to have been a more partisan electorate gave political parties control over candidates. That is, rational candidates considered their electoral fate to be tied to the fate of their party and its presidential candidates, rather than to their own ability to service constituents.

The introduction of the primary as a major nominating vehicle clearly weakened the effect of political parties on the nominating process. As primaries increased in number and media technology became universally available, candidates raised their own money and built their own organizations, which today include pollsters, media managers, and others. The result is that winning candidates are not beholden to party organizations for either their nomination or for their election. Once elected, these congressmen have increasingly turned to nonpartisan service activities as the major component of their reelectoral success. Members nominated, elected, and reelected under these conditions are not likely to be especially amenable to pressure from party leaders, especially when they see differences between the party leaders' positions and those of their constituents. In sum, the changing American electoral universe has clearly aided the decline of party in the House of Representatives. The decline in partisan identification, the changes in ballot forms, the rise of primaries, and an increased reliance on the electronic media have all increased congressmen's ability to manage their own electoral fate. Under these conditions, parties as organizations have lost control over nominations and campaigns.

Such was not true of the partisan alignments in the U.S. House of Representatives from roughly 1854 until the period 1910–1911, which pitted the urban industrial North against the more rural South and Border States. This regional alignment was mapped onto the congressional parties, that is, the North was essentially Republican while the South was Democratic. The election of a Democratic majority in the House in 1910 and the subsequent election of Woodrow Wilson in 1912 broke

Republican dominance of the North until 1918. From 1920 until the period 1930–1932, the Republicans regained dominance in the North. The Franklin D. Roosevelt landslide in 1932 made the Democrats the dominant party in both the North and South until the 1938 House elections allowed the Republicans to become competitive in the North. The Democratic party's control of the House from 1930 until today has resulted from their dominance in northern urban districts combined with their southern contingent. Thus the electoral base of the House Democratic majority from 1938 to at least 1980 has been based on a regional arrangement that was electoral only. The fact that on many issues, especially civil rights (until the late 1960s at least), the congressmen of these regions disagreed also helped to weaken party strength in the House. Relatively safe in their seats, southern Democrats could count on ultimately rising to positions of power within the committee system. Whether this Dixie dominance rested on the southerners' ability to spend time on Capitol Hill or on the fact that certain elections such as 1946 devastated their northern counterparts makes little difference. The facts are that in the 1938–1980 period southerners held a disproportionate share of committee chairmanships. The northern element of the Democratic party dominated presidential politics (with 1976 being the only exception), and southerners dominated congressional politics. In short, in the post-1938 period, the Democratic party in the House was composed of two distinct and often opposed elements, and the consequence of this coalition did not aid party strength in the House. The rise of Republican strength in the South in the Reagan era, however, has brought many conservative districts into the Republican party fold. This development obviously increases party voting since districts formerly represented by conservative Democrats voting with the Conservative coalition are now represented by Republicans voting Republican.

Internal Causes

The major integrative mechanisms in the House over the years have been the congressional parties, especially the majority party. When a congressional party was strong, the House leadership could integrate what the division of labor pulled apart. In an important sense, then, the ability to integrate is a test of party strength. Despite short-term fluctuations, nineteenth-century House leaders had the advantage over their twentieth-century counterparts in this regard. Since 1911, only the three New Deal Congresses (1932–1938) made a point of party strength. From 1938 until 1980, the decline is especially pronounced.

Superior party strength in the nineteenth century stemmed internally from the availability of sanctions to leaders. Kenneth Shepsle makes this point nicely when he argues that legislatures are cooperative games. That is, the stronger the parties' sanctions over members, the higher the level of intraparty cooperation. One reason that European legislatures have high levels of party voting is that their party systems—from local constituencies to party as government—have greater sanctions than do American parties. While levels of party voting in the U.S. House have probably never been as high as they are in European systems, historical analysis shows that the greater the sanctions, the higher the levels of party voting. The greatest sanction available to the congressional leadership has been the power to appoint committees. Party voting in the last century is higher than any period in the post-1915 period with the exception of Roosevelt's first three New Deal Houses. The highest levels of party voting in the history of the House came between 1890 and 1910, when the Speaker had the full complement of floor powers to go with his appointive powers. The Speaker's control of the Rules Committee, his right to recognition on the floor, and his power to count a quorum during the 1890–1910 period increased his ability to discipline dissident members. And Brady and Althoff (1974) have shown that the highest levels of party strength occurred in precisely this period.

In the period 1910–1911, a coalition of progressive Republicans and Democrats booted the Speaker off the Rules Committee and broke his stranglehold on committee assignments. With the weakening of the Speaker began the decline of party in the House (see Figure 1). Although Woodrow Wilson was able to work effectively with the Democratic caucus, the fact that he had to turn to the caucus at all on important votes underscores the point that the decline of party in the House was already underway. Both party voting and cohesion dropped during Wilson's first term. From Speakers Joseph Cannon through Sam Rayburn down to "Tip" O'Neill, the shift in the internal operation of the House is best described as the movement from authority to bargaining. Speakers Thomas Reed and Cannon were the leaders of their party, and their subordinates (majority leader, Whip, etc.) were also committee chairmen. Together they sat like a kind of cabinet government. Cannon's power was extensive enough to permit him to thwart Theodore Roosevelt's legislative package in the Fifty-eighth House. After the Speaker lost the power to appoint committees, the party leadership and the committee leadership diverged. Committee leaders became chieftains with whom the party leaders bargained in order to process and pass legislation. Party leaders since the period 1910–1911 generally have been negotiators and middlemen. Only rarely and under exceptional circumstances have they wielded the kind of power that Reed and Cannon took for granted.

This analysis has shown that from the nineteenth to the twentieth century, changes in the electoral system weakened the connection between party in the electorate, party as organization, and the congressional parties. Internally the loss or sanctions available to the leadership, plus the increasing role of specialization and thus the committee's power, weakened party strength in the House. That these two phenomena are related is not in doubt; however, the state of our knowledge about the specific linkages between these exogenous and endogenous factors is limited and speculative. Still the combination in some fashion of these factors is strongly related to the decline of party strength in the U.S. House of Representatives.

The Policy Consequences of the Decline of Party

The first and most obvious effect of the decline of party in the House on American public policy is that party leaders, in political scientist V.O. Key's words, are forced into a "ceaseless maneuvering to find majorities." When the "majority" party cannot provide a majority for programs—either the president's or the party leaders'—the result is at best incrementalism and at worst stalemate. The one characteristic common to all periods of major policy change (e.g., Jacksonian reforms, the civil liberties and economic legislation of the 1860s and early 1870s, the New Deal) was the existence of a cohesive majority party and a cohesive opposed minority. In none of these periods have the president and his congressional allies been forced to build and continually rebuild an interparty coalition to enact programs. When party strength is high, policy tends to have direction and consistency. Under conditions of party weakness or political flux, leaders are forced to seek votes and compromise policy in order to form ephemeral majorities. This point could be shown over time given sufficient data. Since such data are lacking, the example will have to stand for the whole in an examination of the process of policy formation first in recent Houses, then in the Reed Houses of the period of 1897–1901 (Fifty-fifth and Fifty-sixth).

In the contemporary House, the policy process begins in the committees. Individual bills—presidentially sponsored or otherwise—are assigned to the relevant committee or committees. Normally (especially on money bills), the committees are expected to compromise differences between Republicans and Democrats, liberals and conservatives, North and South, so that the final product is acceptable to a majority of members. The committee's bill then goes to the House Rules Committee for both clearances to the floor and specific rules governing time, amendments, and so on. The committee system thus determines where work is done, and it clearly shapes policy.

This committee system is separate from the party system in the modern House, where seniority normally determines committee leadership. Throughout most of the post-1910–1911 period, the committee leaders' perspectives differed from those of the party leaders, a problem particularly acute in the post-1938 period. Since 1938, the Democrats have controlled the House for all but four years (1947–1949; 1953–1955), and conservative southern Democrats often chaired important committees. Because many committees were chaired by southerners like Graham Barden (N.C.), Howard Smith (Va.), and George Mahon (Tex.), who were neither national nor presidential Democrats, the House Democratic leadership was often frustrated. Even cursory studies of legislative proposals, such as Medicare-Medicaid, aid to elementary and secondary education, and civil rights, will show how committee leaders with different legislative or social views could keep the House party leadership from achieving its desired policy results. The party and committee leadership were from separate and often ideologically opposed power bases, even though they were nominally of the same party. When regular House members could take their cues from either set of leaders, the result was often stalemate. This deadlocked relationship has been further complicated by the recent trend of Republican presidents and Democratic Houses. In the Reagan era from 1981 through 1988, a conservative president faced a liberal House, and under Speaker James Wright the House had its own agenda.

In contrast, the party and committee system in the 1890–1910 period were blended. The Speaker of the House was chairman of the Rules Committee; the majority leader was chairman of the Appropriations Committee; the majority Whip was chairman of either Judiciary or Ways and Means. The Rules Committee, which had no formal meeting room and consisted of only five members, was subject to the Speaker's call to meet wherever and whenever he chose. The Speaker's unilateral right to appoint committees permitted him to staff the Rules Committee with loyal party men. This capability, in essence, gave him absolute control over the management and timing of all bills. Furthermore, the Speaker could and did use his appointive powers to reward the faithful and to punish the mavericks within his own party. His monopoly on appointments and his formal parliamentary powers assured strong party voting on the floor. The practice of selecting committee chairmen to fill important posts in the party organization further served to blur the distinctions between committee and party. During this era, the Republicans never sought Democratic support for tariff, appropriations, money, and other bills. Rather they alone determined policy direction by writing and enacting legislation over strident, but ineffectual, Democratic opposition. In contrast to the modern House where bills come before the body late in the legislative session, many important bills in the Cannon-Reed era were introduced and passed within the first few days. The passage of the Dingley Tariff early in the special session of the Fifty-fifth House is a classic case in point.

In the heyday of the Speaker-dominated House, the majority congressional party could pass legislation with strong partisan majorities. The Speaker's powers plus a belief in party government were sufficient to ensure these majorities. But this party dominance did not hold true for most of the Houses since the period 1910–1911. Party leaders in the post-1910–1911 period have had to rely on bargaining and compromise to achieve limited policy goals. Their predecessors could rely on authority to carry the day. The contrast in leadership styles between "Czar" Cannon and Sam Rayburn is the difference between authority and bargaining.

This comparison between ideal types of partisan and fragmented congressional policy formation demonstrates the difference between parties which stand for something and those that try to offer all things to all voters. Of course, not all nineteenth-century Houses had strong congressional parties, nor have all post-1910 Houses had fragmented, indecisive majorities. Franklin Roosevelt's New Deal Houses and Lyndon Johnson's Eighty-ninth House are proof that undiluted policy innovation is possible in the twentieth century. Yet in both these instances party strength was greater than in periods preceding or following them. In general, then, party strength was greater in the nineteenth century than it has been in the twentieth.

One result of this change is clear: Public policy formulation in the twentieth century has been more incremental. A congressional policy process dominated by bargaining and compromise virtually assures this slowness. Party leaders who could count on their party's support were freer to examine policy alternatives and innovative solutions: Less of their time was necessarily consumed in attempts to build majorities.

Conclusions

Party strength was greater before the period 1910–1911 than since. While no one can adduce a complete answer to why this is so, the following reasons seem important: the decline of party identification in the electorate; the rise of primaries as the major nominating mechanism; the concomitant decline in the role of party organizations in nominating candidates; and the development of highly personalized campaign organizations dominated by media and polling technologists. In sum, these factors have helped to create an electoral system in which individual members view their electoral fate as dependent on their own actions rather than those of the local or national party. Members elected under these conditions have fewer incentives than did their nineteenth-century counterparts to vote with their party.

The decline of party as an electoral force in the twentieth century has been paralleled by both a weakening of the party leadership's sanctions over members and a decentralization of policy making to committees and subcommittees. The shift to committees and subcommittees has resulted in an increase in an individual House member's ability to decide on policy matters relevant to his or her constituents. In short, in the twentieth century, parties can use fewer internal incentives (either positive or negative) for members to support the party leaders' positions. In combination with the changed electoral system, the result is a major decline in party strength in the U.S. House of Representatives.

References

Abram, Michael, and Joseph Cooper. 1968. "The Rise of Seniority in the House of Representatives." 1 *Polity* 52.

Anderson, James E. 1979. *Public Policy Making*. New York: Holt, Rinehart, Winston.

Aydelotte, William. 1966. "Parties and Issues in Early Victorian England." 5 *Journal of British Studies* 94.

Benedict, Michael. 1974. *A Compromise of Principle: Congressional Republicans and Reconstruction, 1863–1869*. New York: Karton.

Brady, David. 1973. *Congressional Voting in a Partisan Era*. Lawrence: U. of Kansas Pr.

———. 1978. "Critical Elections, Congressional Parties and Clusters of Policy Change." 8 *British Journal of Political Science* 79.

———. 1980. "Congressional Elections and Clusters of Policy Change in the U.S. House: 1886–1960." In Richard Trilling and Bruce

Campbell, eds. *Realignment in American Politics: Toward a Theory.* Austin: U. of Texas Pr.

———. 1982. "Congressional Party Realignment and Transformations of Public Policy in Three Realignment Eras." 26 *American Journal of Political Science* 333.

———, and Phillip Althoff. 1974. "Party Voting in the U.S. House of Representatives, 1890–1910: Elements of a Responsible Party System." 36 *Journal of Politics* 753.

———, and Charles Bullock. 1980. "Is There a Conservative Coalition in the House?" 42 *Journal of Politics* 549.

Burns, James. 1963. *The Deadlock of Democracy: Four Party Politics in America.* Englewood Cliffs, NJ: Prentice-Hall.

Clausen, Aage. 1973. *How Congressmen Decide: A Policy Focus.* New York: St. Martin's Pr.

Chambers, William N., and Walter Dean Burnham, eds. 1975. *The American Party System: Stages of Political Development.* New York: Oxford U. Pr.

Cooper, Joseph. 1961. "Congress and Its Committees." Ph.D. diss., Harvard U.

———. 1970. *The Origins of the Standing Committees and the Development of the Modern House.* Houston: Rice U. Publications.

———. 1975. "Strengthening the Congress: An Organizational Analysis." 12 *Harvard Journal of Legislation* 307.

———. 1977. "Congress in Organizational Perspective." In Lawrence C. Dodd and Bruce I. Oppenheimer, eds. *Congress Reconsidered.* New York: Praeger.

———, and David Brady. 1981. "Institutional Context and Leadership Style: The House from Cannon to Rayburn." 75 *American Political Science Review* 411.

———, ———, and Patricia Hurley. 1977. "The Electoral Basis of Party Voting: Patterns and Trends in the U.S. House of Representatives." In Joseph Cooper and Sandy Maisel, eds. *The Impact of the Electoral Process.* Beverly Hills, CA: Sage.

Dodd, Lawrence, and Bruce Oppenheimer, eds. 1981. *Congress Reconsidered.* Washington, DC: Congressional Quarterly.

Fenno, Richard. 1962. "The House Appropriations Committee as a Political System: The Problem of Integration." 56 *American Political Science Review* 310.

———. 1973. *Congressmen in Committees.* Boston: Little, Brown.

————, and Frank Munger. 1962. *National Politics and Federal Aid to Education*. Syracuse: Syracuse U. Pr.

Fiorina, Morris. 1977. *Congress: Keystone of the Washington Establishment*. New Haven: Yale U. Pr.

Formisano, Ronald. 1971. *The Birth of Mass Political Parties: Michigan 1827–1861*. Princeton: Princeton U. Pr.

Ginsberg, Benjamin. 1972. "Critical Elections and the Substance of Party Conflict: 1844–1968." 16 *Midwest Journal of Political Science* 603.

Heclo, Hugh. 1980. *A Government of Strangers*. Washington, DC: Brookings.

Hays, Samuel. 1975. "Political Parties and the Community-Society Continuum." In William N. Chambers and Walter D. Burnham, eds. *The American Party Systems*. New York: Oxford U. Pr.

Huitt, Ralph. 1961. "Democratic Party Leadership in the Senate." 55 *American Political Science Review* 333.

Jensen, Richard. 1971. *The Winning of the Midwest*. Chicago: U. of Chicago Pr.

Jones, Charles O. 1961. "Representation in Congress: The Case of the House Agriculture Committee." 55 *American Political Science Review* 358.

————. 1964. *Party and Policy Making: The House Republican Policy Committee*. New Brunswick, NJ: Rutgers U. Pr.

————. 1968. "Joseph G. Cannon and Howard W. Smith: An Essay on the Limits of Leadership in the House of Representatives." 30 *Journal of Politics* 6.

Jones, Stanley. 1964. *The Presidential Election of 1896*. Madison: U. of Wisconsin Pr.

Kernell, Samuel. 1977. "Toward Understanding 19th Century Congressional Careers, Ambition, Competition and Rotation." 21 *American Journal of Political Science* 669.

Key, V.O. 1964. *Politics, Parties and Pressure Group*. 5th ed. New York: Crowell.

Lowell, A. Lawrence. 1901. "The Influence of Party upon Legislation in England and America." *Annual Report, American Historical Association*.

McConachie, Lauros. 1898. *Congressional Committees: A Study of the Origin and Development of Our National and Local Legislative Methods*. New York: Crowell.

McCormick, Richard. 1966. *The Second American Party System: Party Formation in the Jacksonian Era.* Chapel Hill: U. of North Carolina Pr.

McKitrick, Eric. 1975. "Party Politics and the Union and Confederate War Efforts." In William N. Chambers and Walter Dean Burnham, eds. *The American Party Systems.* New York: Oxford U. Pr.

Mayhew, David. 1966. *Party Loyalty Among Congressmen.* Cambridge: Harvard U. Pr.

———. 1974. *The Electoral Connection.* New Haven: Yale U. Pr.

Orfield, Gary. 1975. *Congressional Power: Congress and Social Change.* New York: Harcourt Brace Jovanovich.

Polsby, Nelson. 1968. "The Institutionalization of the U.S. House of Representatives." 62 *American Political Science Review* 144.

———, M. Gallagher, and Barry Rundquist. 1969. "The Growth of the Seniority System in the U.S. House of Representatives." 63 *American Political Science Review* 787.

Rohde, David W. 1991. *Parties and Leaders in the Post-Reform House.* U. of Chicago Pr.

Rusk, Jerrold, and Phillip Converse. 1974. "Comments in Response to Burnham." 48 *American Political Science Review* 1024.

Shepsle, Kenneth A. 1978. *The Giant Jigsaw Puzzle: Democratic Committee Assignments in the Modern House.* U. of Chicago Pr.

Silbey, Joel H. 1967. *The Shrine of Party: Congressional Voting Behavior 1841–1852.* Pittsburgh: U. of Pittsburgh Pr.

Sinclair, Barbara. 1977. "Party Realignment and the Transformation of the Political Agenda: The House of Representatives, 1925–1938." 71 *American Political Science Review* 940.

———. 1982. *Congressional Realignment: 1925–1978.* Austin: U. of Texas Pr.

Sorauf, Frank. 1975. "Political Parties and Political Analysis." In William N. Chambers and Walter Dean Burnham, eds. *The American Party Systems.* New York: Oxford U. Pr.

Sundquist, James. 1968. *Politics and Policy: The Eisenhower, Kennedy and Johnson Years.* Washington, DC: Brookings.

———. 1973. *Dynamics of the Party System.* Washington, DC: Brookings.

Wilson, Woodrow. 1885. *Congressional Government.* Cleveland: World Publishing.

CHAPTER 9

Partisanship and Group Support over Time[*]

Harold W. Stanley

Richard G. Niemi

Studies of changes in party coalitions (Axelrod, 1972, 1982; Petrocik, 1981) have focused either on overlapping groups, such as blacks and the working class, or on exclusive groups such as white, middle-class Protestants. Neither approach is adequate. Use of overlapping groups makes it impossible to tell which characteristics are the crucial determinants of party support. Reliance on exclusive groups largely predetermines the outcome, because the critical groups have to be defined a priori.

By analyzing the partisanship of individual group members with multivariate methods similar to those applied elsewhere in the study of political behavior, we provide improved insights into the marginal difference made by membership in each group and into the makeup of a party's support coalition. Here we examine the Democratic and Republican coalitions since 1952. Our results strengthen conventional wisdom about individual partisan changes by blacks and southern whites, but they differ significantly with respect to the strength and timing of charges by these and other

---

[*]Reprinted with permission. Niemi, Richard G. and Herbert F. Weisberg, eds. *Controversies in Voting Behavior.* 3/e. Washington, D.C.: CQ Press, 1993. [Original source: American Political Science Review (1986) 80:969–76 and American Politics Quarterly (1991) 19:189–210.]

groups. In addition, our findings lend support to Carmines and Stimson's (1984) conclusion that a realignment centering on race occurred in the mid-1960s.

Party Identification: Measurements of Changes in Group Support

We focus on partisanship over the period from 1952 to 1988, with special emphasis on the extent to which the New Deal coalition supporting the Democratic party has deteriorated. We concentrate on party identification as the more durable indicator of partisanship, estimating a total of seventeen equations—one for each of seventeen presidential or congressional elections from 1952 to 1988.

Our basic model includes the core elements of the New Deal coalition: native southern whites (eleven-state definition), blacks, Jews, the working class, union members (in the household), and Catholics. We also included gender. In order to analyze very recent changes in group support, especially with respect to the Republican party, we added several new groups. The availability of data for these groups dictates three separate models:

Model 1 (1952–1988): New Deal elements, gender, church attendance, income.

Model 2 (1972–1988): New Deal elements, gender, white Protestant fundamentalists, church attendance, income.

Model 3 (1980–1988): New Deal elements, gender, Hispanics, white Protestant fundamentalists, church attendance, income, 1943–1958 birth cohort, 1959–1970 cohort.

Our dependent variables throughout are Democratic identification or Republican identification; learners are not considered partisans, but with one exception the results are very similar if one defines partisans to include those leaning toward the parties. The inclusion of variables tapping religion, income, age, and Hispanic origin merits further comment.

In recent years, evangelicals, the Protestant right, fundamentalists, frequent churchgoers, and others have variously been identified as part of the emerging party coalitions (e.g., Edsall, 1988, pp. 9, 25–27). In Model 1, we use frequency of church attendance, which is available from 1952 on and which appears to have a substantial effect on party preference (Petrocik and Steeper, 1987). We are constrained by a change in the survey question in 1970, so that in order to maintain continuity, frequent churchgoers must be defined as a less exclusive category than we would like (attends church regularly or as often as "once a week"). Because of the coding of Baptists, beginning in 1972 it is possible to select fundamentalist Protestants as a separate category. That variable is added to create Model 2.

Much has been made of the recent attractiveness of the Republican party to the wealthy (Edsall, 1988, pp. 9–11). Income, however, is hardly a new factor, so it is useful to gain the perspective that comes from including it throughout the entire period. The problem of cut-points is solved by dividing respondents into thirds on the income distribution in each year. The top third is less exclusive than one might like, but it is surely better than using a constant dollar figure and defines a group that is large enough to carry real political meaning if it tends toward one party.

In recent years new generations of young people seem to have swung toward the Republicans (Norpoth and Kagay, 1989, though see Petrocik, 1989, p. 15). As birth year is most consistent with generational shifts, we define the young as those born in 1959 and later and baby boomers as those born between 1943 and 1958. The fact that the youngest group only began to enter the electorate in the late 1970s, and then in small numbers, is one reason for defining a third model beginning in 1980.

Hispanics are an important group that emerged in the 1980s and are the other reason for establishing the third model. Hispanics are not a unitary force, with Republicans having appealed especially to Cuban-Americans (e.g., Southwest Voter Research Institute, p. 2). Therefore our Hispanic variable excludes those of Cuban origin, and the expectation is that it will push respondents in a Democratic direction.

We use separate models for Democrats and Republicans. To the extent that the New Deal coalition is breaking up, we want to see whether formerly Democratic voters have gone to the Republican party. In addition, for newer groups, we shall see that the hypothesized connections are not always found, and it is useful to see if such groups lean instead to the other party.

The Results

Overall and Incremental Effects of Group Memberships

Axelrod (1972, 1986) found that between 1952 and 1988 three groups had decreasing loyalty to the Democrats: Catholics, southerners, and individuals in households with union members. The poor, blacks, and those residing in the central cities of the nation's twenty-three largest metropolitan areas showed increasing Democratic loyalty. Petrocik (1981) reported that all groups except blacks shared a marked tendency toward independence and a diminished partisan preference; blacks became much more strongly Democratic.

Our results confirm the sharpest of these movements—especially of blacks and southern whites—but they differ in other respects. First of all, once other variables are taken into account, being poor and residing in metropolitan areas did not incline individuals toward Democratic identification (i.e., they did not achieve statistical significance) in the 1952–1988 period. The tendency of the poor and of metropolitan residents to support the Democrats can be accounted for by their other characteristics. Two indicators of status—education and income—were also not related to Democratic identification, perhaps because subjective identification with the working class better revealed the connections of status to partisanship.

Given the nonlinearity of logic, the original coefficients (not shown) are difficult to interpret. Transforming them into probability values, however, yields two summary values of special significance—the overall predicted mean probability of being a Democrat or Republican for each group, and the incremental probability difference each group membership makes.

Table 1 presents the mean and incremental predicted probability that a group member would claim Democratic identification in each of the nine presidential election years and seven off-years. The mean predicted probability gives the frequency of Democratic identification in each group before imposing any controls for other group memberships. Even these initial figures show the plight of the Democrats. Comparisons of the chronological endpoints, for example, show that only for blacks did the probability of Democratic identification increase. Jews declined the most, with the decline particularly steep in the early 1960s and then again after 1984. White southerners also registered a strong decline, with a twenty-nine-point drop between 1964 and 1970, and a ten-point drop between 1980 and 1984. The probability of Democratic identification for Catholics, females, individuals in union member households, and self-identified members of the working class, although peaking in 1960 or 1964, later declined to levels below those of the 1950s. Even among the newer groups, where the time span available for analysis is much shorter, Democrats had less support in 1988 than in the first year of the series.

The incremental impact of a particular group membership makes equally apparent the strongest movements over the years. The black increase, the southern white decrease, and the Jewish decline are all evident and are of about the same magnitude as in the overall results.

Significantly, the patterns are not identical to what has been observed using other approaches. Axelrod (1972), for example, found that in 1952 blacks were far more likely (by 38 percent) than the general population to vote for Democrats. That Democratic edge declined until 1964, when it rebounded to the same level as in 1952. Our results are not a direct contradiction, because they involve slightly different questions (i.e., the marginal impact and partisan identification), but they suggest that being black did not contribute strongly to being Democratic until 1964; before that, it had less marginal impact than, for example, being Catholic. In 1964 and later, however, the effect of

Table 1: Mean and Incremental Probabilities of Democratic Identification for Members of Each Group

Group	Year																
	1952	1956	1958	1960	1964	1966	1968	1970	1972	1974	1976	1978	1980	1982	1984	1986	1988
Mean Probabilities[a]																	
Black	.54	.51	.51	.44	.78	.63	.85	.75	.67	.71	.74	.66	.74	.82	.64	.71	.65
Catholic	.56	.51	.58	.65	.60	.54	.52	.51	.50	.51	.50	.50	.43	.54	.43	.45	.39
Jewish	.76	.63	.71	.52	.56	.67	.51	.56	.52	.52	.60	.55	.83	.62	.60	.36	.37
Female	.47	.43	.51	.49	.55	.47	.47	.45	.43	.43	.42	.42	.45	.49	.40	.42	.41
Native southern white	.77	.71	.76	.72	.73	.60	.54	.44	.52	.52	.52	.45	.52	.54	.42	.43	.41
Union household	.54	.51	.60	.57	.64	.56	.50	.54	.46	.47	.47	.50	.47	.52	.46	.45	.43
Working class	.54	.49	.55	.51	.61	.52	.52	.47	.45	.43	.47	.45	.47	.51	.41	.45	.44
Regular churchgoer	.50	.47	.47	.49	.54	.48	.47	.45	.44	.40	.43	.43	.40	.47	.37	.43	.39
Income top third	.43	.40	.46	.44	.43	.42	.39	.39	.34	.31	.31	.33	.35	.36	.32	.33	.29
Wh. Prot. fundamentalist	—	—	—	—	—	—	—	—	.45	.44	.42	.42	.54	.48	.41	.39	.36
Hispanic, non-Cuban	—	—	—	—	—	—	—	—	—	—	—	—	.54	.60	.49	.58	.48
Born 1959–1970	—	—	—	—	—	—	—	—	—	—	—	—	.32	.35	.31	.35	.27
Born 1943–1958	—	—	—	—	—	—	—	—	—	—	—	—	.39	.43	.34	.35	.35
Incremental Probabilities[b]																	
Black	.16	.17	.13	.08	.32	.23	.49	.38	.36	.41	.43	.35	.46	.46	.35	.42	.37
Catholic	.20	.19	.22	.31	.18	.16	.18	.15	.20	.21	.21	.20	.14	.20	.14	.15	.10
Jewish	.44	.34	.34	.19	.19	.37	.22	.25	.28	.25	.38	.32	.58	.35	.35	.08	.19
Female	-.01	-.04	.04	.04	.02	.03	.03	.03	.05	.04	.03	.04	.09	.06	.06	.05	.10
Native southern white	.44	.42	.41	.41	.33	.26	.20	.10	.19	.22	.22	.13	.18	.19	.10	.12	.13
Union household	.11	.11	.13	.13	.15	.15	.06	.14	.07	.09	.10	.15	.10	.11	.12	.09	.11
Working class	.12	.08	.08	.08	.08	.09	.08	.03	.05	-.02	.07	.06	.06	.04	.03	.04	.10

Table 1 (continued)

Group	Year																
	1952	1956	1958	1960	1964	1966	1968	1970	1972	1974	1976	1978	1980	1982	1984	1986	1988
Regular churchgoer	.00	.00	-.09	-.03	-.01	.02	.00	.03	.03	-.03	.03	.02	-.04	.01	-.04	.01	.03
Income: top third	-.04	-.01	-.02	-.04	-.12	-.03	-.04	-.05	-.06	-.12	-.09	-.10	-.05	-.11	-.06	-.06	-.05
Wh. Prot. fundamentalist	—	—	—	—	—	—	—	—	.08	.04	.04	.08	.21	.07	.09	.05	.03
Hispanic, non-Cuban	—	—	—	—	—	—	—	—	—	—	—	—	.16	.10	.06	.13	.08
Born 1959–1970	—	—	—	—	—	—	—	—	—	—	—	—	-.17	-.17	-.16	-.16	-.19
Born 1943–1958	—	—	—	—	—	—	—	—	—	—	—	—	-.09	-.06	-.10	-.12	-.10

Notes: All three models described in the text were evaluated. However, presentation is greatly simplified by showing only the following: 1952–1970 values are based on Model 1; 1972–1978 values are based on Model 2; 1980–1988 entries are based on Model 3. Values that can be estimated with more than one model seldom differ by more than .01 from one model to another.
[a]Cells are the mean of the predicted probabilities of Democratic identification for all group members in each year.
[b]Cells are the average of the difference, for each group member, between the individual's predicted probability of Democratic identification and what the individual's probability would have been without the effect of group membership.

being black contributed much more significantly to a Democratic identification than it had at any time in the 1950s.

Similarly, the impact of being Jewish declined between the 1950s and 1960s, but unlike Petrocik's (1981) trend, our results show a rebound, even by 1972, when his series ended. After 1984, the marginal impact declined again, leaving it where it had been in the early 1960s.

Though smaller and therefore less noticeable, a contrast with earlier results is also apparent among Catholics. Axelrod (1972) and Petrocik (1981) found the contribution of Catholics declining by 1972 and 1968, respectively. Our data suggest that, except for the special circumstances of 1960, being Catholic stimulated a Democratic identification to about the same degree until 1980.

The sharpest contrast suggested by our approach occurs for members of union households. Here both Axelrod's earlier results and our overall probabilities suggest a decline in Democratic proclivities. In contrast, the incremental push that comes from this characteristic appears to have changed very little over the last four decades. This difference may be identifiable because we are able to separate the effect of being working class from that of being in a union household. Since many union members consider themselves working class, and since there was a drop in the marginal impact of this variable (except for the partial recovery in 1988), exclusion of the working class measure might erroneously indicate a decline in the effect of being in a union household.

Observe also the contrasting images created by the overall versus incremental probabilities of women. Females were less likely to identify themselves as Democrats in the 1980s than they were in the 1950s; at the same time, being female has given an increasingly larger boost to Democratic identification. Note, however, that this increment is not simply a Reagan phenomenon. Marginal female support for the Democrats goes all the way back to 1960 and has been slowly but steadily increasing since then.

As we turn to newer groups and draw on other models, we note first that none of the above conclusions change with the inclusion of new variables (see note to Table 1). In addition, since several of the new groups are said to be attracted to the Republican party, we shall draw on Table 1 and on a parallel table for the Republicans (Table 2). (Note that the probabilities in Tables 1 and 2 do not sum to 1.0 because they exclude independents and apoliticals.)

The relationship between religion and partisanship was allegedly reinvigorated during the Reagan years as the president supported traditional moral values consistent with fundamentalist Christianity. However, both measures of religiosity yield some surprises. Church attendance has a relatively minor effect on partisanship throughout the entire period, with what appears to be a Reagan effect in 1980 and 1984. Incremental probabilities for the Democrats (Table 1), are mostly insignificant. For the Republicans (Table 2) incremental probabilities are small, straddling statistical significance except for 1958 and for a small but meaningful bulge in the two Reagan election years. The fact that the probabilities return to their usual levels in both congressional years in the 1980s and in 1988 suggests that the religious phenomenon was personal and was not transferred to the party. The overall probabilities tell a slightly different story. Between the 1950s and 1980s there was a small but steady decline in Democratic support among regular churchgoers; combined with steady support for the Republicans among this group, the ratio of Democratic to Republican mean probabilities changed noticeably.

When our measure is affiliation with a fundamentalist religion, the results are contrary to popular rhetoric but in line with most scholarly research. Rothenberg and Newport (1984, chap. 6) found that self-described fundamentalists are little, if any more, Republican than other respondents. Baptists are more Democratic than any other denomination, with "conservative" denominations relatively Democratic as well. Similarly, Smidt (1983, p. 36) found that white southern evangelicals are more Democratic than nonevangelicals.

Our multivariate results indicate that in every election since 1972, membership in a Protestant fundamentalist denomination has pushed whites away from a Republican identification and uniformly inclined them toward the Democrats (incremental probabilities, Tables 1 and 2). These

Table 2: Mean and Incremental Probabilities of Republican Identification for Members of Each Group

Group	Year																
	1952	1956	1958	1960	1964	1966	1968	1970	1972	1974	1976	1978	1980	1982	1984	1986	1988
Mean Probabilities[a]																	
Black	.14	.19	.15	.17	.06	.09	.03	.05	.08	.03	.06	.06	.04	.02	.03	.05	.06
Catholic	.18	.20	.17	.14	.16	.17	.15	.17	.14	.15	.16	.14	.18	.17	.20	.22	.26
Jewish	.00	.12	.12	.08	.06	.05	.05	.05	.09	.12	.09	.05	.00	.19	.10	.21	.12
Female	.29	.31	.28	.31	.24	.25	.23	.26	.24	.23	.27	.23	.23	.23	.28	.26	.28
Native southern white	.09	.12	.11	.12	.09	.11	.09	.17	.16	.12	.15	.16	.15	.18	.22	.22	.22
Union household	.22	.21	.17	.17	.14	.18	.19	.15	.16	.13	.14	.14	.14	.18	.20	.21	.20
Working class	.21	.23	.23	.24	.16	.20	.20	.20	.21	.19	.19	.16	.18	.17	.22	.20	.19
Regular churchgoer	.28	.29	.31	.30	.26	.25	.24	.26	.26	.25	.28	.23	.28	.26	.32	.28	.32
Income top third	.31	.34	.33	.30	.31	.26	.27	.29	.30	.28	.30	.25	.30	.33	.36	.30	.33
Wh. Prot. fundamentalist	—	—	—	—	—	—	—	—	.20	.16	.21	.18	.17	.20	.22	.26	.27
Hispanic, non-Cuban	—	—	—	—	—	—	—	—	—	—	—	—	.14	.05	.09	.14	.13
Born 1959–1970	—	—	—	—	—	—	—	—	—	—	—	—	.14	.28	.25	.27	.29
Born 1943–1958	—	—	—	—	—	—	—	—	—	—	—	—	.20	.20	.28	.25	.26
Incremental Probabilities[b]																	
Black	-.24	-.18	-.24	-.23	-.24	-.22	-.32	-.28	-.24	-.28	-.25	-.22	-.26	-.28	-.35	-.29	-.28
Catholic	-.23	-.19	-.25	-.27	-.20	-.18	-.22	-.17	-.19	-.17	-.17	-.18	-.13	-.16	-.17	-.12	-.09
Jewish	-.43	-.32	-.27	-.34	-.35	-.35	-.34	-.34	-.28	-.21	-.29	-.30	-.35	-.23	-.35	-.15	-.33
Female	.03	.06	-.01	.02	.00	-.01	-.02	.01	.01	.00	.05	.02	-.02	-.03	.00	-.01	-.02
Native southern white	-.34	-.30	-.33	-.35	-.28	-.27	-.29	-.19	-.15	-.18	-.16	-.12	-.14	-.13	-.08	-.10	-.14
Union household	-.06	-.10	-.13	-.14	-.11	-.09	-.07	-.13	-.11	-.12	-.13	-.10	-.13	-.09	-.10	-.07	-.11
Working class	-.13	-.09	-.04	-.11	-.11	-.09	-.04	-.07	-.01	-.01	-.03	-.07	-.04	-.07	-.06	-.07	-.12

Table 2 (continued)

Group	Year																
	1952	1956	1958	1960	1964	1966	1968	1970	1972	1974	1976	1978	1980	1982	1984	1986	1988
Regular churchgoer	.05	.04	.10	.06	.04	.03	.03	.01	.05	.06	.05	.08	.03	.08	.08	.04	.05
Income: top third	.01	.04	.03	-.02	.05	-.03	.02	.03	.08	.05	.04	.07	.09	.08	.03	.03	
Wh. Prot. fundamentalist	—	—	—	—	—	—	—	—	-.06	-.07	-.05	-.07	-.09	-.07	-.13	-.04	-.03
Hispanic, non-Cuban	—	—	—	—	—	—	—	—	—	—	—	—	-.03	-.13	-.11	-.09	-.11
Born 1959–1970	—	—	—	—	—	—	—	—	—	—	—	—	-.06	.04	.02	.04	.04
Born 1943–1958	—	—	—	—	—	—	—	—	—	—	—	—	-.02	-.05	.03	-.01	-.01

[a]Cells are the mean of the predicted probabilities of Republican identification for all group members in each year.
[b]Cells are the average of the difference, for each group member, between the individual's predicted probability of Republican identification and what the individual's probability would have been without the effect of the group membership.

forces were especially strong during the first Reagan term. Note, however, that the overall probabilities in recent years show a strikingly different pattern. Since 1980, the likelihood of fundamentalists identifying with the Republican party has increased steadily, while the corresponding figure for the Democrats dropped steadily and even more sharply. Thus, there is an increased relationship between fundamentalism and Republican identification, but in the sense of the partisan push that comes from specific group attachments, religious fundamentalism is not a powerful partisan force.

A key to the divergent mean and incremental probabilities lies, in part, in changes among native southern whites. One of the major groups of white fundamentalists is Southern Baptists. As native southern whites moved away from the Democrats, this coincidentally moved many Southern Baptists from the Democratic to the Republican fold. But that change appears not to have had religious motivation. In fact, as Table 1 shows, fundamentalism itself still carries with it a small incremental nudge in favor of the Democrats.

A second group thought to be part of a Republican rejuvenation is the well-to-do (Petrocik and Steeper, 1987). Here our results are less at variance with conventional wisdom, though still there are differences. Table 2 shows a clear increase in incremental probabilities of Republican identification in the early 1970s and the early 1980s. There is less consistency in Table 1, but the numbers there also indicate a major change beginning in the 1970s. Note, however, that the push toward Republican identification did not sustain itself past 1984. Incremental probabilities for 1986 and 1988 retreated to a level not seen since 1970. The change appears to be only a bit more stable if one examines the overall probabilities.

Another group thought to be part of the Republican upsurge is young voters, especially those born after 1958 (Norpoth and Kagay, 1989). Our results suggest that the incremental push from being in the youngest cohort is better described as a strong anti-Democratic force. Indeed, none of the coefficients underlying the incremental probabilities of being a Republican are statistically significant, though most are in the "right" direction. Those relating to Democratic identification are consistently significant and strongly negative. The baby boomers are also anti-Democratic, though to a lesser degree, and are neutral with respect to the Republicans. Both of these groups have consistently high positive increments in favor of independents (not shown), most likely a reflection of the dealigning period in which they became adults.

The final group to gain significance in the 1980s is Hispanics (here excluding those of Cuban origin). Group attachments clearly incline them toward the Democratic party and away from the Republican party. There are too few cases and years to make finer distinctions about country of origin or changes over time.

Before moving on, it is useful to take a global look at the overall and incremental probabilities. The first observation is that for all of the New Deal groups, the Democrats maintain a rather wide advantage, even in those instances in which there have been dramatic changes over the past four decades. Among native southern whites in 1988, for example, twice as many identify with the Democrats as with the Republicans.

Differences of comparable magnitude are found in only one of the newer groups. While frequent churchgoers and those in fundamentalist congregations have at times identified with the Democrats by two-to-one margins, the current margin is about four to three for both groups. The well-to-do have never split very unevenly. The youngest cohort has not leaned heavily toward either party even though it is potentially significant that the margin has shifted (barely) to the Republicans as of 1988. Baby boomers are more Democratic, but the margin has declined in the last few years. Only among Hispanics is the margin similar to those for the old-line groups.

Of course the size of the group differences is partly a reflection of the overall numbers of Democrats and Republicans. Because the Democrats are the larger party, it is perhaps not surprising that they hold larger margins in "their" groups than the Republicans hold in theirs. Still, not one of the groups comprising the new elements of the Republican coalition tilts heavily in its direction.

It is worth dwelling on this point for a moment in relation to the concept of partisan realignment. If, as some have suggested, the changes over the past two decades or so constitute a realignment (in the sense of changes in the underlying support coalitions), one can draw at least two inferences. First, the realignment appears to be on shaky grounds because the party that is growing in size lacks a really strong base in any group, old or new. Given the lingering pro-Democratic sentiments in New Deal groups and the absence of similar new Republican support, the Republicans' best hope appears to lie in continuing support from new adults. A generational change is by its nature relatively slow and undramatic; when favorable groups are only marginally so, it will be even slower. The consequence for the Republicans is that, absent a dramatic event or personality, it will take a long time to become a majority party. A consequence for those analyzing group support is that they will find small, sometimes conflicting change until eventually clear trends emerge.

Somewhat contrariwise, one might also conclude that a realignment requires less in the way of "reshuffling" than has been commonly suggested. A significant realignment may occur when there is a major change in only one or two groups (e.g., as occurred among blacks in the 1960s), accompanied by a variety of other changes (Aldrich and Niemi, 1990). In any case, both inferences suggest why the concept of group realignment is so difficult to work with.

It is also noteworthy that the extra push from membership in new groups is generally weaker than that from traditional ones. Note, for example, the 1988 column of incremental probabilities in Tables 1 and 2. Despite the declining force of the New Deal groups, only age—and then only negatively for the Democrats—has an incremental probability as high as those for any of the older groups. Apart from age, what may be happening is not so much a change in the group basis of support for the two parties as a breakdown of group differences altogether. Weakening ties between group attachments and party loyalties, not simply changes in which groups are allied with which party, may be a partial explanation for the widely observed decline of political parties.

Changing Demographics or Changing Support Levels

In addition to our ability to distinguish overall and marginal effects, another way of using our multivariate approach is to ask whether changes in the mix of demographic characteristics have had a significant effect on the probability of claiming Democratic identification. It is possible, for example, that the decline in the number of females identifying with the working class (60 percent in 1952; 50 percent in 1984) and other such changes can largely account for the observed changes. We can apply the coefficients from a later election year to an earlier distribution of individual group memberships and contrast these hypothetical results with the actual ones for the later year. Such a comparison conveys the degree of partisan change arising from shifts in the coefficients (that is, the partisan meaning of group memberships). By similarly varying the distribution of group memberships, one can gauge the degree of partisan change arising from shifting mixes of individual group memberships.

The two sets of coefficients for the endpoints 1952 and 1988 capture the partisan meanings of group memberships for those two years. If we first apply the 1952 coefficients to 1952 or 1988 data, the overall probabilities of Democratic identification are not appreciably different. However, major differences in probabilities result from applying the 1988 coefficients to the data from 1952. The shifts in the meaning of group memberships far outweigh the partisan implications of demographic changes. Changes in the partisan meaning of group memberships, not declines in reinforcing group memberships, account for the decreasing probabilities of identifying with the Democrats.

Group Support and the Party Coalitions

Axelrod's (1972) analysis reveals the extent to which the Democratic coalition is made up of blacks, metropolitan residents, and so on. If one wishes simply to know a group's share of the party's coalition, Axelrod's approach has much to recommend it. However, studying groups within party coalitions does not require us to treat the groups as if they were monolithic. Since most individuals have multiple group characteristics, removing a single characteristic from the mix need not mean that all members of that group desert the party. Axelrod's figures cannot reveal, for example, how many southern whites would remain Democratic if being a southern white gave no nudge toward Democratic identification. Nor can they show what the size of the Democratic coalition would be if that Democratic propensity was lost. Our approach yields both of these results. Such results are hypothetical, of course, but they are what the party strategist would most like to know. If the party stopped appealing to southern whites as such, how many southern whites would remain Democratic, and how much of a loss would the party sustain?

Answers to these questions, along with comparison figures of the type that Axelrod generated, are given in Tables 3 (Democrats) and 4 (Republicans). In the first two sections of the tables we show the proportion of Democratic and Republican identifiers in the United States and, below that, the percentage of the partisan coalition with a given group characteristic. This breakdown of the coalition, is in terms of overlapping groups, making these percentages analogous to those presented for the Democratic vote by Axelrod. Not surprisingly (because of their size in the population), working-class identifiers and females consistently make up the largest shares of Democratic identifiers, although the proportion of working-class identifiers has dropped significantly from what it was in the 1950s. Jews now constitute only one percent of the Democratic coalition, and blacks, thanks to recent increases, now constitute a fifth of the coalition. Of the newer groups, the only striking result is the ragged upward trend in the proportion of the coalition that is Hispanic. With the long-term decline of most New Deal elements and relatively quick, further increases in minority supporters, the Democrats may increasingly be viewed as the party of racial/ethnic minorities and liberal whites (cf. Schneider, 1988, p. 67–68).

As the Democratic coalition lost some of its New Deal elements, one might expect a transfer into the Republican party, either in the form of a direct transfer or by Democrats becoming independents while independents become Republican. Such is the case for no group. Native southern whites come the closest. As the proportion of the Democratic coalition made up of this group dropped by about seven percentage points between 1960 and 1988, the proportion in the Republican party increased by about the same margin (Tables 3 and 4), though the larger Democratic coalition means these similar percentages do not constitute similarly sized groups. In contrast, Catholics now make up a slightly larger proportion of the Republican coalition without having decreased their share of the Democratic coalition. Most striking are the declines in working class and union household support in both coalitions. The explanation of these simultaneous declines is quite simple—fewer respondents now classify themselves as working class and union membership has declined. Nevertheless, it suggests that the parties may be able to reduce their appeal to these groups without fearing the same magnitude of negative response that would have occurred in years past.

The Republican coalition has not increased its proportions of new group members except for the young and possibly those in fundamentalist congregations, where there appears to be an increase of four to five percentage points in the last two elections. Non-Cuban Hispanics are no more a part of the Republican coalition than are blacks. Young people constitute a slightly larger proportion of the Republicans than of the Democrats.

The results in the third section of Table 3 show what would have happened to each group if the Democratic increment due to the group characteristic were removed. Of the New Deal groups, the working class would have been the least affected. Despite the appeal of Reagan and Bush to the workers, other characteristics of working-class individuals are sufficiently pro-Democratic, that even in 1988, 78 percent of this group who identified with the party would have continued to do so if there were no special push due to their class identification. In contrast, less than half of the blacks and Jews would have continued to identify with the party if it lost its special appeal to them as blacks and Jews. Of more interest are the percentages who would remain in the coalition among frequent churchgoers and among those in fundamentalist congregations. The high

Table 3: Size and Composition of the Democratic Coalition, 1952–1988

Group	Year																
	1952	1956	1958	1960	1964	1966	1968	1970	1972	1974	1976	1978	1980	1982	1984	1986	1988
Predicted Probability of Democratic Identification in the U.S.[a]																	
	48	44	50	47	54	46	45	44	41	41	40	40	41	46	38	40	36
Percentage of Democratic Coalition with a Given Group Characteristic[b]																	
Black	10	9	9	7	13	13	16	14	14	15	12	14	16	15	15	21	20
Catholic	25	23	24	24	25	24	21	28	25	27	26	21	23	26	26	23	22
Jewish	4	4	4	3	2	3	3	3	3	3	3	5	2	3	3	1	1
Female	50	50	51	50	52	53	54	51	53	53	50	46	47	48	49	49	53
Native southern white	23	26	25	25	19	18	18	16	19	20	16	13	16	18	16	17	18
Union household	30	29	28	30	27	32	25	25	26	26	23	25	22	22	22	20	20
Working class	65	64	62	64	60	60	55	49	54	50	50	45	43	47	45	46	51
Regular churchgoer	38	43	39	42	41	40	37	36	37	33	34	33	29	35	31	36	34
Income top third	35	26	30	33	27	33	25	30	24	18	23	23	19	23	22	21	27
Wh. Prot. fundamentalist	—	—	—	—	—	—	—	15	16	12	12	12	5	14	13	13	15
Hispanic, non-Cuban	—	—	—	—	—	—	—	—	—	—	—	3	3	2	6	5	8
Born 1959–1970	—	—	—	—	—	—	—	—	—	—	—	—	3	5	10	13	13
Born 1943–1958	—	—	—	—	—	—	—	—	—	—	—	26	26	28	28	28	29
Percentage of Democratic Identifiers in Group Continuing to Claim Democratic Identification After Removing Democratic Tendency of Defining Group Characteristic[c]																	
Black	71	66	75	82	59	64	43	49	46	42	42	48	38	43	44	42	43
Catholic	64	64	63	53	70	70	66	72	61	58	58	59	67	63	68	67	73
Jewish	41	45	53	63	65	44	57	56	45	52	36	41	30	44	41	78	49
Female	103	111	91	91	96	94	93	93	89	91	92	91	79	92	86	88	76
Native southern white	42	41	45	43	55	56	62	77	64	57	58	71	66	65	77	73	67
Union household	80	79	79	77	76	74	88	74	84	80	78	71	78	78	73	79	74
Working class	79	83	85	85	87	82	85	94	88	105	86	87	87	92	93	92	78

Table 3 (continued)

Group	1952	1956	1958	1960	1964	1966	1968	1970	1972	1974	1976	1978	1980	1982	1984	1986	1988
Regular churchgoer	100	101	120	106	102	96	101	93	92	107	94	95	110	97	110	98	93
Income: top third	110	104	104	110	128	107	111	113	118	139	128	129	114	130	119	119	117
Wh. Prot. fundamentalist	—	—	—	—	—	—	—	—	83	90	92	80	71	83	78	87	83
Hispanic, non-Cuban	—	—	—	—	—	—	—	—	—	—	—	—	61	83	87	77	91
Born 1959–1970	—	—	—	—	—	—	—	—	—	—	—	—	153	148	152	145	170
Born 1943–1958	—	—	—	—	—	—	—	—	—	—	—	—	122	114	130	134	127
Relative Size (%) of Democratic Coalition after Removing Group Characteristic																	
Black	97	97	98	99	95	95	91	93	92	92	91	94	91	91	92	88	89
Catholic	91	91	91	88	93	93	92	94	89	90	89	90	93	92	92	92	94
Jewish	97	98	98	99	99	97	99	98	99	99	98	98	96	99	98	100	99
Female	102	105	96	95	98	97	96	96	94	95	96	96	90	94	93	94	88
Native southern white	87	85	87	86	91	92	93	96	93	91	93	96	94	94	96	96	94
Union household	94	94	94	93	94	92	97	94	96	95	95	93	95	96	94	96	95
Working class	86	89	91	90	92	89	92	97	96	94	103	94	94	96	97	99	88
Regular churchgoer	100	100	108	102	101	98	100	97	97	102	98	98	103	99	103	99	98
Income: top third	104	101	101	103	107	102	103	104	104	107	107	107	107	107	104	104	105
Wh. Prot. fundamentalist	—	—	—	—	—	—	—	—	97	98	99	98	94	98	97	99	99
Hispanic, non-Cuban	—	—	—	—	—	—	—	—	—	—	—	—	99	100	99	99	99
Born 1959–1970	—	—	—	—	—	—	—	—	—	—	—	—	102	103	105	106	109
Born 1943–1958	—	—	—	—	—	—	—	—	—	—	—	—	106	104	108	109	108

[a] These estimates, derived from the model, are virtually identical to the actual percentage of Democratic identifiers.

[b] Figures derived from taking the mean predicted probability of Democratic identification for a group in a particular year (Table 1) multiplied by that group's number of respondents, and dividing this product by the number of Democratic identifiers.

[c] Figures derived by recalculating the probabilities of Democratic identification without the effect of, say, working-class identification, and then taking the mean of these probabilities for all respondents who claimed working-class status. The ratio of this revised mean probability to the mean probability that includes the effect of working class gives the ratio of the hypothetical size to the actual one.

Table 4: Size and Composition of the Republican Coalition, 1952–1988

Group	Year																
	1952	1956	1958	1960	1964	1966	1968	1970	1972	1974	1976	1978	1980	1982	1984	1986	1988
Predicted Probability of Republican Identification in the U.S.[a]																	
	28	29	28	29	24	25	24	25	24	22	24	21	23	25	28	26	29
Percentage of Republican Coalition with a Given Group Characteristic[b]																	
Black	4	5	5	4	2	3	1	2	3	1	2	2	1	1	1	2	2
Catholic	14	14	12	8	14	14	13	12	14	13	16	13	16	14	17	18	19
Jewish	0	1	1	1	1	1	1	1	1	1	1	1	0	1	1	1	1
Female	53	55	48	50	48	53	49	51	52	48	56	47	44	42	46	48	46
Native southern white	5	7	6	6	5	6	6	11	10	8	8	9	8	11	11	14	12
Union household	21	18	14	14	13	19	18	12	16	13	12	14	12	12	13	15	12
Working class	43	46	47	46	33	42	40	37	43	39	35	31	30	29	33	32	29
Regular churchgoer	37	39	45	40	41	38	36	36	39	36	39	34	38	36	36	37	36
Income top third	44	33	37	36	40	37	33	40	37	29	39	33	31	39	33	31	39
Wh. Prot. fundamentalist	—	—	—	—	—	—	—	—	12	10	10	10	8	11	10	14	15
Hispanic, non-Cuban	—	—	—	—	—	—	—	—	—	—	—	—	1	0	1	2	3
Born 1959–1970	—	—	—	—	—	—	—	—	—	—	—	—	3	8	11	16	17
Born 1943–1958	—	—	—	—	—	—	—	—	—	—	—	—	24	25	31	31	28

[a]These estimates, derived from the model, are virtually identical to the actual percentage of Republican identifiers.
[b]Figures derived from taking the mean predicted probability of Republican identification for a group in a particular year (Table 2) multiplied by that group's number of respondents, and dividing this product by the number of Republican identifiers.

percentages, often above 90 percent, reemphasize the small incremental push that comes from membership in these categories. Other groups are much more important for the Democrats to worry about. The 145+ percentages for the youngest cohort indicate that Democrats have a lot to gain even from a neutral, rather than negative, appeal to the young.

What effect would such changes have had on the party coalition? The last section of Table 3 shows that the Democrats used to depend more variably and more heavily on limited group appeals. The loss of a given group increment would have reduced the coalition by as little as 2–3 percent or by as much as 14 percent. Recently, however, the overlap among group memberships and the Democratic tendency of each membership has been such that the loss of appeal to any of the characteristics would result in a more uniform 5–12 percent loss in identifiers. This change is significant, but it leaves the Democrats no less vulnerable. The party is no longer so dependent upon a few groups, as it was in the 1950s, but is now almost equally dependent upon six.

Perhaps a bit surprisingly, loss of appeal to Hispanics as such would seem to have very little effect on the coalition. In part this reflects the modest size of the Hispanic group, but it also results from multiple characteristics that push Hispanics toward the Democrats. The number for the post-1958 cohort is as much above 100 as many of the other numbers are below 100. The Democrats could increase their size substantially with direct appeals to the young if those appeals did not somehow undercut the attention they currently pay to their strongest support groups.

Conclusion

At the individual level of analysis, research in the last ten years has altered the way we view partisanship. We no longer think of party identification as immutable or as unchanging except for sudden upheavals (e.g., Franklin and Jackson, 1983). Change is typically slow and limited to small movements along the partisanship scale, but movement there is. Yet we are only now incorporating this view of individual-level partisanship into models of aggregate change (MacKuen, Erikson, and Stimson, 1989). If individuals change their partisanship in response to on-going political events, we need to ask how these changes alter the group composition of the party coalitions. One inference is that if individual changes are slow, small, and partially self-canceling, changes in group support for the parties will more often be glacial than explosive despite the endogeneity of partisanship.

It is this deliberate, halting manner of aggregate change that most strikes us here. Over the past four decades, changes in the composition of each party's coalition have more often conformed to a pattern of secular realignment than to that of a single, critical election. An explanation for this slowness of group realignment can be tied directly back to the individual-level change. Much of the movement has been limited to partisan-independent or independent-partisan shifts rather than moves from one party to the other. Even the movement of blacks toward the Democrats between 1960 and 1968 lowered the incremental probability of being a Republican (or, actually, raised the negative probability) much less than it increased the probability of being a Democrat (from −.23 to −.32 for Republicans and from .08 to .49 for Democrats). The same was true of the propensities away from the Democrats among native southern whites (−.35 to −.29 for Republicans and .41 to .20 for Democrats). Whether a group realignment has occurred has been so heavily debated in part because the deliberateness of the change has made it very difficult to detect.

If a realignment has indeed taken place, the important questions shift to what the new Republican coalition looks like, whether a Republican majority will result, and why it has taken so long for the Republican coalition to solidify. A partial answer to these questions is found in the fact that the Republicans have not yet found strong support among the traditionally Democratic groups. While the New Deal coalition has weakened, we already noted how little increased support there was for the Republicans (as opposed to decreased support for Democrats). Another part of the answer is that among the "newer" groups, it was only among the post-1958 cohort, the well-to-do, and frequent churchgoers that the incremental probabilities in the 1980s were in a Republican direction; even then, the probabilities for the young cohort were very small and those for the rich and religious were largely unchanged from the 1970s. Such loosening of group ties to the parties may reflect as well as partially affect the candidate-centered politics of recent years.

References

Aldrich, John, and Richard G. Niemi. 1990. "The Sixth American Party System: The 1960s Realignment and Candidate-centered Parties." Unpublished manuscript.

Axelrod, Robert. 1972. "Where the Votes Come From: An Analysis of Electoral Coalitions." 66 *American Political Science Review* 11.

————. 1986. "Presidential Election Coalitions in 1984." 80 *American Political Science Review* 281.

Beck, Paul Allen. 1977. "Partisan Dealignment in the Postwar South." 71 *American Political Science Review* 1 477.

Carmines, Edward G., and James A. Stimson. 1984. "The Dynamics of Issue Evolution." In Russell J. Dalton, Scott Flanagan, and Paul Allen Beck, eds. *Electoral Change in Advanced Industrial Democracies*. Princeton: Princeton U. Pr.

Edsall, Thomas B. 1988. "The Reagan Legacy." In Sidney Blumenthal and Thomas B. Edsall, eds. *The Republican Legacy*. New York: Pantheon.

Erikson, Robert S., Thomas D. Lancaster, and David W. Romero. 1989. "Group Components of the Presidential Vote, 1952–1984." 51 *Journal of Politics* 337.

Franklin, Charles H., and John E. Jackson. 1983. "The Dynamics of Party Identification." 77 *American Political Science Review* 957.

Key, V. O., Jr. 1955. "A Theory of Critical Elections." 17 *Journal of Politics* 3.

————. 1959. "Secular Realignment and the Party System." 21 *Journal of Politics* 198.

MacKuen, Michael, Robert S. Erikson, and James A. Stimson. 1989. "Macropartisanship." 83 *American Political Science Review* 1125.

Niemi, Richard G., and Herbert F. Weisberg, eds. 1993. *Controversies in Voting Behavior*, 3rd Edition. Washington, DC: CQ Press.

———, eds. 1993. *Classics in Voting Behavior*. Washington, DC: CQ Press.

Norpoth, Helmut. 1987. "Under Way and Here to Stay: Party Realignment in the 1980s?" 51 *Public Opinion Quarterly* 376.

———, and Michael R. Kagay. 1989. "Another Eight Years of Republican Rule and Still No Partisan Realignment?" Paper presented at the annual meeting of the American Political Science Association, Atlanta.

Petrocik, John R. 1981. *Party Coalitions: Realignment and the Decline of the New Deal Party System*. Chicago: U. of Chicago Pr.

———. 1989. "Issues and Agendas: Electoral Coalitions in the 1988 Election." Paper presented at the annual meeting of the American Political Science Association, Atlanta.

———, and Frederick T. Steeper. 1987. "The Political Landscape in 1988." 10 (5) *Public Opinion* 41.

Rothenberg, Stuart, and Frank Newport. 1984. *The Evangelical Voter*. Washington, DC: Free Congress Research and Education Foundation.

Schneider, William. 1988. "The Political Legacy of the Reagan Years." In Sidney Blumenthal and Thomas B. Edsall, eds. *The Republican Legacy*. New York: Pantheon.

Smidt, Corwin. 1983. "Born-again Politics: The Political Behavior of Evangelical Christians in the South and Non-South." In Tod A. Baker, Robert Steed, and Laurence W. Moreland, eds. *Religion and Politics in the South*. New York: Praeger.

Sundquist, James L. 1983. *Dynamics of the Party System: Alignment and Realignment*, Rev. ed. Washington, DC: Brookings.

CHAPTER 10

Dealignment in the American Electorate

Martin P. Wattenberg

For decades now scholars of American political parties have anxiously searched polls and electoral results for signs of a critical realignment. Given the regular historic patterns of party system change, such a realignment seems long overdue. The last major restructuring of the party system occurred in the 1930s, and many once-controversial aspects of government involvement in the economy have become institutionalized and widely accepted by both parties. At the same time, since the New Deal, new issues have divided the electorate in ways that could potentially realign American voters. None of these issues, however, has had more than a marginal impact on the overall distribution of party identification.

Waiting for a major realignment has been much like waiting for Godot. While many of the signs seem to indicate that it should surely come along any time now, that promise remains unfulfilled. Perhaps the most important sign has been the gradual decaying of the existing party system. As James Sundquist has told us: "[F]luidity, independence, and party-switching—those marks of the turbulent 1960s—also characterized the prealignment and realignment eras of the past." Therefore much of our initial interest in and theorizing about the movement away from the parties in the late 1960s and early 1970s has centered on how such a development might facilitate a new partisan alignment. In order for the system to realign, it would first have to dealign, and such a process was clearly taking place.

The term "dealignment" was apparently first used in print by Ronald Inglehart and Avram Hochstein in their article "Alignment and Dealignment of the Electorate in France and the United States." In this 1972 essay Inglehart and Hochstein contrasted the relationship between age and strength of partisan identification in a decaying American system to that of a rapidly developing French partisan alignment.

However, Inglehart and Hochstein's article was preceded by two years by the publication of Walter Burnham's seminal book *Critical Elections and the Mainsprings of American Politics*. Here, Burnham analyzed what he called the "long-term electoral disaggregation" and "party decomposition" in the United States. While neither of these terms made much of a dent in the common parlance of scholarship on political parties, "dealignment" stuck almost immediately. In contrast to realignment—which refers to a durable change in the distribution of partisan attachments and hence political behavior—dealignment involves a movement away from party affiliation and guidance. Dealignment is thus characterized by a weakening of party identification and a decline in the role of partisanship in shaping individual voting decisions.

What was initially seen as a temporary development, opening the way for a new partisan alignment, has since come to be viewed as an enduring feature of American party politics by many analysts. Burnham has recently gone so far as to label the dealignment period since 1968 as the Sixth American Party System:

> In retrospect, the critical realignment that so many people looked for around 1968 actually happened around that date, but in the "wrong" place. Instead of producing an emergent Republican (or any other) majority, parties themselves were decisively replaced at the margins by the impact of the "permanent campaign" (Burnham, 1985, p. 248).

While the old party alignment continues to fade away, Burnham and others believe that a new alignment will find it very difficult to put down roots in the current dealigned era. Any realignment that does occur will be hollow as long as political parties continue to have a weak image in the public mind and an uncertain role in the future of American government.

The evidence for dealignment can be classified into three broad categories: first, the normative attitudes toward the role of political parties in the United States; second, the trends in party-line and split-ticket voting; and third, the decline of party identification and party images.

American Attitudes Toward Political Parties

Americans have traditionally maintained an ambivalent attitude toward political parties. The Founders wished to avoid the establishment of parties but at the same time viewed them as necessary evils. Initially, they established parties not with the view of creating long-term organizations to compete for power but rather as a means of permanently defeating the opposition. To them, political parties were needed only until a national consensus could be attained. Even after the acceptance of regularized opposition parties in the mid-nineteenth century, Congress was able to weaken the role of parties in American political life. For example, the power of patronage was greatly limited by the implementation of merit-based civil service in the 1880s. Furthermore, the nomination function was largely taken away from parties with the introduction of direct primaries at the turn of the century.

Ironically, in a nation that founded the world's first political party system, parties have been looked upon with much suspicion. Whereas other countries have consciously adopted a political party system in light of experience elsewhere, for the United States, parties were a risky venture in the then-uncharted waters of democratic development. As a consequence, in no other western country are parties as tightly regulated and constrained as they are in the United States. From the European perspective, observers such as Philip Williams are often left wondering "how in the 1980s American political parties can be said to have lost power when they hardly ever had any."

Extensive survey evidence exists to document Americans' lack of concern with partisanship and the role of political parties in U.S. government. Most pervasive is Americans' general belief that they should vote for the man, not the party. Even in 1956, when most voters were in fact voting straight party tickets, 74 percent of respondents in a Gallup poll agreed with this general belief; by 1968 this figure had risen to 84 percent. Most recently, a survey by Sabato found 92 percent agreeing with this statement: "I always vote for the person who I think is best, regardless of what party they belong to."

On the other side of the coin, only 14 percent in Sabato's 1986 survey agreed with the statement that "I always support the candidates of just one party." Such feelings have been shown to be particularly weak in the younger generation. For example, Beck's 1984 analysis of the 1973 wave of the Jennings-Niemi socialization study found that 18 percent of the parents felt "it is better to vote a straight ticket than to divide your votes between the parties," compared to a mere 8 percent of their twenty-five-year-old offspring.

Using such public opinion data, we can now safely say that putting candidate considerations ahead of party considerations in voting has become a part of the American creed. One reason for this consensus has been a sense that political parties are not very meaningful in today's world. For example, in the Jennings-Niemi socialization study, 86 percent of the parents and 92 percent of their children agreed with this statement: "A candidate's party label does not really tell a person what the candidate's stand will be on the issues." Similarly, the 1980 National Election Study found that 52 percent of the public agreed that "the parties do more to confuse the issues than to provide a clear choice."

The most potentially damaging attitude to the political parties' future, however, is the large percentage of the population that sees little need for parties altogether. For example, 45 percent of the 1980 election study sample agreed that "it would be better if, in all elections, we put no party labels on the ballot." An astonishing 30 percent agreed with the extreme statement that "the truth is we probably don't need political parties anymore." And similarly, 37 percent in Sabato's 1986 survey agreed that "political parties don't really make any difference anymore." Indeed, by a 45 percent to a 34 percent margin more people see interest groups as better representatives of their political needs than either of the political parties, according to a 1983 Gallup poll. Patterns such as these have prompted Jack Dennis to write that "we may be called upon in the not so distant future to witness the demise of a once prominent institution of American government and politics," that is, the political party.

In stark contrast to political scientists' hand-wringing about party decline, the public seems blithely unaware of the parties' plight. A December 1985 *New York Times* poll asked people the following question: "Think about how much influence political parties have today. Do they have more influence than they had twenty years ago, less influence, or about the same influence as twenty years ago?" The results revealed that 50 percent actually thought the parties have more influence today, compared to 24 percent who thought their influence was less, 18 percent who said it was about the same, and 8 percent who didn't know. Because the public is so unaware of the problem of party decline, the task of educating people on the need for party revitalization takes on greater importance as well as difficulty. To make people care once again about political parties will require a public conviction that parties can and do fill an important institutional role.

The Decline of Party-Line Voting

Analysis of American voting patterns in the twentieth century clearly reveals a steady trend away from straight party-line voting. Although sample survey evidence is necessarily limited to the relatively recent period for which data are available, we can get a far more extended historical perspective on dealignment and the relationship of partisanship to the vote by examining aggregate election returns over time. We can expect that if party loyalties are closely related to the vote, the results for different offices in the same election will tally faithfully. Therefore, if a Democratic candidate wins the presidential race in a given district, then other Democratic candidates in the district should also win. If, however, voters are casting their ballots on the basis of variables other than party, ticket-splitting may result in victories for some candidates on the ticket and losses for others.

As Burnham (1985) has shown, the squared correlation between a nonsouthern state's vote for president and its vote for Senate, House, and for governor has declined continuously throughout this century. The degree of shared variance with the presidential vote for every fifth election year from 1900 to 1980 plus 1988 is presented below:

	Senate	House	Governor
1900	—	.97	.94
1920	.80	.70	.55
1940	.76	.66	.61
1960	.43	.55	.36
1980	.24	.06	.00
1988	.09	.00	.09

In simple terms, these squared correlations indicate that at the turn of the century, observers could predict almost perfectly how a state would vote for Congress and governor by its vote for president. By mid-century a state would often follow the same pattern in voting for president as for other offices, but with a fair number of exceptions. Finally, knowing a state's presidential vote in 1988 was of virtually no help in predicting its vote for other offices, as the voting patterns were hardly correlated at all.

The results of these patterns have distinct political significance. They clearly demonstrate the unprecedented level of split-party control of both the federal and state governments in recent years. Most visible, of course, has been the division between partisan control of the presidency and the Congress from 1952 to 1992. During this forty-year period, the same party has controlled the presidency and the House for just fourteen years. In addition, for the period between 1981 and 1986, different parties controlled the House and Senate for the first time since 1916.

With the election of President Clinton in 1992, unified party government has now been at least temporarily restored. Whether the 1992 election marks the end of the era of divided government and the beginning of a new Democratic era remains to be seen. If evidence from the state governments is any indicator, then divided government remains an important phenomenon in American politics. As Morris Fiorina (1992) shows, the percentage of states that have unified party control of the governorship and the state legislature has steadily declined for over four decades. Whereas 85 percent of state governments had one party controlling both houses of the legislature and the governorship in 1946, after the 1992 elections, this was the case in only 38 percent of the states. Divided government, once an occasional oddity, has become commonplace.

While such patterns have clear substantive significance, they are somewhat less than definitive indicators of split-ticket voting because of the possibility of aggregate fallacy. Only through analysis of individual-level survey data is it feasible to actually gauge the scope and nature of party-line voting. Examinations of the National Election Study data from 1952 to 1984 confirm the conclusion from the aggregate election returns that the degree of cross-party voting has risen quite sharply over the last few decades. Listed in the following pages are the percentages over time for ticket-splitting between (1) president and House votes; (2) House and Senate votes; and (3) votes for other state and local offices.

It is thus readily apparent that split-ticket voting has at least doubled in every respect over the last three decades. During the 1952–1960 period ticket-splitting was relatively rare as well as fairly stable. Over the next twenty years, however, a steady increase is apparent, with the 1980 election recording the highest levels to date. (Because any vote for Ross Perot is by definition a split-ticket vote, the figure for 1992 may well be higher.) Some analysts have argued that ticket-splitting is simply due to the nomination of presidential candidates whom many party identifiers could not support. Yet secular increases can also be found in measures that do not involve presidential voting.

To recapitulate, one prominent sign of dealignment has been the decline of the parties' ability to structure the vote. Division of party control of both the federal and state governments has become common as split-ticket voting has increased greatly over the last quarter of a century. Furthermore,

given the current state of public attitudes about voting the man
rather than the party, we have good reason to expect that this
element of dealignment will continue for some time to come.
Because the potential for ticket-splitting has consistently been
greater than its incidence, we can reasonably interpret recent
trends as reflecting the tendency for behaviors eventually to
come into line with attitudes.

The Decline of Party Identification and Partisan Images

Accompanying the trend toward greater split-ticket voting
has also been a decline in party identification. Election studies
during the period from 1952 to 1964 consistently found that
approximately 75 percent of the electorate identified themselves
as either Democrats or Republicans, and roughly half of these
identifiers considered themselves to be strong partisans. The
similarity in party identification margins from one sample
survey to another during this period led Philip Converse (1966)
to write of the "serene stability in the distribution of party
loyalties," and later (1976) to call these years the "steady state
period" of party identification. However, after 1964 the picture
changed significantly. By 1972 the percentage of respondents
identifying with one of the parties had dropped from 77 percent
to 64 percent, and the proportion of strong partisans declined
from 38 percent to 25 percent.

At first, these changes in the distribution of party loyalties
were seen as quite a revolutionary development. For example,
Burnham (1970) has argued that the losses in identification for
both parties could very well represent "a dissolution of the
parties as action intermediaries in electoral choice and other
politically relevant acts." In addition, the rise of a "mass base for
independent political movements of ideological tone and
considerable long-term staying power" seemed to be one
possible consequence of the decline, according to Burnham.
Similarly, Gerald Pomper wrote that the continuation of such a
trend "may eventually bring the nation to a free-floating politics,

in which prediction is hazardous, continuities are absent and governmental responsibility is impossible to fix."

More recently, however, revisionist views interpret the decline in party identification as far less cataclysmic. To begin with, the downward trend no longer seems to be a trend at all, but rather a limited period effect in which a rapid decline was followed by the development of a new, somewhat lower level of stability. Since 1972 the proportion of the population identifying with one of the parties during presidential election years has held steady at between 63 percent and 65 percent. In retrospect, the period of most seriously weakened party loyalties—1964 to 1972—seems to be an unusually tumultuous epoch in the history of American politics, which may well never again be duplicated in the severity of the shocks (Vietnam, racial unrest, etc.) felt by the electorate.

Perhaps more important is the analytic argument by Keith et al. (1977) that the decline in party identification has been greatly inflated by classifying as "nonpartisans" those Independents reporting themselves as "closer" to one of the two parties. These so-called "Independent leaners" are not an uncommitted and unmobilized bloc but are instead largely "closet" Democrats or Republicans. Although they may prefer to call themselves Independents rather than Democrats or Republicans, their voting behavior in presidential elections show them to be just as partisan as weak party identifiers. Between 1952 and 1988 the mean defection rate for weak Democrats was 34 percent, compared to 31 percent for Independent Democrats; likewise, weak Republicans defected 15 percent of time on the average, compared to 14 percent for Independent Republicans. If Independent leaners are simply partisans by another name, then the proportion of the population identifying with a party can hardly be said to have declined at all over the years. As Keith et al. tell us, "Most of the growth in Independents has occurred among the hidden partisans, while the high-level speculations have concerned the genuine Independents, whose increase has been rather modest."

This argument was first introduced by Keith et al. in a 1977 convention paper and immediately became influential in the field. Ironically, the book that evolved from the 1977 paper,

Keith et al.'s *The Myth of the Independent Voter* was released for publication in June of 1992—just when Ross Perot was leading in the public opinion polls. If ever there was a solid demonstration of dealignment and the independence of American voters, the Perot phenomenon was it.

Another view of the independent leaners is offered by Sabato, who maintains that "the reluctance of 'leaners' to admit their real party identification in itself is worrisome because it reveals a sea change in attitudes about political parties and their proper role in our society." Even if increased independence is little more than a movement of partisans into the closet, the question of what is particularly attractive about the closet at present must be addressed. In the 1980 National Election Study, respondents who called themselves Independents were handed a list of eleven statements and asked which ones best described why they so identified themselves. The percentages follow:

74.7%	I decide on the person not the party.
59.0%	I decide on the issue not the party label.
36.3%	The parties almost never deliver on their promises.
29.5%	I support both Democrats and Republicans.
20.2%	I'm not much interested in politics.
17.0%	I don't know enough to make a choice.
14.8%	Neither party stands for what I think is important.
13.5%	I like both parties about the same.
12.6%	I'm Independent because of the way I feel about what Jimmy Carter has been doing.
4.7%	My parents were Independent and I am too.
4.2%	I dislike both parties.

The primary reasons are thus normative values: Voters should decide on the basis of person and issues rather than on the party. Such findings support the notion that parties are presently seen as lacking in relevance to the large majority of Independents.

In contrast, we have relatively little evidence for Nie, Verba, and Petrocik's hypothesis postulating a lack of voter confidence in the parties. The negative statement most frequently mentioned was that "the parties almost never deliver on their promises," checked by slightly over one-third of the Independents. Yet such an opinion could conceivably reflect a perception that parties have become so institutionally irrelevant that they no longer have the power to keep their promises. A far better test of the alienation hypothesis is the statement that "neither party stands for what I think is important," checked by only 14.8 percent of the Independents. And finally, the purest measure of dissatisfaction with the parties follows from the statement that "I dislike both parties," checked by a mere 4.2 percent. All told, even if we accept a party's inability to deliver on promises as a negative performance statement, less than 20 percent of the reasons checked for independence indicate a lack of satisfaction with the two political parties.

Indeed, when asked what they like and dislike about the two major political parties in an open-ended fashion, very few Americans make an overall negative evaluation of both parties. Even at the high point of negative feelings toward the parties in 1968, only 10 percent of the public expressed more dislikes than likes about both the Republicans and Democrats. For 1984 and 1988 this figure was down to a miniscule 3 percent—just what it was in 1952 and 1956.

Rather than expressing negative attitudes toward the parties, the dealignment era has been characterized by an increasing proportion of the mass public—that is, neutral toward both parties. From 1952 to 1984 the percentage who can be classified as neutral toward both parties gradually increased from 13.0 percent to 35.8 percent. Virtually all of these "neutrals" exhibit this response pattern to the four open-ended questions about the parties in the National Election studies:

Q. Is there anything in particular that you like about the Democratic Party?
A. No.
Q. Is there anything in particular that you don't like about the Democratic Party?
A. No.

Q. Is there anything in particular that you like about the Republican Party?
A. No.
Q. Is there anything in particular that you don't like about the Republican Party?
A. No.

In the 1950s such a response pattern reflected general political ignorance. Most of these "neutrals" had little to say about candidates as well and were of little political importance because of their apathy and consequent low turnout. Today, this group is apathetic about parties, but not about candidates and politics in general. Indeed, these "neutrals" are often considered the most important group in American electoral politics, and they are known collectively as "the floating voters."

Compared to the decline of party identification, the rise of neutrality in party images has occurred over a much longer period of time and has been a far more pronounced trend. This discrepancy occurs because party identification involves a process of self-labeling and is thus likely to be far more stable than most other political attitudes. Yet such stability can be seen as a theoretical weakness of the measure as well as a strength. While the label may survive intact from year to year, the meaning associated with it may change considerably over time. If parties have become less relevant to the public in recent decades, then attitudes toward people's support of one party and/or opposition to the other will have become less clear— even among those whose party affiliation remains unchanged.

The best possible test for this hypothesis requires an examination of what people have replied to the party "likes/dislikes" questions over time, controlling for party identification. The comparison of the level of neutrality toward the parties in 1952 and 1984 reveals that the increase is evident for each category of the party-identification scale (see following table).

In particular, the proportion of weak partisans and Independent leaners who can be classified as neutral toward both parties has increased from hardly more than one-tenth in 1952 to nearly two-fifths by 1984. The similarity over time between the

	1952	1984
Strong Democrats	4.8%	14.2%
Weak Democrats	14.5	37.4
Independent Democrats	13.3	38.0
Pure Independents	23.3	70.2
Independent Republicans	9.5	40.8
Weak Republicans	13.5	36.8
Strong Republicans	4.6	14.4

two supports the contention of Keith et al. that Independent leaners are generally quite similar to weak partisans. However, their basic point is to show that the decline of party identification is not so serious as some maintain, whereas the above data indicate just the reverse. Indeed we know of little reason to be alarmed that more people are calling themselves Independent leaners given their similarity to weak partisans. However, the fact that both categories are now far more neutral toward the parties themselves is cause for genuine concern.

Thus, the rise of neutrality does not really account for the decline of party identification: Rather it indicates that the decline in party relevance is even sharper than the rise in independence would lead us to expect. The "likes/dislikes" measure reveals greater neutrality over time among strong partisans, weak partisans, Independent leaners, and pure Independents alike, thereby showing that strength of party identification no longer has the depth of meaning attached to it that it once did.

Conclusion

Evidence of dealignment, then, is readily apparent most everywhere one looks in public attitudes and behavior. The belief that one should vote the man and not the party has now become part of the American consensus, and split-ticket voting has risen markedly. Fewer people now identify with parties, and the percentage who have neither likes nor dislikes for the two parties has more than tripled since the 1950s. As the candidate-centered age reaches maturity, these dealigning trends will probably not be substantially reversed in the near future. Even the Reagan-Mondale contest of 1984, pitting a traditional Democrat against the most partisan president in recent memory, did little to undo the dealigned state of the American electorate.

During the early stages of the dealignment, many analysts were concerned that parties were on the verge of disappearing from the political scene. As dealignment has progressed, however, a more realistic view has been that parties will continue to play an important but significantly diminished role in American electoral politics. For example, Leon Epstein writes that "frayed" strikes him as "an apt word for what has happened to party identification during the last three decades. . . . The word connotes a wearing that need not mean disintegration or abandonment." Epstein concludes that the parties will "survive and even moderately prosper in a society evidently unreceptive to strong parties and yet unready, and probably unable, to abandon parties altogether."

The data concerning normative attitudes toward the parties reviewed in this article indicate that most voters now view parties as a convenience rather than a necessity. However, regardless of whether the public recognizes it or not, the fact of the matter is that parties are necessary for structuring the vote. Political scientists have long recognized the indispensable functions performed by parties, and dealignment has not changed this view. As Dalton, Flanagan, and Beck tell us, "Unless elections become purely contests of personalities, parties are likely to continue to play an important role in structuring political choices, even in a purely dealigned and issue-oriented electorate."

Consequently, political parties will doubtless survive in an atmosphere of dealignment, but will parties still be able to perform many of their key functions in such an environment? If many voters no longer pay much attention to party labels, why should elites pay more than lip service to the concept of party unity in government? As Burnham (1985) writes, "[the dealigned electorate] can and does elect people, but it cannot and does not give them the power to govern with the kind of coherence and cross-institutional will that effective state action will come to require." If a political party wants to play like a team in office, then it must achieve office as a team. The crucial point to note about dealignment is therefore that such a scenario has become increasingly unlikely.

References

Beck, Paul Allen. 1984. "The Dealignment Era in America." In Russell J. Dalton et al., eds. *Electoral Change in Advanced Industrial Democracies: Realignment or Dealignment?* Princeton: Princeton U. Pr.

Burnham, Walter Dean. 1970. *Critical Elections and the Mainsprings of American Politics.* New York: Norton.

———. 1985. "The 1984 Elections and the Future of American Politics." In Ellis Sandoz and Cecil V. Crabb, Jr., eds. *Election 84: Landslide Without a Mandate?* New York: Mentor.

———. 1987. "Elections as Democratic Institutions." In Kay Lehman Schlozman, ed. *Elections in America.* Boston: Allen and Unwin.

Converse, Philip E. 1966. "The Concept of a Normal Vote." In Angus Campbell et al., eds. *Elections and the Political Order.* New York: Wiley.

———. 1976. *The Dynamics of Party Support: Cohort-Analyzing Party Identification.* Beverly Hills, CA: Sage.

———, and Gregory B. Markus. 1979. "Plus ça change . . . The New CPS Election Study Panel." 73 *American Political Science Review* 32.

Dalton, Russel J., Scott C. Flanagan, and Paul Allen Beck, eds. 1984. *Electoral Change in Advanced Industrial Societies.* Princeton: Princeton U. Pr.

Dennis, Jack. 1975. "Trends in Public Support for the American Party System." 5 *British Journal of Political Science* 187.

Epstein, Leon D. 1986. *Political Parties in the American Mold.* Madison: U. of Wisconsin Pr.

Fiorina, Morris P. 1992. *Divided Government.* New York: Macmillan.

Inglehart, Ronald, and Avram Hochstein. 1972. "Alignment and Dealignment of the Electorate in France and the United States." 5 *Comparative Political Studies* 343.

Jennings, M. Kent, and Gregory B. Markus. 1984. "Partisan Orientations over the Long Haul: Results from the Three-Wave Political Socialization Study." 78 *American Political Science Review* 1000.

Keith, Bruce E., David B. Magleby, Candice J. Nelson, Elizabeth Orr, Mark Westlye, and Raymond E. Wolfinger. 1977. "The Myth of the Independent Voter." Paper presented at the annual meeting of the American Political Science Association.

———, et al. 1986. "The Partisan Attitudes of Independent Leaners." 16 *British Journal of Political Science* 155.

———, et al. 1992. *The Myth of the Independent Voter*. Berkeley: U. of California Pr.

Nie, Norman H., Sidney Verba, and John R. Petrocik. 1976. *The Changing American Voter*. Cambridge: Harvard U. Pr.

Pomper, Gerald. 1975. *Voter's Choice: Varieties of American Electoral Behavior*. New York: Dodd, Mead.

Sabato, Larry J. 1988. *The Party's Just Begun: Shaping Political Parties for America's Future*. Glenview, IL: Scott, Foresman.

Sundquist, James L. 1983. *Dynamics of the Party System: Alignment and Realignment of Political Parties in the U.S.* Rev. ed. Washington, DC: Brookings.

Wattenberg, Martin P. 1987. "The Hollow Realignment: Partisan Change in a Candidate-Centered Era." 51 *Public Opinion Quarterly* 58.

———. 1990. *The Decline of American Political Parties, 1952–1988*. Cambridge: Harvard U. Pr.

CHAPTER 11

Party Organization in Historical Perspective

David R. Mayhew

For much of American history, the subject of parties has meant, first of all, a distinctive American brand of patronage-based party organization. These structures have caught the eyes of observers and provoked hypotheses about relations among the public, parties, government, and policy. Thus, for example, the classic *American Commonwealth* by James Bryce (1888), *Democracy and the Organization of Political Parties* by Moisei Ostrogorski (1902), D.W. Brogan's *The American Political System* (1933), and E.E. Schattschneider's *Party Government* (1942).

Such structures have flourished at all three levels of government, though at different times. State-level organizations grew throughout the nineteenth century and peaked, in general, around 1900. At the federal level the leading decades were the 1830s through the 1880s. Local organizations, including city machines, grew in importance during the last half of the nineteenth century and stood up remarkably well during the first half of the twentieth until the 1960s. Relations among the three levels have to be kept in mind. Patronage and influence have flowed among them as a matter of routine; furthermore, organizations at one level have sometimes been shaped or generated by entrepreneurs from another.

At the local level, political organizations like these lasted into a time when hundreds of scholars became available to take a close look at them. Numerous works from the 1950s and 1960s are especially useful. They permit a good fix on the geography of local patronage-based organizations as of the late 1960s, after which came a steep downhill slide in their fortunes. (See David Mayhew, *Placing Parties in American Politics* [1986] for a bibliographic essay on the subject; this work also tracks the geographic incidence-cum-prominence of such local organizations, as of the late 1960s, through application of a definition of "traditional party organization" [TPO].)

A "traditional party organization" has the following properties: (1) It has substantial autonomy. That is, its existence does not depend on the incentive structure of an organization operating mostly outside electoral politics (e.g., a union or a private corporation). The TPO might get resources from nonlocal levels of government, but it can operate as a substantially independent power base in dealing with such other levels. (2) The TPO lasts over decades or generations rather than over months or years and can survive leadership changes. (3) Its internal structure has an important element of hierarchy. In fact, it is apt to be known by its leader's name, as in the case of Chicago's Daley organization or Albany's O'Connell organization. (4) The TPO regularly tries to nominate candidates for a wide range of public offices, ordinarily including state assembly, state senate, and local or municipal offices, and sometimes judgeships and congressional and statewide offices. A TPO routinely tries to nominate convention or primary slates. (This definitional move excludes, from the TPO rubric, incumbent officials who use job patronage to their own end but do not impinge on nominating for other offices. They run their own shows, which come to an end when they leave office. Some mayors of Boston and Denver offer good instances, as do county commissioners' positions in Oklahoma.) (5) A TPO relies substantially on "material" incentives and not much on "purposive" incentives to get people to work for or to support the organization. Particularistic awards of jobs, contracts, tax abatements, statutory variances, among other things, amount to a distinctive political currency. Job patronage, in particular, in exchange for election work, makes possible the organizational hierarchy that in turn permits control of nominations.

Finally, for later purposes here, a "machine" can be said to be a "traditional party organization" that is able to exercise overall control over government at a city or county level. Not all TPOs have enjoyed that success. Some, for example, have been successful only in city wards or have channeled candidates into some public offices but not into mayoralties.

Given this five-pronged definition, thirteen states supported arrays of strong "traditional party organizations" as late as the 1960s: Rhode Island and Connecticut in southern New England; New York, New Jersey, Pennsylvania, Maryland, and Delaware (for which the evidence is notably scanty) in the Middle Atlantic area; Ohio, Indiana, and Illinois in the southern Midwest; and the noncoastal Border States of West Virginia, Kentucky, and Missouri. The pattern is substantially specific to each state. That is, all other sorts of variables held equal, knowing that a "traditional party organization" occurs somewhere locally in a state helps to predict whether it will turn up elsewhere in the same state—in urban, suburban, or rural areas. In Maryland, West Virginia, Kentucky, Missouri, and Indiana, TPOs have commonly taken a "factional" form. That is, local politics has featured competition for office and its effects between two or more TPOs operating in the same party in the same city or county. Places sustaining such factional-TPO politics have included Jackson County (Kansas City), Missouri; Jefferson County (Louisville), Kentucky; Vanderburgh County (Evansville), Indiana; Kanawha County (Charleston), West Virginia; the city of Baltimore; and rural Queen Annes County in Maryland.

Outside these thirteen states, "traditional party organizations" were, as of the 1960s, rare, weak, nonexistent, or at least quite recessive in the politics of their states. The other TPO outcroppings worth mentioning, mostly rural, appeared in Hispanic New Mexico, Mexican-American southern Texas, Francophone southern Louisiana (including the wards of New Orleans), and the southern Appalachian chain.

What accounts for this geographic pattern of the 1960s? Certainly not "regionalism" in any simple sense. The thirteen prime TPO states do not constitute a "northeastern" or a "northeastern quadrant" bloc. Massachusetts, northern New England, Michigan, Wisconsin, and Minnesota showed no trace of such organizations in the 1960s. Relative size of immigrant populations offers little help. All of the states just named, and also New Hampshire, drew relatively more late-wave immigrants than any of the Border States or, for that matter, Ohio, Indiana, or Illinois. Relative size of urban population helps somewhat, not surprisingly, at least if all fifty states are taken as a comparison. But West Virginia, Kentucky, and Indiana are really not very urban.

History, going back at least two centuries, seems a better bet than cross-sectional analysis for explaining this late-1960s organizational map. Strikingly, on the one hand, all thirteen "organization states" grew into polities early enough to win statehood by 1821 (West Virginia as part of its parent state). This date was well before statehood came for Michigan, Wisconsin, Florida, or California, to give some geographically scattered examples. Nearly a necessary condition, though hardly a sufficient one, it seems, for TPO politics to have existed in a state in the 1960s is some set of factors associated with the state before 1821 or their resonance since. "Nearly," because the Hispanic- or Mexican-background areas of Texas or New Mexico are not parts of pre-1822 states, though the U.S. electoral politics of both does date to the 1840s or 1850s. "Hardly a sufficient one" because even though seven of the original states appear on the list of 1960s organization states, six do not: New Hampshire and Massachusetts to the north of the contiguous bloc of such states, and Virginia, North Carolina (some mountain-area outcroppings notwithstanding), South Carolina, and Georgia to the south.

Tracing the historical background of modern party organization is not easy, since most of the considerable recent scholarship on party history has dealt with voter cleavages rather than party structure. The work that addresses structure, moreover, has only sometimes looked into institutional-maintenance features, patronage-based or otherwise. But enough pertinent work now exists to make possible a broad outline of the rise, incidence, and fortunes of patronage-based organization over the last two centuries or so. The story wends its way among local, state, and national levels of government, and it points to the antecedents, at least, of the 1960s geographic pattern of organization. The strict 1960s definition of "traditional party organization" need not be imposed beyond its time or (local) level, but the earlier lines of party structure to be discussed here follow more or less the same logic. Particularistic goods or favors produce organization hierarchy, which in turn allows influence over nominations and of public offices that generate goods and favors.

No one doubts that on the East Coast, the modern New England (or Massachusetts, at least) versus Middle Atlantic versus southern Atlantic pattern of party organization has deep eighteenth-century roots. New York, New Jersey, and Pennsylvania, according to recent accounts, stood out as colonies and then as revolutionary-era states for their ethnic, religious, and economic heterogeneity. They generated exceptional conflict. These states had no dominant socioeconomic hierarchies, as was notably the case in Massachusetts, Virginia, and South Carolina, that could handle political matters relatively harmoniously and ward off a polarizing mobilization of the public. In the Middle Atlantic area, deference politics broke down. Professional political management, competing tickets of candidates, and statewide campaigns seem to have set in as standard features of politics by 1789. The three core Middle Atlantic States seem to have set the pace. But Rhode Island also was riven by a vigorous, mobilizing, two-sided factional politics throughout much of the middle and late eighteenth century. Delaware held excited and violent elections. And Maryland conducted statewide campaigns and pioneered in electioneering practices such as parades, speeches, and rallies.

The Middle Atlantic area developed in these early years some distinctive elite-level political practices. Was it generating a distinctive "political culture?" Not necessarily, if that term is taken to mean attitudes ingrained in the minds of the general population about how politics should be conducted. Only the elite-level practices can be documented. Still, these practices may be the whole story, or most of it, in the eighteenth century and later. Individual-level phenomena (e.g., the political outlook of the typical Pennsylvania German or Quaker) did not bring about political practices; the causative factors were evidently society-level phenomena (i.e., societal heterogeneity and the lack of a more or less unified ruling social hierarchy). And elite political practices once in place could be very tenacious.

Scholarship covering the period just after 1800 pins down another development in the Middle Atlantic area. State-centered spoils systems, tied to the organizational needs of electioneering, became prominent in the contemporary political universe. Evidence of spoils is especially good for New York and New Jersey, though Pennsylvania evidently had about the same. In these states at this time, electoral contesting took place between preparty "factions" rather than what are now called "parties." But to dwell on the distinction would probably be a mistake. Doing so can obscure the relatively seamless evolution of political practices from the eighteenth century into the nineteenth.

From here, the politics of the Middle Atlantic area progressed into the distinctively organization-centered mode, with a larger popular base than earlier, described by Richard P. McCormick in *The Second American Party System* (1973) for the Jacksonian period. (On New Jersey, see Levine 1974.) In New York, through something of a Darwinian process, Martin Van Buren's state-level Albany Regency moved to the fore first as a leading faction and then as a party in the 1820s and 1830s. It is the classic archetypal instance of a disciplined, job-awarding, electioneering enterprise. Thurlow Weed's Whig organization emerged in New York in the late 1830s as a carbon copy.

Organizations at lower levels show different patterns. When we think of twentieth-century parties in New York, New Jersey, Pennsylvania, and Maryland, we think at least of their distinctively powerful county organizations. Not much work has been done on the origins of these states' county systems, but what there is suggests that their foundations were laid in the decades before the Civil War as state governments spun off powers and allocational authority to local governmental units, as happened in Maryland, for example, in the 1850s. New York City and Philadelphia, the two American municipalities with the longest continuous histories of city- or ward-level organizations based substantially on patronage, evidently had installed those institutions by Jacksonian times.

Parties, of course, along with some sorts of attendant mobilizing mechanisms, grew to prominence throughout most of the country during the Jacksonian period. But outside the

Middle Atlantic area writ large, almost no state-, county-, city-, or ward-level party organization comes to light that had the hierarchy, discipline, material incentive structure, durability, and overall influence of the Albany Regency or early Tammany Hall. The chief exception seems to be New Hampshire's Hill Regency of the 1830s, which had much in common with the Albany organization, except its staying power; we do not know that the Hills outlived the friendly national administrations of the 1830s or had recognizable progeny. Massachusetts notably resisted a full-blown spoils system in pre-Jacksonian times, and in Ronald Formisano's recent treatment (1983) of that state's parties of the Jacksonian era, Albany Regency-like structures are notable for their absence.

Historians would pay less attention to Martin Van Buren's Albany Regency had it not played a leading role in two moves of national importance in the 1820s and 1830s. The first was to present a resonant ideological justification for building parties as disciplined, patronage-based organizations. In effect, new Jacksonian ideas were grafted onto old practices. An apparatus of such considerable substance, it was argued, could serve as a democratic battering ram against the socioeconomic privilege that controlled the political sector. And a spoils system, interpreted as the rotation-in-office principle, could embody the democratic statement that anybody is good enough to hold an appointive job.

The second move was the "Middle Atlanticization," more or less, of American national politics through the incorporation of the political practices of fast-growing New York and Pennsylvania into the federal parties and government. From the 1830s through the 1870s, after which came a tailing off, the Jacksonian Democrats, the Whigs, and then the Republicans built and tended nationally centered party organizations that drew considerable strength from the use of federal job patronage. Post offices and customhouses, in particular, served as nodes of party activity down in the cities and states.

Organization during this time commonly took the form of intraparty factions, rather than a leadership apparatus that enjoyed unified control of a party at some level of government. Such factions typically drew resources from, and operated at, federal levels but also at lower levels. By the 1870s, U.S. Senators had moved into the role of chief dispensers of federal patronage. Financial assessments of federal employees as well as kickbacks from private contractors (notably mail carriers) and duty payers (notably the liquor trade) brought the party in power considerable income for electioneering purposes. This particularistic fundraising, in contrast to the corporate financing that came later, may have allowed the parties to be relatively independent of broader societal interests. Federal patronage politics seems to have reached a high tide in the Stalwart Republican coalition of the 1870s that flourished under President Ulysses Grant. Its bases were the southern and Border State parties plus New York, Pennsylvania, and Illinois—"the home states of the three most prominent Republican machine politicians."

All three nineteenth-century American mass parties—the Jacksonian Democratic, Whig, and Republican—are instances of "internally mobilized" as opposed to "externally mobilized" parties. They took shape at times when their leaders held positions of governmental authority in a combination of federal (e.g., the Republicans after 1860) and state holdings (e.g., all three parties had strong bases in New York). A further condition, a lack of institutionalized bureaucracies, permitted the particularistic use of government resources to build patronage-based organizations. As a general proposition, these are evidently the circumstances in which such organizations are likely to arise.

J.G.A. Pocock has noted the irony that Americans waged a revolution against a patronage-based "connections" regime in the eighteenth century, the English system shaped by Walpole, only to build one themselves in the next century when the English were getting rid of theirs. The American system, however, in accord with federalism, remained relatively decentralized. And the strong civic base of the American regime probably put a limit on how much politics could hinge on material-incentive transactions. "Reform" grew as a tradition too. At presidential nominating conventions, parties ordinarily found it wise, for electoral reasons, to nominate blue-ribbon candidates. Consequently no national "boss" arose. And the system's national-cum-state party factions bolstered by patronage ties commonly had identifying policy tendencies as well.

During and after Jackson's presidency the new patronage-oriented style of the national parties intruded downward into states where before it had been unimportant or absent. One of the interesting stories of the nineteenth century is the extent to which this intrusion, in some places at least, was resisted. In post-Civil War Massachusetts, Benjamin F. Butler drew on federal patronage to build a considerable organization in the Republican party. But unlike comparable entrepreneurs in, say, Pennsylvania and Illinois, Butler failed to build a dominant, patronage-based state organization. No such organization was ever built. Massachusetts's influential Brahmin class of Republicans joined ranks to close Butler out. The elite remained committed to an idealistically individualistic style of politics that shied away from disciplined organization and featured, though the term sounds musty in 1870s Massachusetts, deference.

As in Massachusetts, so in the South. Democratic party elites in the South Atlantic and Gulf Coast states (but not in Maryland, Kentucky, and Tennessee) balked at the rotation-in-office principle of the Washington-centered spoils system. They largely stayed clear of the game from Jackson's presidency through Buchanan's. Particularly in the Carolinas and Virginia, elite gentries, expressing a republican ethic of individual public service, dominated politics until the Civil War. By New York standards, southern party organizations remained despised and underdeveloped.

Even if Whigs and Democrats competed closely at the state level, the picture below could be rather different. In North Carolina, relations of deference to notables built up large, safe majorities for one party or the other even at the county level. Alabama's Whigs, in their Black Belt strongholds of the 1840s, nominated candidates in direct primaries rather than in convention-generated slates. Alabama's hill-country Democrats ran against one another in considerable numbers in general elections in the 1840s just as they were running against one another in Democratic primaries a century later. All in all, the mechanism of spoils and slating seems to have failed to "take" at the local level in the coastal South even when Whigs rivaled Democrats at the state level. Political scientists err in so easily crediting the idiosyncratic structure of the South's parties to Democratic one-party dominance that grew in the late nineteenth century.

Especially in the southern Atlantic states, political elites kept up their resistance during and after Reconstruction, which was, among other things, an effort by Republicans to graft a national party style onto the South. In reaction, a *political* ethos as well as simply race or economics animated the defeated elites of Virginia and the Carolinas. Virtue—as measured by wealth, position, education, character, and manners—was supposed to prevail in politics, and in certain areas it did. The Democratic gentries of North Carolina and Virginia fought thirty-year battles against the intrusion of ordinary, popular, mobilizing, patronage-based American parties, and around 1900 they won. In both cases, though more strikingly in Virginia, the result in the twentieth century was a distinctive kind of strong state Democratic party organization that fended off the outside world and preserved local relations of deference through low suffrage. Progressivism, in these two states, is hard to disentangle from gentry restoration.

The trajectory differed in South Carolina, where deference politics attracted the opposition of turn-of-the-century "demagogues" like "Pitchfork Ben" Tillman (who assaulted the "aristocratic oligarchy") and Cole Blease. Much of the rest of the Deep South generated similar figures sooner or later. But the particularly revealing analogy is Massachusetts, a New England state that produced instructive counterparts to Tillman and Blease in the versatile Benjamin F. Butler (who orated as well as organized) and later the "Brahmin Baiter" James Michael Curley. These were distinctive one-man oppositions that arose to oppose deference-politics regimes surviving well beyond the age of Jackson. But at this time in these environments, hierarchical, patronage-based parties could not easily be built. Massachusetts, like the Deep South, carried into the twentieth century an individualistic style of politics in which politicians seek and hold office on their own rather than as agents of disciplined party organizations. Boston had some influential ward organizations around the turn of the century, and Curley's later mayoralties were corrupt, but no Tammany-style organization has ever succeeded in dominating Boston or, so far as one can tell, any other sizable Massachusetts city.

As the federal government's material nourishment of the parties fell off after the 1870s, corporate money partly took up the slack, and organizational strength shifted downward to the states and cities. United States senators, who until 1913 still needed the votes of state legislators to get elected, assembled and headed most of the exceptionally strong state party organizations that operated around 1900. New York, Pennsylvania, and Maryland—continuing the Middle Atlantic tradition—set the standard with their authoritative, material-incentive-based, statewide organizations that incorporated powerful city and county units and could ordinarily control state nominations and command state legislative majorities. Private corporations in this region normally played the roles of allies and something like equals. City or county machines figured importantly in the state party systems, united or faction based, of New Jersey, Ohio, Indiana, and Illinois. In general, outside the Middle Atlantic region and the Ohio Valley, strong turn-of-the-century state party organizations were extensions of private business—as in North Dakota, or in Michigan and Wisconsin—that lacked dominant city machines in Detroit or Milwaukee to serve as organization bases. California and New Hampshire went further yet: Railroad companies, not parties, quite directly organized the chief political hierarchies at the state level (e.g., in nominating conventions). Elsewhere, particularly in most of the South, no sort of party or party-like organization managed to dominate state electoral politics during the early years of the twentieth century.

At the local level, as these instances suggest, a geographic pattern of party organization had coalesced by 1900, one that resembled the later "traditional party organization" map of the 1960s. In general, significant material-incentive-driven organizations operated at ward, city, or county levels in the Middle Atlantic area and in the older states of the Ohio and Mississippi valleys—particularly in old sea and river ports. Cincinnati, Indianapolis, Louisville, New Orleans, Chicago, and

Kansas City, Missouri, are examples west of the Appalachians. Not much is known about the pre-Civil War roots of such organizations west of Pennsylvania, but by about 1900 they emerge clearly in the records. Organizations arose, or would later arise, in many of the newer northern industrial cities of the older Ohio Valley states (e.g., in Cleveland, Toledo, South Bend, and Gary) but not, evidently, in similar new industrial cities a tier farther north (e.g., in Kenosha, Racine, or Grand Rapids), or at least such organizations would have less strength and durability farther north. It is true that TPOs flourished around 1900 in a few places where all traces of them would be gone by 1950 (e.g., in San Francisco and in some of the wards of Omaha and Boston). But in general the 1900 map looks like the 1960s map.

"Reform," of course, infused cities all over the country after 1900, but reform could occur and widely did without a city "machine" as an incumbent enemy. Often the target instead was, to use a distinction advanced by Raymond Wolfinger, "machine politics," or particularistic exchange relations without any party organization in the picture. In Milwaukee and Detroit, for example, private utilities and the liquor industry nickel-and-dimed individual city councilors whatever their party. Reform like this also occurred, to cite some well-documented instances, in Galveston, Beaumont, and Grand Rapids.

Most of the powerful state party organizations fell victim to Progressive reform, but city machines, surprisingly, had more of a future than a past in 1900. For one thing, *factional* party organizations, which had been the norm at the city level in the nineteenth century, gave way starting around 1900 to *unified* party organizations. Some of these were powerful enough to amount to machines, and they certainly became statistically more common. Tammany Hall, to give an example, was not able to consolidate its control over the Manhattan Democratic party—putting down other nonreform factions—until 1890. Similar consolidations evidently occurred around 1900 in Philadelphia and New Orleans. And the geographic domain of material-incentive-based urban organization would shrink very little during the first half of the twentieth century, even as the factional variant gave way to the unified variant. Hence, most of the strong, memorable American city machines—Jersey City, Memphis, New Orleans, Kansas City, Albany, Gary, Providence, and Chicago—have been largely or entirely twentieth-century creations. The city machines of the Democratic party were to lead an important late life as elements of ruling national coalitions under Franklin Roosevelt, Harry Truman, John F. Kennedy, and Lyndon Johnson. The most prominent of the last considerable array of material-incentive-based organizations was, of course, Chicago's Daley machine of the 1950s and 1960s.

At local, state, or national levels, what are the overall effects of having parties based substantially on material incentives? In the American case, three arguments are often presented. First, leaders have thereby often built the significant support needed to govern fractious and heterogeneous populations. This is an argument about aggregation of coalitions. It has figured, for example, in interpretations of Lincoln's rule during the Civil War and the Democratic machine's control over Chicago. Second, since one, if not the only, alternative to "material" incentives in politics is "purposive" incentives, some argue that issues, ideologies, and causes have played a less significant role in American material-incentive-driven environments than perhaps otherwise. City machines, for example, have been relatively uninterested in issues. Third, other analysts maintain that patronage politics has delayed or diminished the growth of American governmental programs and, in general, the state. The long-term effect of patronage, stemming mostly from nineteenth-century political experience but echoing well beyond that, has been to undermine public belief in the administrative capacity of government, and to stave off or delay the growth of European-style bureaucracies that have their own expansionary dynamic.

References

Abrams, Richard M. 1964. *Conservatism in a Progressive Era: Massachusetts Politics, 1900–1912.* Cambridge: Harvard U. Pr.

Baker, Jean H. 1973. *The Politics of Continuity: Maryland Political Parties from 1858 to 1870.* Baltimore: Johns Hopkins U. Pr.

Banfield, Edward C. 1961. *Political Influence: A New Theory of Urban Politics.* New York: Free Press.

Barnes, Brooks M. 1981. "The Congressional Elections of 1882 on the Eastern Shore of Virginia." 89 *Virginia Magazine of History and Biography* 467.

Barnes, Samuel H., and Giacomo Sani. 1974. "Mediterranean Political Culture and Italian Politics: An Interpretation." 4 *British Journal of Political Science* 289.

Benedict, Michael Les. 1985. "Factionalism and Representation: Some Insight from the Nineteenth-Century United States." 9 *Social Science History* 361.

Bonomi, Patricia U. 1973. "The Middle Colonies: Embryo of the New Political Order." In Alden T. Vaughan and George A. Billias, eds. *Perspectives on Early American History.* New York: Harper & Row.

Bourke, Paul F., and Donald A. DeBats. 1978. "Identifiable Voting in Nineteenth-Century America: Toward a Comparison of Britain and the United States Before the Secret Ballot." 11 *Perspectives in American History* 259.

Brogan, D.W. 1933. *The American Political System.* London: Hamish Hamilton.

Brown, M. Craig, and Charles N. Halaby. 1987. "Machine Politics in America." 17 *Journal of Interdisciplinary History* 587.

Bryce, James. 1959. *The American Commonwealth.* 2 vols. New York: Putnam's.

Carman, Harry J., and Reinhard H. Luthin. 1943. *Lincoln and the Patronage.* New York: Columbia U. Pr.

Christian, Ralph J. "The Folger-Chatham Congressional Primary of 1946." 53 *North Carolina Historical Review* 25.

Clark, E. Culpepper. 1980. *Francis Warrington Dawson and the Politics of Restoration: South Carolina, 1874–1889.* Tuscaloosa: U. of Alabama Pr.

———. 1983. "Pitchfork Ben Tillman and the Emergence of Southern Demagoguery." 69 *Quarterly Journal of Speech* 423.

Cole, Donald B. 1970. *Jacksonian Democracy in New Hampshire, 1800–1851.* Cambridge: Harvard U. Pr.

———. 1984. *Martin Van Buren and the American Political System.* Princeton: Princeton U. Pr.

Cooper, William J., Jr. 1968. *The Conservative Regime: South Carolina, 1877–1890.* Baltimore: Johns Hopkins U. Pr.

Dinkin, Robert J. 1977. *Voting in Provincial America.* Westport, CT: Greenwood Pr.

———. 1982. *Voting in Revolutionary America.* Westport, CT: Greenwood Pr.

Dorsett, Lyle W. 1977. *Franklin D. Roosevelt and the City Bosses.* Port Washington, NY: Kennikat.

Escott, Paul D. 1985. *Many Excellent People: Power and Privilege in North Carolina, 1850–1900.* Chapel Hill: U. of North Carolina Pr.

Ettinger, B.G. 1985. "John Fitzpatrick and the Limits of Working-Class Politics in New Orleans." 26 *Louisiana History* 341.

Fish, Carl Russell. 1905. *The Civil Service and the Patronage.* New York: Longmans, Green.

Formisano, Ronald P. 1983. *The Transformation of Political Culture: Massachusetts Parties, 1790s–1840s.* New York: Oxford U. Pr.

Freehling, William W. 1966. "Spoilsmen and Interests in the Thought and Career of John C. Calhoun." 52 *Journal of American History* 25.

Greenberg, Douglas. 1979. "The Middle Colonies in Recent American Historiography." 36 *William and Mary Quarterly* 396.

Greenberg, Kenneth S. 1985. *Masters and Statesmen: The Political Culture of American Slavery.* Baltimore: Johns Hopkins U. Pr.

Harmond, Richard. 1968. "The 'Beast' in Boston: Benjamin F. Butler as Governor of Massachusetts." 55 *Journal of American History* 266.

Harrison, Robert. 1982. "Blaine and the Camerons: A Study in the Limits of Machine Power." 49 *Pennsylvania History* 157.

Heintzman, Ralph. 1983. "The Political Culture of Quebec, 1840–1960." 16 *Canadian Journal of Political Science* 3.

Isaac, Paul E. 1975. "Municipal Reform in Beaumont, Texas, 1902–1909." 78 *Southwestern Historical Quarterly* 409.

Jaenicke, Douglas W. 1986. "The Jacksonian Integration of Parties into the Constitutional System." 101 *Political Science Quarterly* 85.

Josephson, Matthew. 1938. *The Politicos: 1865–1896.* New York: Harcourt, Brace.

Kass, Alvin. 1965. *Politics in New York State, 1800–1830.* Syracuse, NY: Syracuse U. Pr.

Key, V.O., Jr. 1948. *Politics, Parties, and Pressure Groups.* 2nd ed. New York: Crowell.

———. 1949. *Southern Politics in State and Nation.* New York: Knopf.

Kruman, Marc W. 1983. *Parties and Politics in North Carolina, 1836–1865.*
    Baton Rouge: Louisiana State U. Pr.

Levine, Peter. 1974. "The Rise of Mass Parties and the Problem of
    Organization: New Jersey, 1829–1844." 91–92 *New Jersey History*
    91.

Luthin, Reinhard H. 1954. *American Demagogues: Twentieth Century.*
    Boston: Beacon.

McCormick, Richard P. 1973. *The Second American Party System: Party
    Formation in the Jacksonian Era.* New York: Norton.

McKitrick, Eric L. 1967. "Party Politics and the Union and Confederate
    War Efforts." In William Nisbet Chambers and Walter Dean
    Burnham, eds. *The American Party Systems: Stages of Political
    Development.* New York: Oxford U. Pr.

Macy, Jesse. 1904. *Party Organization and Machinery.* New York: Century.

Mallam, William D. 1960. "Butlerism in Massachusetts." 33 *New England
    Quarterly* 186.

Mayhew, David R. 1986. *Placing Parties in American Politics:
    Organizations, Electoral Settings, and Government Activity in the
    Twentieth Century.* Princeton: Princeton U. Pr.

Mayo, Edward L. 1979. "Republicanism, Antipartyism, and Jacksonian
    Party Politics: A View from the Nation's Capital." 31 *American
    Quarterly* 3.

Nelson, William E. 1976. "Officeholding and Powerwielding: An
    Analysis of the Relationship Between Structure and Style in
    American Administrative History." 10 *Law and Society Review* 187.

Ostrogorski, Moisei. 1902. *Democracy and the Organization of Political
    Parties.* Vol. 2. New York: Macmillan.

Perman, Michael. 1984. *The Road to Redemption: Southern Politics, 1869–
    1879.* Chapel Hill: U. of North Carolina Pr.

Peskin, Allan. 1985. "Who Were the Stalwarts? Who Were Their Rivals?
    Republican Factions in the Gilded Age." 99 *Political Science
    Quarterly* 703.

Pocock, J.G.A. 1980. "1776: The Revolution Against Parliament." In J. G.
    A. Pocock, ed. *Three British Revolutions, 1641, 1688, 1776.*
    Princeton: Princeton U. Pr.

Prince, Carl E. 1964. "Patronage and a Party Machine: New Jersey
    Democratic-Republican Activists, 1801–1816." 21 *William and
    Mary Quarterly* 571.

Pulley, Raymond H. 1968. *Old Virginia Restored: An Interpretation of the Progressive Impulse, 1870–1930.* Charlottesville: U. Pr. of Virginia.

Rice, Bradley R. 1975. "The Galveston Plan of City Government by Commission: The Birth of a Progressive Idea." 78 *Southwestern Historical Quarterly* 365.

Schattschneider, E.E. 1942. *Party Government.* New York: Rinehart.

Shefter, Martin. 1977. "Party and Patronage: Germany, England, and Italy." 7 *Politics and Society* 403.

———. 1978. "The Electoral Foundations of the Political Machine: New York City, 1884–1897." In Joel H. Silbey, et al., eds. *The History of American Electoral Behavior.* Princeton: Princeton U. Pr.

Skowronek, Stephen. 1982. *Building a New American State: The Expansion of National Administrative Capacities, 1877–1920.* New York: Cambridge U. Pr.

Sorauf, Frank J. 1963. *Party and Representation: Legislative Politics in Pennsylvania.* New York: Atheneum.

Stone, Clarence N. 1963. "Bleaseism and the 1912 Election in South Carolina." 40 *North Carolina Historical Review* 54.

Strum, Harvey. 1981. "Property Qualifications and Voting Behavior in New York, 1807–1816." 1 *Journal of the Early Republic* 347.

Summers, Mark W. 1987. *The Plundering Generation: Corruption and the Crisis of the Union, 1849–1861.* New York: Oxford U. Pr.

Tanner, Mary Nelson. 1963. "The Middle Years of the Anthony-Brayton Alliance, or Politics in the Post Office, 1874–1880." 22 *Rhode Island History* 65.

Thompson, Margaret S. 1982. "Ben Butler versus the Brahmins: Patronage and Politics in Early Gilded Age Massachusetts." 55 *New England Quarterly* 163.

Thornton, J. Mills, III. 1978. *Politics and Power in a Slave Society.* Baton Rouge: Louisiana State U. Pr.

Travis, Anthony R. 1974. "Mayor George Ellis: Grand Rapids Political Boss and Progressive Reformer." 58 *Michigan History* 101.

Tregle, Joseph G., Jr. 1960. "The Political Apprenticeship of John Slidell." 26 *Journal of Southern History* 57.

Tunnell, Ted. 1984. *Crucible of Reconstruction: War, Radicalism and Race in Louisiana, 1862–1877.* Baton Rouge: Louisiana State U. Pr.

Van Noppen, Ina Woestemeyer, and John J. Van Noppen. 1973. *Western North Carolina Since the Civil War.* Boone, NC: Appalachian Consortium Press.

Wallace, Michael. 1968. "Changing Concepts of Party in the United States: New York, 1815–1828." 74 *American Historical Review* 453.

Watson, Harry L. 1981. *Jacksonian Politics and Community Conflict: The Emergence of the Second American Party System in Cumberland County, North Carolina.* Baton Rouge: Louisiana State U. Pr.

Wilson, James Q. 1973. *Political Organizations.* New York: Basic Books.

Wolfinger, Raymond E. 1974. *The Politics of Progress.* Englewood Cliffs, NJ: Prentice-Hall.

Wright, James. 1987. *The Progressive Yankees: Republican Reformers in New Hampshire, 1906–1916.* Hanover, NH: U. Pr. of New England.

CHAPTER 12

Political Parties in a Nonparty Era: Adapting to a New Role

L. Sandy Maisel

Just after 3:00 a.m. on June 25, 1993, Vice-President Albert Gore cast his first tie-breaking vote in the United States Senate, the first cast by a vice-president in six years, allowing President Clinton's deficit-reduction package to survive. That a Democratic president's economic package passed a democratically controlled Senate—or that a differently constructed compromise had narrowly been saved in the House about a month earlier—was viewed as evidence that the gridlock of twelve years of divided government, of a Congress controlled by one party and a White House by the other, had been broken.

Such an interpretation is simplistic and misses important lessons about American government at the end of the twentieth century. Political parties do not play the role in contemporary politics that they did in earlier times. In fact, as they adjust to new forms of politics, they are seeking a role that is relevant for the times.

To be sure, these votes were "party" votes. Every Republican in both houses voted against the president's program; almost all Democrats supported their party leader. More than one Democrat was quoted as saying that he or she supported the program because the president could not be allowed to fail.

The narrow margins were somewhat deceptive. In the House twenty Democrats voted against the president in the last minute and a half on the roll call clock; it can be assumed that at least some of these representatives had promised their votes to Speaker Foley (D., Wa.) if those votes were needed. In the Senate six Democrats voted against the president. Richard Shelby (D., Al.) has opposed President Clinton's program from the start; Sam Nunn (G., Ga.) and J. Bennett Johnston (D., La.) are conservative southern senators who have frequently sought to demonstrate independence. The three others—Richard Bryan (D., Nev.), Dennis DeConcini (D., Az.), and Frank Lautenberg (D., N.J.)—all faced reelection in 1994, each in a state in which voting for a tax-increasing bill would trigger sure opposition. But in the Senate, as in the House, it seems likely that some of those voting against the president's program had promised support if that support had been needed.

But gridlock is not necessarily broken because a president can command the support of his copartisans who control the legislature on one key vote. Another way to look at gridlock is that the system envisioned by the Founders and defended in the *Federalist Papers* still works. Gridlock is a manifestation of separation of powers, of separate institutions made up of individuals representing different constituencies and having different views of what is best for the American people. Far-reaching policy change results when a consensus not only for change but for specific kinds of change has been forged. That consensus is expressed in electoral mandates and converted into public policy by newly formed legislative majorities supporting the president who has articulated the emerging view. When such a consensus has not been forged, when there may be dissatisfaction with the status quo but no agreement on alternatives to be pursued, separation of powers guarantees that radical policy change will not occur.

Such a situation followed the 1992 election. Bill Clinton may have been a self-professed candidate of change, and his party may have retained its majority in both houses of the Congress; but one should not lose sight of the fact that Clinton won the election with 43 percent of the vote, that Ross Perot polled more votes than any third party candidate since Teddy Roosevelt ran on the Bull Moose ticket in 1912, or that the voters were expressing dissatisfaction with government policy much more than excitement about a new policy direction.

How does political party fit into this picture? What is the role of party in American politics as we turn to the twenty-first century? In the Introduction to this book, William Shade talks about stages of party development; what stage of party development are we in now? As Shade mentions, Joel Silbey and others have argued that the two centuries of American history can be divided into epochs according to the centrality of political parties for the political process: a preparty period ending in the late 1830s; a party era for the next six decades; a post-party era ending in the 1950s; and a nonparty era since. No one could argue that the role of party is more central now than it was fifty years ago. But parties continue to exist and candidates seek major party endorsements. Major party candidates win a vast majority of all partisan offices sought; the major parties organize the national legislature and the legislatures of forty-nine of the fifty states. (Nebraska is the sole exception, with a unicameral nonpartisan legislative branch.) In this final chapter the role of political parties in the modern context, in the post-New Deal era and in Silbey's nonparty era, is examined.

One of the most interesting aspects of American politics has been the existence of political parties. Unwanted by our Founders, modern parties were invented by those same men as a necessary tool to achieve policy preferences. After a half century of domination, political parties were scorned by the progressive reformers. They may have lost their central role, but they reformed and persisted. Seemingly made obsolete by changes in campaign technology and advances in information transferal, in recent decades parties have floundered, often demeaned but never ignored, looked on as dinosaurs from another era, but struggling to avoid extinction. The following examines the adaptation of political parties as they seek to define their role in this new era.

Shade's introductory chapter also talks about the tripartite division of political parties as party organization, party in the electorate, and party in the government. The definition of political parties (Maisel, 1993, p.10) as organizations, at times loosely organized, that persist over time, that run candidates for office, that have earned support for those candidates because some portion of the electorate is drawn to those candidacies because of allegiance to the party, and that therefore link the governors to the governed, may be useful here. The key aspect of this definition is the intermediary role between the citizenry and elected public officials, and it allows us to identify separable venues in which party must play a role—campaigning and governing—which will be discussed separately.

The Role of Parties in Campaigns in a Nonparty Era

The heading of this section reads like an oxymoron, an irony that must first be explained since Silbey and those who follow his theory of epochs are clearly right that we are in a nonparty era. The evidence is familiar and overwhelming: Parties have lost control of the nominating process; candidates form their own organizations to seek nominations and use these in general election campaigns; some candidates, such as Phil Gramm (R., Tex.), successfully switch from one major party to the other, a move unheard of in a strong party era; voter allegiance to political parties has declined; fewer voters use party as the key to determining how to vote and more split their tickets. The list can go on and on.

But candidates do still seek major party endorsements, and major party candidates do win most often. Voters claim that "they vote for the man, not the party," but party allegiance, while weakened, is not dead. Political party leaders strive to find a role for their organizations that holds both candidate and voter allegiance.

Political parties have adapted least well to changes in the nominating process. The reforms of the progressive era took absolute control over nominations for state and local office away from party officials and gave it to the party electorate in direct primaries. This change happened at different times in different states, with Connecticut, in the 1950s, holding out as the last state to permit primaries.

Primaries for local and state office come in various shapes and sizes. They can be distinguished by (1) who is eligible to vote (all citizens or only a subset [defined differently in different jurisdictions] affiliated with one political party); (2) who is eligible to run (anyone, those with some previous party history, those who meet certain qualifications such as having obtained a number of signatures [of any citizen or only of party members] or who have received the endorsement of some party meeting or convention); and (3) who wins (a plurality winner in most jurisdictions, but a majority winner, with a run-off possibility in others). What is clear is that party organization plays a minor role in most jurisdictions, that the number of areas which retain a major role is decreasing, and that the role that does exist in other areas continues to diminish.

The first response of political parties to this diminution of their role was to attempt to dominate primaries. Except for in those areas with strong traditional party organizations (stereotypically viewed as political machines), this effort met with minimal success. The areas in which machines have been able to dominate nominations have become fewer and fewer.

In recent years political parties have tried to play a slightly different role. Various party organizations have attempted to define the candidate field for primaries, either recruiting candidates thought to be strong or discouraging those who might cause harm to the party's chances in the general election. This effort began with the Republican party seeking candidates for Congress during the Reagan administration; they were successful in recruiting challengers to incumbent Democratic representatives in the early elections, but these candidates mostly lost—and the recruitment effort lost steam, though it did not disappear. In more recent years leadership committees in state legislatures in both parties have played similar roles. Anecdotal evidence suggests that the parties have had limited, though not inconsequential, success in this effort.

For presidential nominations, the most important changes followed the reforms of the McGovern-Fraser Commission, set up after the 1968 election to respond to charges that the nominating process was undemocratic, untimely, and unrepresentative. The end result of these reforms—debated seemingly without end in the political science literature—is that control of nominations has been taken out of the hands of party leaders and put into a system that is held in high regard by just about no one.

The first response of Democratic party leaders to the McGovern-Fraser reforms was to structure the rules within the new guidelines in order to advantage particular candidates. The series of reform commissions after subsequent presidential nominations and elections was aimed in part at producing a system that would have predictable results. The architects of these post-reform rules changes were notably unsuccessful in producing changes that had the desired results. Though some have not abandoned this effort, few are sanguine about future success. Republicans have been much less interested in reform of their party's nominating rules, though some changes in the Republican process have been necessitated by changes in state law brought about as a consequence of changes wrought by the Democrats, e.g., more states now hold presidential preference primaries, in both parties, and fewer hold caucuses to select delegates to national conventions.

In recent years the principal role that national party organizations have been able to play has been to attempt to limit damage caused by intraparty competition. During the 1992 nominating campaign, Democratic National Chairman Ron Brown saw his responsibility as keeping the party together so that the eventual nominee would not be too weak to run an effective November campaign. His efforts—encouraging early round losers to drop out and endorse front-runner Clinton as well as cajoling the remaining candidates to work together in planning the convention—were largely successful and were credited with helping the Clinton campaign. Republican party leaders had played similar roles in 1980, when President Reagan was first nominated, and in 1988, when President Bush won his first nomination. However, in 1992, Republican operatives were less successful in muting criticism of President Bush by Pat Buchanan and those who opposed him from the party's right wing. The party did not really help the Bush-Quayle campaign at all in this stage of the process.

What can one conclude about the role of parties in the nominating process? Boss Tweed of Tammany Hall is reported to have claimed, "I don't care who does the electing, just so I do the nominating!" If the corollary is that loss of the control of nominations means loss of everything, then parties seem to be in a bad way. But, as we will see, the parties have found other ways to play the role of intermediary between those seeking office and the voters.

Perhaps the easiest change to observe is how political parties have adapted to the cash economy of political campaigns. In an era of strong parties, the coin of the realm was workers who could get loyal party supporters to the polls. Again the litany of activities is familiar: Party workers provide services, often tangible services, to citizens in their precincts and wards. Providing such services—food, shelter, clothing for immigrants and the poor, jobs, assistance in obtaining government services, etc.—builds bonds of loyalty between the party workers and their "constituents." On election day the party workers call in their debts, not with threats but with reminders of the reciprocal nature of the relationship that has been built. "We can only do favors for you if we stay in office." In oversimplified terms, that was the nature of the incentive-reward system in the strong party era. Citizens developed strong ties to parties; party workers, who had bound those ties, made certain that the faithful turned out to vote on election day. Those elected knew that they owed office to the party faithful and helped the workers build the ties that guaranteed future support.

But that system gradually eroded, and that type of intermediary role between the citizens and those who governed them faded away. Services that had been provided by the party came to be provided by the government. As the party could no longer guarantee even nominations, candidates had to build their own organizations in order to compete in primaries. Campaigning became less and less a retail business with personal contact on a door-to-door basis. More and more was performed wholesale, through radio and television, directed mailings, and other less personal modern campaign techniques. Loyalty was to individual candidates, not to candidates of parties, as officeholders worked hard to build personal followings, and the coin of the realm became cash. The value of party workers decreased as campaigns switched from a retail to a wholesale business. Candidates found that they could raise money from individuals or from political action committees and that parties had relatively little to offer.

How did the parties respond to this erosion of their role and influence? First they sought to become a source of the new valued commodity, money. However, they had to do this within limits defined by the reform effort that sought to control the influence of money in politics.

Total campaign spending, the extraordinary amounts of money certain individuals contributed to campaigns, the lack of public information about campaign financing, and the ways in which candidates for office spent their campaign dollars led to widespread dissatisfaction with and eventually a major reform of the federal campaign financing system. In 1971 Congress passed the Federal Election Campaign Act (FECA), which took major steps toward controlling media expenditures and set up the mechanism for publicly financed presidential campaigns. That law was amended substantially in 1974; the theory that governed the reform effort centered around disclosure of all contributions and expenditures and limits on the amounts that individuals, political action committees, and parties can give to candidates for the House and the Senate. The law was amended again in 1976, after the Supreme Court ruled large portions of the 1974 amendments unconstitutional in *Buckley v. Valeo* (424 U.S. 1 [1976]). With minor revisions, that act stayed in effect until the reforms of the Clinton administration. The system within which the parties had to work was one of federally financed presidential campaigns and privately financed congressional and senatorial campaigns, with extensive disclosure requirements and limits on contributions from individual, political action committee, and party sources.

The two major political parties struggled to find a way they could play an influential role in campaigning within this system. Their role in presidential campaigns was essentially eliminated. At the national level, then, they turned to campaigns for the House and the Senate. The four Hill committees—the National Republican Senatorial Committee (NRSC), the National

Republican Congressional Committee (NRCC), the Democratic Senatorial Campaign Committee (DSCC), and the Democratic Congressional Campaign Committee (DCCC)—increased their fundraising capabilities and thus their ability to aid candidates for Congress. The Republicans took the lead in this under Republican National Chairman Bill Brock in the late 1970s. The Democrats soon found themselves at a competitive disadvantage but, under DSCC Chair George Mitchell (Maine) and DCCC Chair Tony Coehlo (Cal.), made huge gains in the first half of the 1980s. The goal of the Hill committees was to develop fundraising arms so that they could raise enough to contribute the maximum allowed under the law to as many campaigns as possible.

The four Hill committees are made up of members of the House and Senate who supervise campaign staffs. Not surprisingly, the first priority for these committees traditionally has been to protect incumbents. In fact, for many years incumbents received money from their parties' congressional campaign committee regardless of whether they were challenged or not. In more recent elections, however, the committees have allocated their money more strategically, protecting threatened incumbents, but also contributing in open seats and to challengers thought to have a good chance of upsetting those already in office. The Hill committees thus represent an effort by the parties to adapt to a new political situation. They raise money from the party faithful, stressing the importance of seats in the Congress. They give to candidates for the Congress who need the money, building at least some tie to the party. In addition, and because of contribution restrictions perhaps more importantly, the parties serve as financial brokers. They advise potential contributors as to which candidates for Congress they would be wise to support; they help put candidates in touch with those who might support their campaigns. They have essentially defined a new kind of intermediary role. The extent of this linkage will be explored below. But it can be noted here that the chairs of the Hill committees are now listed among their parties' leaders in the House and Senate, positions that would have seemed uncalled for two decades ago.

As was the case with candidate recruitment, this effort to play a meaningful and strategically important role in campaign financing started at the national level; in recent years state legislative leadership committees have copied the techniques of their congressional counterparts. While the exact mechanism has varied from state to state and from party to party, and while no one has a firm fix on the extent of this activity—largely because reporting requirements and the accessibility of data make systematic analysis at the state level all but impossible—it seems clear that party as a funding source has assumed greater importance in recent elections. This prominence is enhanced because state legislative races typically cost much less than do congressional and senatorial campaigns. As state party leaders learn from each other, one can only assume that this practice too will spread in the years ahead.

FECA restrictions mean that the parties cannot be major contributors to federal campaigns that often run into the millions of dollars. The brokering role is one way in which they have expanded their role, but the two major parties have continued to seek ways to expand their influence. Another means they have devised is to provide services for candidates. Both national party headquarters now have state-of-the-art communications capabilities, computer facilities, and targeted mailing lists. Each party employs pollsters, political researchers, and regional political experts, whose facilities and expertise the parties are willing to share with those running for office under the party label. Candidates for local, state, and federal office take advantage of party expertise. Former Speaker of the House Thomas P. "Tip" O'Neill often is quoted as claiming that "All politics is local." The national parties have discovered that what works in one locality often works, sometimes with a little twist, in another. Using economies of scale, therefore, the national parties have been able to supply to state and local parties and candidates campaign expertise, technology, and capabilities that the local units would not be able to afford. Again, the parties are developing a new role for a new era.

Campaigning is not just about techniques of reaching the voters, it is also about how the voters respond to the choices presented to them. In this area the parties have made some effort to remain an important part of the electoral process, but they have met with only limited success. Their effort has been two-pronged. First, each party has used opportunities presented by vagueness in the campaign finance laws to mount unified, coordinated campaigns throughout the country and thus the national parties have been able to finance local efforts. From the perspective of the national parties, the advantage is that they can spend more money to aid candidates for federal office, whereas for the local parties, the advantage is that they have increased opportunities to campaign actively within their communities. The hope is that these opportunities will aid all candidates for office.

In addition, on recent occasions the two national parties have run commercials—and essentially orchestrated campaigns—aimed at helping all of their party candidates. The Republicans, seeking to take advantage of citizen dissatisfaction with the government, ran a campaign with the theme "Vote Republican—for a change!" The Democrats countered with "It's not fair! It's Republican!" Generic national advertising certainly has had the effect of irritating the party under attack, but whether it has also had an impact on the voters is less certain.

What is certain is that the leaders of the two major political parties understand that their parties no longer have the appeal to the citizens they once did. That approximately one-fifth of the voters in the 1992 presidential election voted for Ross Perot sent shock waves through both Republican and Democratic party headquarters. On the one hand the response has been to reach out to the Perot voters—each party has polled Perot voters to see exactly what they are looking for in candidates for office. On the other hand the response has been to reach out, tentatively at least, to Perot himself. But in point of fact, the parties are not certain how to handle the Perot phenomenon; they are clear that it is a threat but do not know how to respond. The reason may well be that the appropriate response does not deal with campaigning, but rather with governing, to which we now turn.

The Role of Parties in Governing in a Nonparty Era

Few will be surprised to hear the refrain echoed that the United States does not have a responsible party system. In a responsible party system, the argument goes, a political party is elected based upon a specific set of platform promises, which, once in office, it is able to implement. In the American system, however, representatives and senators are elected separately from the president, and from each other. They represent different constituencies and have different policy preferences. It is not at all unusual for the same geographic area to vote for a Democratic candidate for president, a Republican candidate for United States senator, and a Democratic candidate for the House. In those circumstances, it is difficult to tell what policy mandate the citizens intended to give.

In an era of strong party government, one could claim that legislators were elected on presidential coattails, that the parties were in fact differentiated on key policy questions, and that the party in power was capable of implementing its program. Similarly, one can argue that the party winning what V.O. Key referred to as a critical election, the one in which the citizens realign their allegiance between the major parties on the most salient issues of the day, should be capable of implementing those parts of the party platform that in fact distinguish the winners from the losers. But in a nonparty era, the role of political party in governing is less clear. If citizens vote for the candidate and not for the party, if candidates strive to build ties to their constituents based on personal service and personal appeal, if voters cast their ballots for candidates of different parties for different offices, if officeholders are concerned about their own ability to win reelection more than about the fate of their party, how can political parties make a difference in the governing process? This basic question confronts contemporary political party organizations.

In some ways the question is even more difficult, because citizens evaluate their government based, in part at least, on its ability to solve the problems facing the polity. If each legislator takes the narrow view of looking at what is best for his or her geographic constituency or of how a vote will or will not appeal to those who will decide on whether or not that legislator will be returned to Washington (or by extension to the state capital), then who is going to take the broader view? Who is looking out for the national interest?

The difference between local and national interest might well have been less consuming in an era of growth, or of an expanding governmental pie, an era in which those in power had to decide how the government would expend its vast resources. But as the country enters the twenty-first century, the questions are different. For the first time since the massive expansion of the federal government with the New Deal, the national government must learn to live within its means and to restrict its activities. The huge annual deficits and the debt that seems to be galloping out of control mean that citizens must learn to expect less, not more from their government. To form a national consensus on how needed cuts must be made requires convincing legislators to vote against programs that benefit their constituents, which is not an easy task.

A new type of leadership is necessary that explains policies to the citizens and accepts short-term unpopularity of programs in order to gain long-term benefits and that builds coalitions by convincing people they must take some actions and accept some consequences that they otherwise would find objectionable. It is a new kind of intermediary role between the governors and the governed in which political parties are struggling to play a role.

Recent evidence leads one to conclude that political party organizations within the Congress have accepted this role. As discussed above, Democrat after Democrat in the House and the Senate voted for President Clinton's economic package while saying that he or she did not like it, but that it was a step in the direction of doing what was necessary. Political scientists have begun to comment on rising party unity on key votes in Congress. The president spends inordinate amounts of time conferring with party leaders in the Congress as he deals with pressing issues of the day.

On the other hand, much evidence also indicates that President Clinton realizes he has to build a coalition that crosses party lines. While the Democrats control both houses of the Congress, their control is not overwhelming. If even a few Democrats desert their party positions, or if the Republicans hold their positions and filibuster in the Senate, President Clinton's programs will not pass. The Republicans realize this and have put up a united front against early Clinton initiatives in order to be consulted in formulating programs later on. Other groups in Congress—the Congressional Black Caucus is an obvious example—realize that their power is enhanced because no Democratic program can be passed if they withhold their support. The separation of powers and the independent electoral bases of legislators make party government a pipe dream. Yet the American public wants solutions to problems. President Clinton and his advisors clearly realize that they will be judged on their ability to produce, and since the American people feel that gridlock should have ended with the end to divided government, the nuances of why the president cannot pass his programs will fall on deaf ears among the electorate.

Perceiving this dilemma, party organization has begun to play a new kind of intermediary role. That role is to carry the message of the party's president to the people, and convince the voters to support him, so that these citizens, in turn, will convince their legislators to do so. In the first months of the Clinton administration, some Democratic legislators did not support aspects of the president's program because they feared electoral reprisals if they did so; many Republican legislators opposed the Clinton initiatives not only because of differences in philosophy, but also because they thought they would gain at the polls by taking such a stance—defeat of the president's program would spell defeat for the Democratic party. Therefore, the Democrats had to find a way to convince legislators that their perceptions of the consequences of their votes against the president were wrong. The role of persuading legislators by persuading their constituents was one the party came to by necessity, not design.

In 1993, the Democratic National Committee, and especially DNC Chair David Wilhelm, began to take on this new role of lobbyist for the administration's program. First on President Clinton's economic package and later on his health care proposal, the Democrats, as a party organization, orchestrated national campaigns to convince the citizens that these plans were in their best interest—and to convince voters to tell their legislators to support the president. This policy-oriented role is a new one for the national organization and is decidedly appropriate for the times.

The Democrats did not happen upon this vision of the party's new role on their own. Their actions were a response to near solid Republican opposition to early proposals and to the fear that a few wayward Democrats could doom policy initiatives and, as a consequence, put President Clinton's administration in a difficult position. The experience of the first six months of "unified" government demonstrated that the citizenry was unhappy with a president who did not produce. The Democrats took some time to find an appropriate way to counter the perception of the president as an inept leader, which had been fostered by continuous sniping and opposition by the Republicans in the Congress. Campaigning for the Clinton program and lobbying with the people and indirectly with legislators to give the new president a chance to implement his ideas—even those that might be against certain individual's short-term interests—is a new role for party organization. Again, it is an effort by the party to define a new intermediary role in a nonparty era. In the era of strong parties, the government was involved in far fewer policy debates; philosophical differences on those debates distinguished the major parties. In today's political environment in which government in involved in many more aspects of citizens' lives and in which the policy coalitions on various issue dimensions do not necessarily parallel partisan lines, political party leaders have found a new policy-oriented role to play. It is far too early to assess its success or failure, much less its transience or permanence as a role for parties.

Conclusion

Organization theory holds that large organizations can change only incrementally in the short run; that is, an organization's capabilities at time *t* is only incrementally different from its capabilities at time *t–1* or at time *t+1*. The theory also holds that large organizations strive to find means of self-preservation. These rather simple notions go a long way toward explaining the behavior of political parties in recent decades and toward predicting the role they will play as we enter a new century.

Thirty years ago Cornelius Cotter and Bernard Hennessy wrote an influential book on the Democratic and Republican National Committees entitled *Politics Without Power*, which described the lure of the service on the two national committees, and the sense of involvement at the center of the political arena without commensurate objectively observable power. Cotter and Hennessy wrote before the decline in the role of political parties had been widely perceived. However, the forces that led to that decline were already in place and the direction of that movement was inexorable. But the national party committees head organizations that were not about to disappear. The history of these organizations since Cotter and Hennessy's book has been one of struggle to find a role in a new political environment in which the national parties had some important advantages.

First, while parties were no longer central to the political process, while the political environment continued to change in a way deemed detrimental to parties recapturing their influence, and while other political actors were taking over some of the roles party had played, the tradition of two-party competition was deeply imbedded in the American body politic and was reinforced by institutional mechanisms that all but guaranteed the continued presence of the major parties, even in the absence of influence. Thus the major parties are guaranteed places on the ballot for virtually every election in every state. The Federal Election Campaign Act mandates funding of the two major party national conventions and of their presidential candidates' campaigns. Legislatures throughout the nation are organized by political parties since no other mechanism for structuring broad-based coalitions has emerged to supplant them.

Second, even though citizens' allegiance to political party is not what it once was, even though voters traditionally split their tickets and elected divided governments to rule in both Washington and many of the state capitals, many citizens still have some allegiance to one party or the other and have a perception of party that helps them to structure their choices in the absence of other information.

Third, the media looks to the two political parties as the "teams" that are competing in the "game" of national politics. The media can legitimately be criticized for oversimplifying politics for the American people. One aspect of this oversimplification is the presentation of every situation as Republicans versus the Democrats. When the Democratic president poses a new policy initiative, the television networks turn to the Republicans for the opposition's reaction. Legislative coalitions often cross party lines; but the networks infrequently present the complex picture of shifting cross-partisan coalitions to the public. Thus, from the public's point of view, the parties still play a meaningful role in structuring policy debates. It is ironic that the mass media both presents an image of parties that contributes to public dissatisfaction and continues to structure political discussions in terms of Democrats versus Republicans so that the major parties remain the prime focus of public attention.

The newly evolving role of the political parties continues to be one of an intermediary between citizens and elected public officials, between the governed and the governors, a linkage that can be seen in all aspects of the political process, in campaigns and elections and in governing. The first order of business for the parties was to find a role they could play that was useful to candidates for office, to aid personal campaign organizations. No longer are campaigns run by political parties, but today the parties are able to offer their party's candidates valuable services. Not surprisingly, the role revolves around financial services. Parties cannot provide much money to campaigns directly—though they do provide as much as they are able—but parties can and do reduce the cost of campaigning by providing direct campaign services, and, even more importantly for more visible offices, they help candidates raise the money they need by serving as a broker between candidates and those contributing large sums to campaigns.

In so doing, they provide a link between elected public officials and the public in two ways: They link the contributing public most attuned to and involved in politics directly to candidates; and, indirectly, they help candidates acquire the tools to reach out to the voters. Both roles represent an adaptation to wholesale politics by organizations whose strength once was retail politics. Movement in this direction is well established and understood by all involved.

In governance, parties also seem to be moving in a more policy-oriented direction, again providing a new link between those in power and the general citizenry. The policymaking process seemed to be at an impasse as legislators pursued particularistic goals and national priorities were left with advocates without a constituency. By the 1992 election a consensus that citizens were dissatisfied with the output of the national government was apparent. Ross Perot spoke eloquently to that consensus, as did Bill Clinton in his call for change; George Bush was its victim. However, no national agreement on a new direction for government was in evidence. Legislators seemed comfortable reflecting the public's anger without feeling the necessity of responding to its cause.

Within a few months of taking office, however, the new president saw the public turning against him, just as it had against President Bush, because he was not producing, and he could not produce a legislative program without party support. So he turned to Democratic legislators, and they responded, recognizing the extent to which their fate was tied to his. As this situation was evolving, the party organization began to see a new intermediary role that it could play, linking the president's program to the public and in so doing convincing recalcitrant legislators that their best interest was in supporting the president. This programmatic role of lobbying for the presidential legislative agenda is a new one for national party organizations. It is unclear how successful it will be and how it will be developed.

What is evident, however, is that party organization is doing something in 1993 that it was not doing in 1992. The political parties are finding new ways to fill their role in the American political system, serving as an intermediary between voters and those elected to office. The parties are adapting to a new political environment in which many of the activities that once were their prime focuses are now performed by others and in which they, as organizations, are viewed by many as anachronistic. As we have seen, the parties are taking these steps in ways that are consistent with American political traditions and with their own desires to preserve themselves and their continuing place in American political history.

References

American Political Science Association, Committee on Political Parties. 1950. *Toward a More Responsible Two-Party System.* Washington, DC: American Political Science Association.

Cotter, Cornelius P., and Bernard C. Hennessy. 1964. *Politics Without Power: The National Party Committees.* New York: Atherton.

Fiorina, Morris P. 1977. *Congress: Keystone of the Washington Establishment.* New Haven: Yale U. Pr.

———. 1992. *Divided Government.* New York: Macmillan.

Herrnson, Paul S. 1988. *Party Campaigning in the 1980s.* Cambridge: Harvard U. Pr.

Key, V. O., Jr. 1952. *Politics, Parties, and Pressure Groups.* 3rd Edition. New York: Thomas Y. Crowell.

———. 1955. "A Theory of Critical Elections." 17 *Journal of Politics* 3.

Maisel, L. Sandy. 1993. *Parties and Elections in America: The Electoral Process.* 2nd Edition. New York: McGraw-Hill.

———. 1994. *The Parties Respond: Changes in American Political Parties and Campaigns.* 2nd Edition. Boulder, CO: Westview Press.

Mayhew, David R. 1986. *Placing Parties in American Politics.* Princeton: Princeton U. Pr.

Rohde, David W. 1991. *Parties and Leaders in the Post-Reform House.* Chicago: U. of Chicago Pr.

Sabato, Larry J. 1988. *The Party's Just Begun: Shaping Political Parties for America's Future.* Glenview, IL: Scott, Foresman.

Silbey, Joel H. 1991. *The American Political Nation, 1838–1893.* Stanford, CA: Stanford U. Pr.

———. 1994. "The Rise and Fall of American Political Parties, 1790–1992." In L. Sandy Maisel, ed. *The Parties Respond*. Boulder, CO: Westview Press.

Sorauf, Frank, J. 1964. *Political Parties in the American System*. Boston: Little, Brown.

———. 1992. *Inside Campaign Finance: Myths and Realities*. New Haven: Yale U. Pr.